S

fo

S

ir

Se

Ed

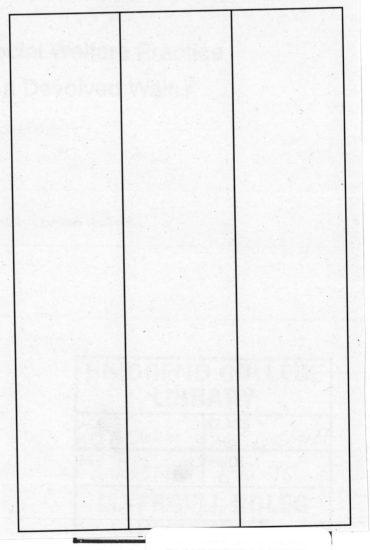

Published by
VENTURE PRESS
16 Kent Street
Birmingham
B5 6RD
www.basw.co.uk

British Library Cataloguing-in-Publication Data
A catalogue record for this book is available from the British Library

ISBN: 978-1-86178-087-4 (paperback)

Printed by:
Hobbs the Printers Ltd
Brunel Road
Totton
SO40 3WX

Printed in Great Britain

FSC
www.fsc.org
MIX
Board from
responsible sources
FSC® C020438

ii

Contents

List of tables, figures and boxes

Tables

Figures

Boxes

List of abbreviations

AM	Assembly Member
CCW	Care Council for Wales
CEPL	Continuing Professional Education Learning
CMHT	Community Mental Handicap Team
CPA	Care Programme Approach
CSPRD	Centre for Social Policy Research and Development
DfES	Department for Education and Skills
DMFT	Decayed, Missing & Filled Teeth
EMA	Educational Maintenance Allowance
FSM	free school meals
GCSE	General Certificate of Secondary Education
GP	general practitioner
HBAI	Households Below Average Income
IASSW	International Association of Schools of Social Work
IFSW	International Federation of Social Workers
LHB	Local Health Board
LHG	Local Health Group
MEDC	more economically developed countries
MOU	Memorandum of Understanding
NHS	National Health Service
NQF	National Qualifications Framework
PFI	Private Finance Initiative
PISA	Programme for International Student Assessment
UAP	Unified Assessment Process
UK	United Kingdom
UNCRC	United Nations Convention on the Rights of the Child
UNCRCC	Committee of the UNCRC
YOT	Youth Offending Team
YPP	Young People's Partnership

Acknowledgements

My thanks to all the contributors to this book who found time within their busy schedules to work on this second edition.

Thanks also to those at BASW/Venture Press for their continued support of this project.

Notes on contributors

Ian Butler is Professor of Social Work at Bath University. He is a former social worker and social work manager with experience in both the statutory and voluntary sectors. Since 2005 he has been a special adviser to the First Minister of Wales. He was Editor of the *British Journal of Social Work* between 2000 and 2003. He was elected as a member of the Academy of Social Sciences in 2004. He has published widely on social work policy and practice with children and families.

Anne Crowley is Senior Policy Adviser with Save the Children. She coordinates Save the Children's advocacy and public policy work aimed at influencing decision makers and duty bearers for the rights of children in Wales. Anne has worked with marginalised young people in both the statutory and the voluntary sectors in Wales. She took up her current post with Save the Children in 1999, seeing the creation of the National Assembly for Wales as a key opportunity to develop made-in-Wales policies to benefit the nation's youngest citizens. In 2004/05 she was an adviser to the Parliamentary Welsh Affairs Select Committee for their enquiry into *Empowering Children and Young People in Wales*. In 2006, she co-edited *Righting the Wrongs*, a report reviewing progress on implementing the United Nations Convention on the Rights of the Child in Wales.

Elaine Davies is a graduate of UCW Aberystwyth and Jesus College Oxford and worked for several years as a social worker and team manager in Dyfed and in the London Boroughs of Islington and Hillingdon. More recently she has fused her interest in language and social care issues and has published and developed training workshops in the area of language-sensitive practice. She now works for the language consultancy, *Cwmni Iaith*.

Mark Drakeford is a former probation officer, community development project leader and youth justice worker. He was elected the Assembly Member for Cardiff West in the 2011 Assembly elections and is currently Professor of Social Policy and Applied Social Sciences at Cardiff University. Since 2000 he has been the Cabinet's health and social policy adviser at the Welsh Assembly Government. A former editor of the *British Journal of Social Work*, he has published widely in the fields of poverty, youth policy and social policy in Wales.

Lee Gregory is a PhD student at Cardiff University currently researching the use of time banks to develop co-production in health and social care. Previous research has been into Child Trust Funds, the Welsh Credit Union movement and the relevance of social policy for social work practice.

Hefin Gwilym is Acting Director of Social Work Studies in the School of Social Sciences, Bangor University. He is also the Course Coordinator for the MA Advanced Social Work degree. Before becoming a social work academic, he had extensive experience of working in social care settings in Wales, including as a team manager for a voluntary residential learning disabilities service in Ceredigion, working as a social worker in the field of mental health for Gwynedd Social Services and as a member of Dwyfor Community Mental Health Team. He has published on a wide range of subjects, including service user involvement in social work education and mental health.

Jayne Neal completed her PhD thesis on the welfare needs of young offenders in Wales in 2008. She has wide practical experience of working with children, young people and families within the voluntary and public sectors in family and childcare and youth justice services. After completing postgraduate study at Bangor University, employment with the Communities First team in Tudno & Mostyn has enabled a move back into working with local youth community as Youth Development Worker.

Richard Pugh is Emeritus Professor in Social Work at Keele University and has worked as a residential and field worker in the UK and the USA. He has published widely on minority language issues, child care, social work theory and rural social work. He has extensive international links with academics and practitioners in Europe, North America and Australia, and is a member of the International Advisory Board of *Portularia* – The Spanish Journal of Social Work – and a trustee of the Institute of Rural Health.

Michael Sullivan is Professor of Policy Analysis at Swansea University. He has advised the Welsh Assembly Government on matters of health policy and, between 2007 and 2010, was seconded as special adviser to the First Minister on public policy and then as a specialist policy adviser. He has written widely on the politics of social policy and, latterly, on devolution and social policy. He has acted as an adviser to the Organisation for Security and Cooperation in Europe on the development of public policy frameworks in Serbia and Montenegro.

Charlotte Williams OBE is Professor of Social Justice at Keele University. She began her career in welfare practice working as a housing officer and later worked as a local authority social worker and finally in social development projects in Guyana, South America before returning to the UK to take up an academic post. She worked as a senior lecturer in social work at Bangor University for over 15 years. She is currently Head of the School of Public Policy and Professional Practice at Keele University. She has researched and published widely on issues of race and ethnicity in welfare practice, more latterly in the context of devolution.

Introduction

Charlotte Williams

Devolution has changed the parameters of welfare practice. There is mounting evidence in terms of legislation, policy and practice that key differences have emerged between Welsh social policies and those that exist elsewhere in the United Kingdom (UK). For example, Wales created a Children's Commissioner well ahead of Scotland and England, smoking was banned in public places in Wales before it was banned in England, Welsh pensioners have enjoyed free bus travel and Welsh school children free swimming for some years, and all people in Wales benefit from free prescriptions, which is not the case in England. Devolution has had an impact in countless ways across the UK and in ways much more fundamental than these apparent policy shifts. Issues of Welsh distinctiveness, identity and nationality have been revitalised following devolution, with the concomitant effect of a resurgence of English nationalism. There is the assertion that Welsh and Scottish social welfare policy reflects a strong commitment to social democracy, by contrast with the neo-liberal agenda of Westminster, creating differences in the style and principles underpinning political choices in the different parts of the UK. It is increasingly claimed that devolution has produced a more inclusive politics, engaging with and empowering a much higher level of involvement by local communities and the general public in matters that affect their well-being. In this way, devolution has opened up both a new politics of the UK and the potential for new forms of governance and varying models of citizenship to emerge. Social welfare practice is being and will continue to be transformed by these changes.

All the while, anxieties have grown about the extent to which this policy divergence foreshadows the break-up of the UK. On the one hand, there are those who argue that we are witnessing an acceleration of this process. They suggest that policy differences that affect our everyday lives are now substantively different across the UK (take student tuition fees as just one example), leading to growing inter-regional and intra-regional inequalities. By contrast, there are those who suggest that these arguments are overstated and point to the fact that the Scottish Parliament and Welsh Government have variously limited powers, that the public have little appetite for full independence and that despite the differences in policy there is still much more that unites rather than divides the nations of the UK. There is little doubting that these debates will continue to engage those of us concerned with the fortunes of the traditional welfare state.

The Welsh Assembly was established in 1999 under the Government of Wales Act 1998, following a slim win on the Yes vote in the referendum of 1997. Now, following the referendum in 2011, the affirmation of self-government has been fully endorsed by a positive vote; the Welsh Government's powers have been extended as has its tangible presence in the everyday lives of the people of Wales. It has £16 billion to spend flexibly in ways that reflect Welsh priorities and needs and crucially, given its brief, on largely social policy concerns. There is little doubt that differences in policy context across the UK will widen and as social welfare practitioners the responsibility will grow to engage proactively with this policy development and change.

This text arose from the need for students, practitioners and other policy actors in Wales to be attentive to and involved in the creation of indigenous policy making and shaping. In this second edition, leading academics and practitioners in the field outline and review the policy framework and political philosophy and values underpinning core areas of welfare practice. They reflect on over a decade of devolution, tracking and assessing developments. What is evident is that devolution represents an evolutionary process in terms of policy development, welfare practices and public engagement. The contributors bring considerable knowledge and experience from their own first-hand experience of practice in the Welsh context and/or work with the Welsh Government. They draw extensively on research and literature from Wales in compiling their chapters and aim to highlight in an accessible way the emerging policy framework shaping practice.

An overriding theme of the contributions is the Welsh Government's ambition to develop a distinctive Welsh approach to policy making – a 'Welsh way' – which reflects particular values, principles and a style of engagement with service users. The chapters are linked by their shared concern with the Government's stated aim to produce a fairer society. Chapter after chapter focuses on the potential of the Welsh Government to translate into concrete practices its ambition to achieve social justice for all. The chapters outline the policy framework and the political philosophy and values underpinning them.

The book is divided into three parts. In Part 1, three chapters set the scene for the book by discussing key aspects of the devolution project. In Chapter 1, I set out to critically explore some of the key assumptions of devolution, arguing that as much as it is a *hurrah* word for many of us, there is a need to move beyond attention to policy differentiation to ask questions about discourses and ideologies that are constructed and mobilised in this process of change and that shape how social problems are identified, articulated and selected for policy attention. As students of social policy and practitioners, we need to develop a healthy scepticism to political projects in order to question their synergy or otherwise with the core values of the social welfare professions. In Chapter 2, Drakeford and Gregory take us further by outlining the development of the Welsh Assembly, its role and remit and indicating the core values and approach that the Welsh Government has taken. Sullivan and Drakeford's concern in Chapter 3 is to indicate, using the example of health policy, the nature, extent and implications of policy divergence. In Part 2, key themes fundamental to service delivery in Wales – the Welsh language, poverty, rurality and equalities – are explored and their implications for practice are signalled. Finally, Part 3 in a broad sweep looks at children's, youth and adult policy, highlighting the distinctive nature of the policy framework in Wales. The book concludes by looking at the aspirations of the Welsh Government to create a coherent and empowering framework for social work practice. Evaluating the outcomes of policy is a complex enterprise but 10 years on, some evidence is emerging that can be reviewed and assessed. This makes it even more compelling to engage social welfare practitioners' awareness of the policy framework and their potential to evaluate and compare policy directions.

It has often been said that devolution is not to be understood as a single event marked by a transfer of powers from Westminster to Cardiff, but as an ongoing and dynamic process. There is little doubt that devolution is a contested terrain, a terrain in which we as writers and academics – but also as citizens of Wales – doubtless have a vested interest. It is easy to emphasise the gains and overlook those nagging questions and puzzles that the devolution project brings in its wake: concerns that it may act to undermine universal or minimum standards across the UK and create territorial inequalities; concerns that it may operate as a countervailing force to solidarity and social cohesion as ethnic-nationalism gains a greater foothold; and concerns that in the search for a coherent unity branded as a 'Welsh way' or a 'Welsh social policy', new and old exclusions may be compounded. There is also the danger that we may become overly introspective rather than outward looking and comparative in our policy development. Thus, the call is for welfare professionals to critically engage with the devolutionary process based on an understanding of the policy framework and policy developments. This book has evident appeal to students of social work, to the nursing profession, those engaged in health and social care roles, youth and community studies and childcare as well as students of social policy, sociology and applied social sciences – all of which have a major contribution to make to the process that is devolution.

Charlotte Williams
September 2011

Section One

Understanding Devolution

Chapter 1

What is Wales?

Charlotte Williams

Introduction

The question of the distinctiveness of Wales has engaged historians and social scientists alike. In his compelling account of the development of the nation, *When was Wales?*, the eminent historian Gwyn Alf Williams provides us with the thought-provoking assertion that 'Wales is an artefact which the Welsh produce' (Williams, 1991, p 304). This statement invites us to understand Wales as a dynamic entity that is constantly in the process of change and remaking. Since devolution, this process of remaking Wales as somehow distinct from other places has taken on a new urgency. Pragmatic questions of how to respond appropriately to the specific needs of the Welsh population now engage policy makers as does fostering the renewed sense of national identity. In this sense we are experiencing a Wales that is in the process of being remade or, in sociological terms, being *socially constructed*. In speech after speech on the opening of devolution, the-then First Minister, Rhodri Morgan, appealed for 'doing things the Welsh way' (Morgan, 2002) and the idea of 'Welsh solutions for Welsh problems' was established as the mantra of the policy makers to come. In over a decade of devolution we have seen these types of ideas crystallise and gain widespread support. The 2011 referendum strengthened the institutions of devolution in terms not only of its powers but also its relationship with the people of Wales. The powerful mandate provided by the popular vote in the referendum confirmed devolution as not only here to stay but also a firmly accepted part of the life of the nation.

These kinds of ideas are not, however, without contention, and beg questions such as:

- What are Welsh problems?
- Are they somehow distinct from problems elsewhere?
- What is special – or indeed different – about Wales?
- What is Wales?

The devolution project begins with the assumption of Wales as a unique entity that displays its own particular characteristics and its own particular needs that require specific responses. It is this type of assumption that this chapter seeks to critically explore. It opens by considering the idea of Wales as socially constructed; it explores the arguments related to the notion of policy divergence and distinctiveness; and it concludes by challenging some of the central assumptions of the devolution project.

Constructing a 'Better Wales'?

In his book, *Making Sense of Wales*, Day (2002) offers a contemporary questioning of the idea of Wales, suggesting that it is a construction based on competing understandings, myths and visions about what is and what is not Wales, and who is and who is not Welsh. He reviews a variety of stereotypical images of Wales and Welshness that vie with each other in sociological and popular imaginings: depictions such as the Celtic imagery of the tourist brochures and the craft artefacts that hark back to an ancient Celtic ancestry; images of a traditional industrial working-class Wales, best symbolised by photographs of the Welsh coal miner; or images of a scenic rural Wales based on ideas about the intimacy and cohesion of small-scale communities (Day, 2002). In doing so, Day is problematising the assumption of any comforting consensus on what Wales might be, or indeed any standardised view of what we would like Wales to be. He is suggesting that there are 'multiple realities, intelligible from differing standpoints and anchored in different sets of social experiences and positions' (2002, p 11). Accordingly, different perspectives and experiences of Wales are mediated through factors of class, place and location, gender, ethnicity or age, as well as other structured social locations. There are, indeed, many ways of viewing Wales, which suggests a complex heterogeneity of positionings rather than any singular reality. Day takes this further, however, by suggesting that these images or constructions have significant import for the ways in which social problems are identified and become the subject of research or not.

Social policy is not divorced from these constructions. How social problems are identified and defined, whether they are responded to and by whom, are not neutral activities but suffused with values that produce competing and contrasting explanations as to what should or should not be done. In any analysis of social policies, it is possible to identify value judgements and specific visions about what steps might be taken to produce a better society. For example, the early strategy document of the Welsh Assembly Government, *Wales: A better country* (WAG, 2003, p 1), set out a vision of 'a fairer, more prosperous, healthier and better educated country, rooted in our commitment to social justice'. More recently, *Fulfilled Lives, Supportive Communities* (WAG, 2007, p 6) is referred to as 'a major programme of change, which will contribute to a *better* Wales and to improving the lives of the people who live here' and envisions services at that local level that are:

- strong, accessible and accountable;
- focused on citizen, family and community needs;
- focused on social inclusion and the rights of individuals;
- concerned with good outcomes;

- delivered in a joined-up, flexible and efficient way to consistently high standards and in partnership with service users.

It is also possible, when considering what policies emerge, to identify a variety of stakeholders and interest groups vying in the public arena to set the agenda on policy priorities, some of which are more powerful than others in shaping outcomes. It is important, therefore, to consider the way in which some ideas about what Wales is, what it should be and what issues require intervention, come to prevail while others do not. As key actors, social welfare professionals are implicated in this process – and increasingly so as opportunities for their direct involvement in policy-making have been opened up in an unprecedented manner by devolution (see Chapter 11, this volume).

Since devolution there has been a tendency to contrast an old Wales with a vision of a new and better Wales and to attempt to define some of the essence of traditional Welsh society and Welsh characteristics on which to develop the devolution project. *Wales: A Better Country* (WAG, 2003, p 3), for example, offers some references to those characteristics considered to be part of the distinctive nature, needs and values of Wales. Wales is regarded as having a unique identity as a small nation and factors such as 'our strong sense of local community', 'our heritage', 'our creative industries and artists' and its own particular language and culture are highlighted (2003, p 3). The report flags the ambition to strengthen Wales' cultural identity and create 'a truly bilingual nation' (2003, p 3).

These ideas about Welsh community life, the national character and national values are all important in fostering a sense of collective spirit and social solidarity. They are also, of course, contestable and relate to the specific mobilisation of sets of ideas that help shape everyday views and promote particular discourses of what a new or better Wales might be. The idea of making and remaking a Wales that appeals to the populace is central to the politicians' task. Delineating a Wales as a point of pragmatic policy interventions is one thing, but this clearly is not the whole story in any discussion of a nation as old as this. Wales is not simply a region; it did not simply come into existence for want of administrative convenience or pragmatic policy making. It is also a product of a history, a culture and a language. It has a collective sense of self as a small nation that is both centuries old and at the same time the product of contemporary re-formation. As citizens and key definers of policy and practice, social welfare professionals in Wales are actively engaged in this process of remaking.

Devolution and divergence

The story of contrasts and comparisons is growing as devolution matures and each version carries its own selection of supporting evidence. Some commentators argue that the degree of divergence in social policy since devolution has been significant (Chaney and Drakeford, 2004; Greer, 2005; Chaney, 2009) while others would suggest that discontinuity with the past is not as striking as it may first seem (Rees, 2005).

It is possible to suggest three key ways of thinking about Welsh distinctiveness post devolution, all of which are intimately interrelated:

- policy divergence as a pragmatic response to specific challenges in the Welsh context;
- policy divergence as based on a particular ideological set of beliefs about welfare delivery and citizenship that are somehow different and reflect 'a Welsh way' of doing things;
- policy divergence as an expression of self-determination based on ideas about national distinctiveness and national identity.

As already mentioned, these perspectives are not distinct but interrelated and together provide the underpinning rationale for devolution. Devolution was secured on the basis of claims to more accountable, responsive and inclusive policy making but it also reflected in part a longstanding expression of ethno-nationalism. On a purely pragmatic level, the socio-economic profile of Wales suggests that there are particular needs and challenges in the Welsh context and these demand specific kinds of responses. It may also be that Wales is different because the values, ideas and beliefs about how we should relate to one another, how we should relate to the state and what we view as a good society, are somehow distinct from other parts of the United Kingdom (UK). In addition, the desire to be self-governing and assert Wales as a distinct national entity and somehow experientially different acted a driver for change. These types of factors combine to produce support for policies, institutions and practices that diverge from elsewhere in the UK.

Welsh distinctiveness

The demographic profile of Wales presents some very particular challenges for social policy. Historically, the absence of data specifically disaggregated for Wales limited the production of evidence to guide policy. So comprehensive was social policy analysis based on 'England and Wales' as the organising principle that an immediate challenge for Welsh Government was the development of a rigorous evidence base. This situation has significantly improved in over a decade of devolution with the Welsh Government providing detailed and comprehensive statistics in a number of policy fields (see National Statistics Online).

Wales is a small nation and it is also very diverse. These divisions are often described in rather stark terms such as north/south, urban/rural, Welsh speaking/non-Welsh speaking, Anglicised/non-Anglicised, white people/black people and so on. This typification, however, misses the detail of complex differentiation across Wales both within and across its counties and even within wards. The population of Wales in mid-2008 was estimated at 2,993,000. The population is expected to increase by 11% to 3.3 million by 2031, having crossed the 3 million mark prior to the 2011 census (www.clickonwales.org). The rural population counts for one third of this total. More than 60% of the Welsh population are resident in the industrial belt of South Wales, between Chepstow and Swansea, with 694,626 (23.2%) in the three coastal cities of Cardiff, Newport and Swansea. Almost a quarter of the population are Welsh speaking. Speaking Welsh and indeed identifying as Welsh even without being able to speak the language forms an important interface with issues of welfare (see Chapter 4, this volume) as do the more generalised and perhaps nebulous notions of 'ways of life' or 'Welsh culture' (Mooney and Williams, 2006).

Wales is also a multicultural society. Traditionally, it has been difficult to assert that issues of race, ethnicity and religion demand a specific response in the Welsh context. Ethnic diversity in Wales is a factor that has been slow to be acknowledged in public policy terms, hampered by the assumption that relatively low numbers means relatively low need (Williams et al., 2002). The majority of people living in Wales (almost 97%) describe their ethnicity as White, with the remaining 3% being from a broad mix of ethnic backgrounds including those of mixed ethnicities. The largest non-White ethnic group in Wales is the Asian grouping, although this comprises just 1.2% of the Welsh population (Annual Population Survey 2008/09).

There are a number of factors that single out the experiences of the minority ethnic population in Wales from the picture elsewhere in the UK, perhaps the most important feature being the degree of dispersal, which has meant that few concentrated communities exist outside the crescent of cities in the south. Cardiff has the largest percentage of minority ethnic people, with 11.8%, followed by Newport (7.0%) and Swansea (4.5%) (WAG, 2006a). Yet there is no authority in Wales that does not have a minority ethnic presence.

Since the accession of the Eastern European countries to the European Union in 2004 (the so-called 'A8' countries), Wales experienced a major demographic change. Poles, Lithuanians, Estonians and others became residents and workers in many towns and cities across Wales and in particular the more rural areas (Wales Rural Observatory, 2006; Cam, 2007). Areas in Wales such as Llanelli and Wrexham had not previously experienced such large-scale migration or the concomitant pressures placed on local services, for example in terms of housing requirements or extra assistance needed for migrant children in schools. It is apparent, however, that the early wave of migration from the A8 countries has slowed and generally subsided as many migrants only stayed for short periods.

It may well be that communities are no more diverse than ever they were (Day, 2002) but the diversity is now becoming more visible and complex and raising new issues for public services. Religious diversity is in the mix since its first enumeration in the 2001 Census which remains the most reliable source of information to date. Beyond the more debated issue of faith schools, faith-based community and welfare organisations play a key role in service delivery and individual preferences in care-giving and care-receiving practices can be shaped by religious affiliation. Nearly three-quarters of the Welsh population (74%) describe their religion as Christian. After Christianity, Islam is the next most common faith. Cardiff has the largest Muslim population (4% of the local population) but in the country overall, Muslims account for 1% of the population (clickonwales.org). Most Muslims are from Asian backgrounds, although at the last census nearly 3,000 White people also describe themselves as Muslim. Among other faiths, the next largest groups are Hindus and White Buddhists followed by White Jews and Indian Sikhs (clickonwales.org). The rapidly changing profile of many communities, and in particular rural communities in Wales, presents a number of challenges to welfare practitioners, not least because of the complex patterning of diversity relating to ethnicity, gender, age, nationality and class among other lines of difference.

The Welsh population has been steadily growing, increasing by some 300,000 people since the post-war period, and it is forecast to grow slowly but surely over the next 20 years. These changes in population size relate to changes in the ratio of births to deaths and to flows of inward and outward migration. In common with most European countries, Wales has an ageing population, and it has the highest proportion of people of pensionable age for any part of the UK (17.3%). Currently, 44% of the Welsh population are over 45. In the 10 years between the 1991 Census and the 2001 Census, the number of people over working age increased by nearly 2% while the number of children under 16 decreased by 0.5%. In the first two decades of the 2000s, the number of older people in Wales is projected to increase both in absolute terms and as a proportion of the overall population. By 2018, the number of children is projected to fall by around 6.0% while the number of people aged 85 and over is projected to increase by 47.4%, from 60,000 in 2004 to 88,000 in 2018. The number of people aged 65 to 84 is projected to increase by 27% (WAG, 2007). By 2021, one in three households in Wales will include a person aged over 65 and over 50,000 households will be headed by a person aged 85 or older. In some areas of Wales, such as Conwy Unitary Authority, over a quarter of the population are now of pensionable age. This changing population structure has far-reaching implications for policy making, not least in relation to the 'dependency ratio' – the proportion of people over pensionable age to those under the age of 16. Falling fertility rates to below the level for the population to replace itself and increases in life expectancy will have important implications for the demand for social care services in Wales.

Many of those of pensionable age live alone. Wales has a high number of one person-households (29%) and just over half of those living alone are pensioners (15%). The tendency to live alone increases sharply with age. Almost half of those aged over 75 live alone. Over 20% of pensioners live in poverty (100,000) and poverty is especially high among single pensioners (JRF, 2007). The implications of this profile for health and social services are perhaps obvious (see Chapter 10, this volume, on social services for adults) particularly in relation to the care and support of older people and their well-being. Expectations of social services are constantly raised as people's rights awareness grows;

as more careful assessment of services highlights gaps in delivery, or the need for more sophisticated responses; and as awareness of new social problems and needs is increased. The number of people in Wales receiving a social service grew by 50% (from 100,000 to 150,000) between 2001 and 2005. Alongside publicly provided services, an army of some 340,000 people provide unpaid care for family members, one in five of the population and including some 7,000 children (WAG, 2007). The Welsh Assembly Government report *Fulfilled Lives, Supportive Communities* (WAG, 2007, p 12) acknowledges that these demographic trends will mean a number of vulnerable adults requiring increased support from social services, but it also suggests that the scale of increased demand could be reduced if services could be changed to reduce dependency and work more effectively.

Another issue related to the dependency ratio that has attracted somewhat contentious debate in Wales, and has been subject to competing constructions, is the problem of migration. By far the biggest migration issue facing Wales is the out-migration of young people and yet, in the popular mind, in-migration and the challenge this poses to small Welsh-speaking communities across Wales is perceived as the problem While in-migration from the rest of the UK has accounted for 85% of total migration into Wales, migration to the rest of the UK has accounted for 87% of total migration from Wales, the largest outward migration being in the 16–24 age group (www.clickonwales.org). Rural depopulation (see Chapter 6, this volume) poses challenges for policy makers in responding to issues of social integration and welfare provision.

One of the most critical issues in the demand for social services relates to the poor health of the nation. In Wales, 23% of all adults report having a limiting lifelong illness compared with 18% in England and 20% in both Scotland and Northern Ireland (WAG, 2007). Trends indicate that by 2018 there will be an increase of 12% in the number of adults with at least one chronic condition. Black and minority ethnic groups are particularly prone to ill-health: the evidence that exists shows that they tend to have poorer health and poorer access to care than the majority population (Winkler, 2009).

Welsh distinctiveness is also marked out by the high number of disabled people in the population in comparison with elsewhere in the UK, with 22% (one in five) of the working-age population having a work-limiting disability (Davies et al, 2011). Deep and persistent economic inequalities persist for this sector of the Welsh population. Jones (2011) pertinently points out the additional indirect economic effects that disabled people experience by virtue of the fact that they may require care from family and friends who themselves have to give up paid work or work less hours so that they can provide the care. She suggests that this contributes to a higher incidence of poverty in disabled households and interestingly notes the comparative high levels of informal care provision in Wales compared with the UK average (Jones, 2011, p 165).

Perhaps the state of the nation's health is a factor that has attracted the most headline news of all the demographic features of Wales. The legacy of heavy industries and the facts of poverty combine to produce some of the poorest regions in the whole of Europe, with two-thirds of the Welsh population covered by Objective One status for the period 2001 to 2006 and with all areas of Wales covered by European Structural Funding. Seventeen (almost 10%) of the poorest areas of the UK are in Wales. The low level of earnings in Wales contributes directly to the low Gross Domestic Product (GDP) and hence the need for European Structural Fund help (Brooksbank, 2006). Wales remains a low-pay economy. The historical productivity gap relative to the UK is continuing to widen (Davies et al, 2011). This impacts directly on employment opportunities for individuals and on rates of pay. The proportion of employees who are low paid is higher in Wales than in the UK as a whole. Thirteen per cent of male full-time workers and 18% of women full-time workers are in the low-paid sector, about a quarter higher than the figures for England (JRF, 2007). The issue of in-work poverty is often masked by a focus on unemployment figures. The first systematic examination of economic inequality in Wales came with the publication of *An Anatomy of Economic Inequality in Wales* (Davies et al, 2011). This report indicates that approximately one-fifth of the Welsh population live in poverty and that being in work does not necessarily provide a route out of poverty, with 13% in-work households in Wales living in poverty. The Joseph Rowntree Foundation report *Monitoring Poverty and Social Exclusion in Wales* (JRF, 2009) notes unemployment as a major risk factor for low income in Wales, that risk rising from 5% for a full-working family to over 60% for a workless one. However, even when another adult in the family remains in work, the family's risk of low income still rises to 25%. Even before the current recession, the problem of low income was rising sharply to the extent that half of the previous improvement in child poverty had already been lost (see Chapter 5, this volume).

What this overview of the demographic profile of Wales reveals is a relatively poor country characterised by visual contrasts and detailed differentiation by class, colour, age and other social locations as well as by differences in locality and identities. Deep patterns of inequality are also evident, which are proving resistant to change (Chapter 6, this volume). The gap in the life chances of particular groups means that social justice concerns would inevitably come high on the agenda of the Welsh Government keen to make real citizenship rights. These issues present core challenges for social services in Wales, a sector where concerns about variable standards of delivery, increased expectations and gaps in the skills mix and size of the social care workforce have prompted a comprehensive modernisation strategy (see Chapter 11, this volume).

A Welsh way?

It is now not too difficult to accumulate a body of evidence to demonstrate a measure of policy divergence in Wales from elsewhere in the UK. The First Minister, Carwyn Jones, in his speech to the Labour Party conference in 2010 stated:

[W]e do it differently in Wales. We do it our way – and we make no apologies for that. In Wales, we are proud to remain true to our principles on such things as comprehensive education. We are proud that the NHS [National Health Service] in Wales is a market-free NHS. We are proud that we have free prescriptions for all. We are proud that we have free hospital parking. We are proud that we will keep our free bus travel for our pensioners. We are proud that during the darkest days of the recession, we intervened with wage subsidies for those companies in greatest danger to keep 10,000 workers in jobs. Workers who remain employed to this day. These are the things we do differently. These are things that make us proud. (Jones, 2010)

To this list there are now numerous other distinctive policy directives, including the Welsh Baccalaureat, the absence of school league tables, and Assembly Learning Grants (see Chaney, 2009). In addition to these policy areas, the Welsh Assembly Government has also taken a number of actions that signal differences of approach, such as reforms of public services to achieve better coordination and cooperative working (see Chapter 2, this volume), a rejection of the managerialist performance culture imposed on local government, a greater emphasis on collaboration and the establishment of new-style regulatory bodies such as the Care Standards Inspectorate for Wales.

These apparent differences in policy, however, belie more complex questions about the nature of change. Adams and Robinson (2002, p 199) refine the blanket assumption of distinctiveness by offering a framework for considering divergence. Their argument is that divergence 'is not all of the same character' and suggest a useful way of considering differences along five trajectories: 'Values, Structures, Decision-Making, Changes to Policy, Outcomes'. This framework invites a consideration of different values and ideologies that may exist between the different nations of the UK. It raises questions about the nature of change to administrative structures, to the institutional framework and to the processes of decision making. It asks: 'What new policies are emerging and is devolution producing different outcomes in various policy areas?'. This leads us to more detailed questions about the nature of the divergence and its implications in terms of a distinctively Welsh approach.

The issue of values and ideology is one taken up by Drakeford and Gregory (Chapter 2, this volume) and is a theme that permeates many chapters of this book. It is often suggested that Wales, like Scotland, has adopted a more social-democratic style of politics that significantly marks it out from the strategies and approach of New Labour. It is argued that this reflects a strong Welsh social-democratic tradition, which is collectivist and communitarian, upholding strong support for the public sector as opposed to English neoliberal modernism. As such, the claims are made that Welsh politics represents a defence of the traditional welfare state and it is the English who are diverging from it. This positioning was clearly articulated by Rhodri Morgan, First Minister between 2000 and 2009 as follows:

> *The actions of the Welsh Assembly Government clearly owe more to the traditions of Titmuss, Tawney, Beveridge and Bevan rather than those of Hayek and Friedman. The creation of a new set of citizenship rights has been a key theme in the first four years of the Assembly – and a set of rights which are as far as possible: free at point of use, universal and unconditional.* (Morgan, 2002)

This statement was made in what became known as the 'Clear Red Water' speech, delivered just prior to the Assembly elections for the second term of office. This speech has become probably the most cited reference point for the value base underpinning the direction of Welsh social policy. The speech sets out what Morgan refers to as 'clear red water' between policy in Wales and policy emanating from Westminster. In this speech, Rhodri Morgan described himself as 'a socialist of the Welsh stripe' and constructed his argument around what he identified as three particular 'ideological fault lines' in approaches to social welfare: universalism versus means testing, equality versus choice and equality of opportunity versus 'the fundamentally socialist aim of equality of outcome' (see Chapter 2, this volume):

> *Our commitment to equality leads directly to a model of the relationship between the government and the individual which regards the individual as citizen rather than consumer. Approaches which prioritise choice over equality of outcome rest, in the end, upon a market approach to public services, in which individual economic actors pursue their own best interests with little regard for wider considerations.* (Morgan, 2002)

Major policy strategies such as *Making Connections* (WAG, 2006b) and *Fulfilled Lives, Supportive Communities* (WAG, 2007) open with vision statements reiterating this commitment to a model of public service delivery that differs markedly from the market-oriented approach of Westminster. The language of policy papers in Wales stresses citizenship, equality of outcome, universality and collaboration rather than competition and consumerism.

There are, however, a number of caveats worth considering in relation to this forthright positioning. While there are many examples to support the universalist direction, there are also many examples of the limitations of universalism. Assembly Learning Grants are means tested, Communities First (the anti-poverty strategy) is geographically determined (disadvantaged areas) and some would argue that initiatives such as free swimming and free breakfasts for primary school children are hardly revolutionary. Wyn Jones and Scully (2004) have pointed to the fact that the Clear Red Water speech stopped short of discussing redistribution as one of the fundamental pillars of the traditional welfare state. In addition, universal policies cost money and there are obvious limitations posed by the Welsh funding formulae, as the anomaly of 'Scandinavian-style' politics on an 'Anglo-

American tax funding base' will be difficult to square (see *Agenda*, 2007). Holtham (2010) sets out what he calls the 'five fallacies of devolution', arguing that legislative devolution without tax-raising powers will continue to represent a limiting factor on the accountability and responsibility of Welsh politicians. The issue of reform of the Welsh block grant and moves to greater fiscal autonomy is likely to come to the fore in political debate now that devolution has come of age. Notwithstanding this, the general ideological orientation is marked and the collectivist *aspirations* are a core feature of social policy-speak in Wales.

This raises a second issue. The coherence of this ideological differentiation must also be open to debate. The new politics of Wales is characterised by a much more open and pluralist decision-making process, with a shift from government, top-down policy making to governance based on networks of policy making (see Chapter 2, this volume). In this respect, it is difficult to see how one *big* idea can hold sway without an emphasis on the top-down, bureaucratic and centralised social-democratic stateism that became the focus of such criticism in old-style welfare politics. Perhaps more telling is what might appear to be a mismatch between this political orientation and public sentiment. The basis of the ideological rift argument rests on the assumption of a particular version of the Welsh radical tradition, which may not be borne out in reality. The idea that the people of Wales have a more progressive or more left-wing set of values than those in England is clearly unfounded (Jeffery, 2005). In their empirical test of this sentiment, Wyn Jones and Scully (2004) found little evidence to suggest widespread public radicalism underpinning the policy agenda committed to 'Clear Red Water' and concluded that the Welsh might not be as radical as they like to believe. It appears that the Welsh or indeed the Scots are not more left-wing than the English; indeed, the evidence suggests the Welsh as the least left-wing (Jeffery, 2005).

Others have suggested that what is more apparent in devolved politics is a change of *style* rather than a clear shift away from the overarching neoliberal agenda of Westminster politics (Mooney et al, 2006). Welsh Labour has continued to fight shy of the market-driven solutions favoured by central government but it remains important to critically examine whether many policies of the Welsh Government more truly reflect pragmatic responses rather than a distinct *Welsh way*. Laffin (2004) has suggested that Welsh policy overall is much more willing to demonstrate ideological divergence than the Scottish who he argues are moving closer to Westminster policy. The ability to hold a steady course on the ideological bent of policy in Wales has been assured by three successive Labour administrations and may now be more tested with coalition governments in both Wales and Westminster (see Chapter 3, this volume, for an example of this in relation health policy). In the new context of extended powers for the Welsh Government, however, we may well witness an increasingly forthright positioning on a distinctive *Welsh way* of doing social policy.

Structures, decisions and outcomes

Other changes are everywhere in evidence. In terms of structures, while there has been a radical departure from the pre-devolution situation, it is important to note that Wales has had a degree of administrative devolution for some time. Early in the development of the Welsh language policy in education, for example, Wales-specific structures were set up to oversee Welsh education practice. A Secretary of State for Wales was established in the 1950s and in 1964 the Welsh Office was set up to manage Welsh affairs. Unlike Scotland, however, Wales did not have its own legal system and areas such as social work were not independent of the English system in the way that they were in Scotland. Devolution has now brought considerable changes to institutions in Wales even beyond the formal departmental structure of the Welsh Government itself.

Wales has a relatively small institutional infrastructure. For example, there are just 22 local authorities, seven health boards, 220 secondary schools, four police forces and six regional areas as identified by *People, Places, Futures: The Wales Spatial Plan* (WAG, 2004). These six distinctive regions provide the framework in which the Welsh Government delivers on its vision for the economic, social and environmental development of Wales. A regional approach to collaboration between the 22 local authorities is mooted in 2011 and it is likely that while major restructuring of local government is resisted, greater efforts will be made by the Welsh Government to ensure that economies of scale are produced by cross-authority collaborative working. This follows the trend in health where 22 local health boards were replaced in 2007 by seven combined organisations, bringing together the former Local Health Boards and Trusts into single bodies. Proximity and familiarity characterise inter-agency working within such a small country. There are close and informal relationships between many public agencies and the extent of collaboration is being formally encouraged by the Welsh Government initiative *Making Connections* (WAG, 2006b).

The Welsh Government has also been instrumental in creating and funding a number of new bodies with a Wales-wide remit, particularly consultative bodies such as the Interfaith Council, the All Wales Ethnic Minority Association and the Wales Women's Coalition. In 2006, it disbanded the so-called quangos or associated public bodies such as the Children and Family Court Advisory and Support Service (CAFCASS) and the Welsh Development Agency, bringing them within the Welsh Government structure. In 2007, it opened offices in North Wales. Many of these developments are aimed at making decision making more transparent and bringing decisions closer to the people. In turn, a significant degree of institutional realignment with the Welsh border has occurred in the voluntary and private sectors. Organisations previously managed from England restructured their administrative arrangements and functioning to reflect a focus on Wales as a distinct entity. Organisations such as Citizen's Advice Wales, Stonewall Cymru, Barnardo's and others manage their affairs on a distinctly Welsh basis.

In terms of decision making, much has been made of the Welsh Government's ambitions towards greater inclusivity and a new, more open style of politics (Chaney et al, 2001; Chaney, 2009). A number of innovations indicate the shift towards governance (discussed in Chapter 2, this volume), including the creation of consultative bodies, civic forums, public consultations, the use of statutory partnerships with the voluntary sector and the deliberative nature of the committee system of the Welsh Government which, has a greater degree of power than its counterpart in Westminster (Chaney, 2009). A wide range of stakeholder groups from the voluntary sector and from business are actively invited into the policy-making process in a way not possible prior to devolution (Day, 2006). Task and finish groups have been used during the life of the Welsh Government such as the Older People's Strategy Task Group (2003) and the Child Poverty Task Group (2005), which were made up of a range of professionals and included lay experts. The ability of the Welsh Government to engage successfully with citizens is seen as something of a triumph (Chaney, 2009).

Has devolved government paid dividends? Outcomes are inevitably a more tricky issue to assess. Outcomes such as lower waiting lists, lower rates of morbidity and greater social inclusion are notoriously difficult to attribute to specific public policy measures. No assessment can be made here about particular policy fields, although later chapters provide some evaluation of developments. The point should be made, however, that it takes a number of years for policy changes to realise into measurable outputs and outcomes for people in Wales. For example, *From Vision to Action: The report of the Independent Commission on Social Services in Wales* (Independent Commission on Social Services in Wales, 2010) argues that progress has been slow in realising the transformational change required to realise the aspirations of the strategy outlined in *Fulfilled Lives, Supportive Communities* (WAG, 2007); service standards are seen as too uneven and the report recommends among other things better prioritisation and more high-profile leadership to effect change (see Chapter 11, this volume). What is clear is that in terms of policy prioritisation, Wales has a highly permissive divergence, achieved by block grant funding rather than ring-fenced funding. It has £16 billion to spend and can use its money as it sees fit, reflecting its own priorities, approaches and styles of working.

The focus on divergences in policy alone is to take too simplistic an approach to thinking about policy in post-devolution Wales. What is more likely is that we are experiencing a complex patterning of both divergence and convergence of policies across the nations of the UK. As much as we can identify divergences, there are equally a number of forces of convergence shaping policy preferences. Public opinion is an important factor in limiting policy divergence as expectations of a measure of common standards across the UK shape priorities (Jeffery, 2005). An example of this might be concerns over health service waiting lists for treatments such as breast cancer or hip replacements, which often make headline news. The interdependency between the labour market in the UK and its largely common tax regime is another factor prompting convergence. The portability of qualifications and their relevance across the UK and beyond is yet another example. And the amount of policy transfer and policy learning between areas of the UK means roughly common approaches to common issues, for example in child poverty strategies (Lohde, 2005). Convergence in policy strategies can be a good thing as policy experimentation in one part of the UK can provide important lessons that can be transferred elsewhere. It may also allow for strategic responses to issues that cut across national boundaries, for example in responding to the needs of asylum seekers or migrant workers, or it may standardise good practices, for example in relation to equalities.

A contested devolution

There is little doubt that devolution has brought considerable change to policy and practices across the UK. It heralds a greater democratisation in welfare delivery, with a plethora of new points of engagement for ordinary citizens in shaping policies that impact on their well-being. Novel approaches to ensuring citizenship rights are being tested out in attempts to produce a much more deliberative democracy. It has provided an arena for policy experimentation and policy learning and perhaps above all an increased sense of ownership on the part of the Welsh public in the running of their own affairs.

Gradually, the public in Wales have warmed to the idea of self-governance and the Yes vote in the 2011 referendum must stand out as a historic turning point in devolved government being recognised as part of the settled will of the people of Wales. There are, however, a number of critical lines of inquiry to be pursued in thinking through the devolution project. This is not to suggest that devolution is a 'good thing' or a 'bad thing' but to offer it as a dynamic process, one that is evolving and one that is worthy of critical reflection.

As has been suggested, the idea of policy divergence is central to the devolution project. The notion that particular circumstances require particular policy responses is a given and by implication the suggestion that policy making is somehow new and novel. This assumption is, as the starting point, itself contestable. I have indicated how a degree of administrative devolution was present prior to constitutional change. Several policy commentators have identified deep continuities with past policy-making or influences that stretch forward to ensure that specific policy paths are maintained such that policy innovation might not be as great as it seems. Rees (2005, p 34) refers to 'assumptive worlds' and 'conventional ways of thinking' that shape debates on educational policy and relationships between the Welsh Office and institutions in Wales that have lain down particular 'policy pathways' that will be hard to shake off. Greer (2005) has suggested the important influence of established policy communities on the nature of contemporary restructuring of the health service and Wincott (2005) notes the history of abuse scandals in Wales, which have led to much more rights-based approaches to early childhood education and care policies for children. These all suggest a measurable degree of continuity in the practices of policy making that shape and constrain policy development.

When thinking about policy developments, therefore, it is useful to consider the extent to which they are derivative of what has gone before rather than radically distinctive or innovative. Perhaps more importantly, in the endeavour to construct a sense of a new and better Wales, there is a tendency to obscure continuities with the past that reflect deep inequalities, divisions and polarities. In the search for what Rhodri Morgan (2002) called the 'powerful glue of social solidarity', it is easy to overlook what has long been recognised: that social policies can structure, sustain and even promote social inequalities.

Devolution has become a *hurrah* word for many of us in Wales and there is indeed much to be proud of. However, there are a number of issues that devolution raises in relation to social justice that must be of critical concern to welfare practitioners. Jeffery (2002), for example, raises the point that devolution could be seen to lead to the lowering of standards across the UK as opposed to pushing them up. Rather than the four-nation UK reflecting 'virtuous circles' of policy making, policy learning and policy transfer, one view suggests that a fragmented UK might slide into a 'race to the bottom' where restraints and cutbacks in one part of the UK become the justification for constraints and cutbacks in another (Adams and Robinson, 2002, p 212). There is concern that policy divergence may lead to different standards of public services across the UK and serve to undermine citizenship rights and a sense of solidarity fostered by UK-wide institutions such as the NHS or lead to different models of social citizenship (Greer and Matzke, 2009). In this sense, some would argue that devolution undermines the idea of the British welfare state and the principles on which it is based. Further, it has been pointed out that devolution raises a number of concerns about widening economic disparities, territorial inequalities and two-tier systems across the UK. Is it reasonable to expect free prescriptions in Wrexham but not Warrington, which are just 35 miles apart, or to have long-term support for older people in one area of the UK and not another? For these reasons, the question must arise: is devolution as progressive as might be suggested in social justice terms?

This important question is not easily answered in the absence of any constitutionally agreed set of common standards or formal minimum standards set by the UK centre, or indeed any set of institutions charged with 'holding the ring'. There is arguably an important role for Westminster politics in maintaining the balance between diversity and equality, between the demands of subsidiarity, autonomy and particularity on the one hand and solidarity, standardisation and universalism on the other. These, of course, are longstanding tensions in welfare delivery but ones that are now being felt more acutely under devolution.

Overall, there has been no real evidence of resistance and conflict between the centre and the devolved nations that could be seen to threaten the solidarity of the UK. Scotland is flexing its muscles and there is much policy-speak of independence. In Wales, the effect of divergence is more benign. While these tensions may become more evident if the dominance of Labour administrations across the nations is weakened, as in the recent change of government in Scotland and as the powers for indigenous policy making increase as in Wales, it is also clear that devolution was never intended to produce different sets of citizenship rights across the UK and a number of mechanisms, including most importantly the electorate themselves, operate as a countervailing force.

Perhaps the focus on policy divergence itself should be held up for critical inspection. While the norm has been to compare things happening in Wales with things happening in England, this centre–periphery axis is but one dimension for comparison. England is just one of four constituent parts of the UK and not the 'norm' against which all are contrasted. Wales can now look to international influences in the development of its policies. There are also points of comparison to be made within as well as across the nations. Wales' longstanding concerns about a north–south divide have come to the fore post devolution and, in response to this, Chaney and Drakeford have argued that devolution is not simply about a transfer of power from London to Cardiff, but from Cardiff outward to the whole of Wales (2004).

All this begs the important question as to whether nation itself is the appropriate unit for welfare delivery (for a broader discussion of this, see Clarke, 2004) and brings us full circle in our consideration of the question: what is Wales? Increased globalisation and associated migrations across nations pose a number of challenges for any social policy and social welfare practice based on provision ring-fenced by national borders. National boundaries by definition involve inclusions and exclusions and as a key instrument of nation building, social policies reflect particular sets of assumptions about who is insider and who is outsider. For this reason it is important to look beyond a focus on traditional policy domains and beyond a focus on institutional structures towards an assessment of the social relations of welfare that emerge within these new regimes. Mooney and Poole (2004, p 479), writing in the context of Scotland, argue that the focus on 'institutional approaches' is limiting in terms of assessing the potential for a distinctively Scottish social policy and suggest that 'divisions and relations of welfare matter more'. Adopting such an approach allows those of us involved in welfare delivery to ask, who is being included and who is not?, but more critically to turn the lens towards constructions of the Welsh nation and ask, inclusion into what? What is Wales?

References

Adams, J and Robinson, P (eds) (2002) 'Divergence and the centre' in Adams, J and Robinson, P (eds) Devolution in Practice London, Institute for Public Policy Research

Agenda (2007) 'Editor's introduction' Agenda Winter, Cardiff, Institute of Welsh Affairs, p 13

Brooksbank, D (2006) 'The Welsh economy: a statistical profile' Contemporary Wales 18, pp 275–97

Cam, S (2007) *Migrant Workers in Wales: A comparison between Wales and the rest of Britain* Working Paper No 94, Cardiff, School of Social Sciences, Cardiff University

Chaney, P (2009) *Equal Opportunities and Human Rights: The first decade of devolution in Wales* London, Equality and Human Rights Commission, www.equalityhumanrights.com/uploaded_files/equal_opportunities_and_human_rights_the_first_decade_of_devolution_in_wales.pdf

Chaney, P and Drakeford, M (2004) 'The primacy of ideology: social policy and the first term of the National Assembly for Wales' in Ellison, N, Bauld, L and Powell, M (eds) *Social Policy Review 16* Bristol, The Policy Press, pp 121–42

Chaney, P, Hall, T and Pithouse, A (eds) (2001) *New Governance, New Democracy?* Cardiff, University of Wales Press

Clarke, J (2004) *Changing Welfare, Changing States* London, Sage Publications

Davies, R, Drinkwater, S, Joll, C, Jones, M, Lloyd-Williams, H, Makepeace, G, Parhi, M, Parken, A, Robinson, C, Taylor, C and Wass, V (2011) *An Anatomy of Economic Inequality in Wales* London, Equality and Human Rights Commission, www.equalityhumanrights.com

Day, G (2002) *Making Sense of Wales: A sociological perspective* Cardiff, University of Wales Press

Day, G (2006) 'Chasing the dragon? Devolution and the ambiguities of civil society in Wales' *Critical Social Policy* 26(3), pp 642–55

Greer, S (2005) 'The politics of health–policy divergence' in Adams, J and Schmuecker, K (eds) *Devolution in Practice 2006* London, Institute for Public Policy Research, pp 98–120

Greer, S L and Matzke, M (2009) 'Introduction: devolution and citizenship rights' in Greer, S L (ed) *Devolution and Social Citizenship in the UK*, Bristol, The Policy Press

Holtham, G (2010) 'The five fallacies of devolution' *Agenda* 42, pp 24–6

Independent Commission on Social Services in Wales (2010) *From Vision to Action: The report of the Independent Commission on Social Services in Wales* Cardiff, Independent Commission on Social Services in Wales

Jeffery, C (2002) 'Uniformity and diversity in policy provision: insights from the US, Germany and Canada' in Adams, J and Robinson, P (eds) *Devolution in Practice: Public policy preferences within the UK* London, Institute for Public Policy Research, pp 176–97

Jeffery, C (2005) 'Devolution and divergence: public attitudes and institutional logics' in Adams, J and Schmuecker, K (eds) *Devolution in Practice 2006* London, Institute for Public Policy Research, pp 10–28

Jones, C (2010) Speech to the Labour Party Conference, Manchester, 26 September

Jones, M (2011) 'Disability and disadvantage in Wales' in Davies, R, Drinkwater, S, Joll, C, Jones, M, Lloyd-Williams, H, Makepeace, G, Parhi, M, Parken, A, Robinson, C, Taylor, C and Wass, V (2011) *An Anatomy of Economic Inequality in Wales* London, Equality and Human Rights Commission, www.equalityhumanrights.com

JRF (Joseph Rowntree Foundation) (2007) *Monitoring Poverty and Social Exclusion in Wales* York, JRF

JRF (2009) *Monitoring Poverty and Social Exclusion in Wales* York, JRF

Laffin, M (2004) 'A brand that binds' *Agenda* Autumn, Cardiff, Institute of Welsh Affairs, p 15

Lohde, L (2005) 'Child poverty and devolution' in Adams, J and Schmuecker, K (eds) *Devolution in Practice 2006* London, Institute for Public Policy Research, pp 172–95

Mooney, G and Poole, L (2004) 'A land of milk and honey? Social policy in Scotland after devolution' *Critical Social Policy* 24(4), pp 458–83

Mooney, G and Williams, C (2006) 'Forging new "ways of life"? Social policy and nation building in devolved Scotland and Wales' *Critical Social Policy* 26(3), pp 608–29

Mooney, G, Scott, G and Williams, C (2006) 'Introduction: rethinking social policy through devolution' *Critical Social Policy* 26(3), pp 483–97

Morgan, R (2002) Speech to the University of Wales, Swansea, National Centre for Public Policy Third Anniversary Lecture, 11 December

National Statistics Online, www.statistics.gov.uk/STATBASE/ssdataset.asp?vlnk=5955

Rees, G (2005) 'Democratic devolution and education policy in Wales: The emergence of a national system?' *Contemporary Wales* 17, pp 28–43

WAG (Welsh Assembly Government) (2003) *Wales: A Better Country* Cardiff, WAG

WAG (2004) *People, Places, Futures: The Wales Spatial Plan* Cardiff, WAG

WAG (2006a) *Local Labour Force Survey* Cardiff, WAG, www.statswales.wales.gov.uk/TableViewer/tableView.aspx?ReportId=3091

WAG (2006b) *Making Connections* Cardiff, WAG

WAG (2007) *Fulfilled Lives, Supportive Communities* Cardiff, WAG

Wales Rural Observatory (2006) *Scoping Study of Eastern and Central European Migrant Workers in Rural Wales* Cardiff, Wales Rural Observatory, www.walesruralobservatory.org.uk

Williams, C, Evans, N and O'Leary, P (2002) *A Tolerant Nation? Exploring ethnic diversity in Wales* Cardiff, University of Wales Press

Williams, G A (1991) *When Was Wales? A history of the Welsh* (third edition) London, Penguin Books

Wincott, D (2005) 'Devolution, social democracy and policy diversity in Britain: the case of early-childhood education and care' in Adams, J and Schmuecker, K (eds) *Devolution in Practice 2006* London, Institute for Public Policy Research, pp 76–97

Winkler, V (ed) (2009) *Equality Issues in Wales: A research review* Research Report 11, Cardiff, The Bevan Foundation

Wyn Jones, R and Scully, R (2004) *Devolution in Wales: What does the public think?* Devolution Briefings No 7, Aberystwyth, Institute of Welsh Politics, Aberystwyth University, www.devolution.ac.uk/pdfdata/Scully_RLJ_Briefing7.pdf

Chapter 2

Governance and Social Policy in a Devolved Wales

Mark Drakeford and Lee Gregory

Introduction

For anyone involved in social welfare services in Wales, the nature and pattern of governance in the post-devolution era has to be a matter of continuing interest. Other than to those directly involved in such issues, much of what makes up the landscape of public administration has little intrinsic fascination. The reason why social workers and other social welfare practitioners need to know these things is different. It is because, boring and arcane as some of the detail may be, effective practice depends on being able to navigate a path through these developments in a way that delivers the best possible outcomes for users. In the post-devolution era, change has been rapid and multifaceted. The relationships between different tiers of government has altered; the basic foundations of the National Assembly for Wales itself have been radically reformed; the underlying approach to public service provision, particularly as regards Wales and England, has become increasingly divergent; and different practical policies have emerged as a result.

Other chapters in this volume will provide the necessary detail of these changes in relation to specific services – health, social services and so on. Here, our aim is fourfold:

- to set out an account of the changing powers, responsibilities and internal arrangements of the National Assembly itself;
- to explore the relationship between the Welsh Assembly Government and local authorities in Wales, particularly as far as social welfare services are concerned;
- to suggest some of the ideological distinctiveness of social policy making in a post-devolution Wales, again concentrating on those aspects that make a difference to social work and social welfare;
- to explore future issues for consideration based on the current devolution settlement.

The developing Assembly

The unsteady origins and troubled birth of Welsh devolution have been well traced by a variety of different authors (Andrews, 1999; Osmond, 2003). After 18 years of Conservative administration, in which Welsh voters consistently rejected Conservative candidates in increasingly large numbers, the Labour Party Manifesto at the 1997 General Election promised the establishment of a Scottish Parliament, and a Welsh Assembly, provided that such a proposal was confirmed in a post-election referendum. The 'democratic deficit' had been exposed in a series of examples where either policies had been imposed on Welsh voters despite their clear rejection of them – water privatisation and the Poll Tax, to cite just two examples – or where policies that were widely embraced in England – such as grant-maintained schools and fundholding general practitioners – were largely ignored, despite some hefty financial inducements to do so.

It was largely this experience that appeared to have brought about a major shift in Welsh public opinion. The 1979 referendum, in the dying months of the Callaghan government, had seen devolution proposals rejected in Wales by a landslide. Even the most enthusiastic supporters of the idea concluded that it had been settled for a generation or more. Yet, less than 20 years later, the proposition was put again to the voters. In some ways, this history ought to have served as a warning that devolution was always going to be a more contentious proposition in Wales than in Scotland. The Labour Party itself continued to hold both devo-enthusiasts and devo-sceptics, as they came to be known. The 1997 proposals, on which the referendum was held, were a careful balancing act in which the principle of an Assembly was hedged about by a series of limitations on its powers. The close-run nature of the September 1997 referendum vote was claimed, by both sides, as a vindication of their views. Enthusiasts believed that the second-best nature of the Welsh proposals had blunted voters' willingness to support devolution. Sceptics regarded the vote as a vindication of their caution, believing that voters were largely unconvinced of devolution, with the scale of doubt growing in proportion to the scale of change.

Essential elements of the 1999 Assembly

Despite the narrow margin of victory, the referendum provided the go-ahead for preparation of the Bill that was to become the Government of Wales Act 1999. The main features of the Assembly it created were for 60 members (smaller, therefore, than most Welsh councils), elected by a form of proportional representation (and thus a self-denying ordinance, stripping Labour of the built-in majority that it would have enjoyed through a first-past-the-post form of election). The Assembly was to represent a form of 'new politics', in which old, tribal dividing lines were to give way to fresh forms of less partisan dialogue and debate, in which the best talents of all parties would combine to put Wales first. The Act set out the 'functions', or areas of policy responsibility, which were to be devolved to Wales. Essentially, these comprised the great domestic agenda of health, education, housing, social services, local government, sports and arts, the Welsh language and agriculture. There were substantial areas of responsibility, also, in the field of economic development. These did not include, however – as was the case in Scotland – an ability to vary taxation levels. Indeed, the whole of the macro-economy – taxation, social security, interest rates, government borrowing and so on – remained the responsibility of the Westminster administration. All matters relating to defence and foreign policy were similarly un-devolved. By chance, rather than by design, the result has been that total public expenditure in Wales has been divided more or less evenly between Westminster and the Assembly.

For social workers, and others involved in welfare professions, the main conclusion to be drawn from this division of responsibilities under devolution is that the National Assembly is, overwhelmingly, a *social policy* body. Anyone in Wales engaged in asserting the rights to essential services of the most disadvantaged citizens – surely one of the core purposes of social work – needs to understand that the rule book for access to such services – in health, education, housing and so on – is now written in Wales. Progress towards rebalancing the social contract in favour of the least well off thus depends on the policies adopted, the financial decisions taken and the legislation passed at the National Assembly. Dry, dusty and detailed as matters of governance often are, they remain an essential focus for any social welfare worker with a serious interest in social change and a practical, rather than simply rhetorical, commitment to addressing discrimination and disadvantage.

Other chapters in this volume will look in more detail at the Welsh Assembly Government's record in relation to policy development. At this stage, it is important to emphasise that, from the outset, the Assembly has been provided with substantial legislative powers, through which the statute book in Wales has departed from that which applies in England. Because, in the terms used by lawyers and parliamentary drafters, these have been 'secondary' powers, it has often been assumed that 'secondary' must mean 'insubstantial'. In fact, a 50-year trend in United Kingdom (UK) law making means that, more and more, Acts of Parliament passed at Westminster have set out principles and frameworks, leaving the detail of policy development and implementation to 'secondary' legislation. Thus, when, in Wales, means-testing was abolished for Disabled Facilities Grants for children, or when prescription charges were abolished or when additional payments are made to the Child Trust Funds of looked-after children, then these measures – which apply only in Wales – are the result of secondary legislation in action. This has changed as a result of the 2011 referendum, discussed in more detail below.

Early days

The earliest days of devolution in Wales were marked by uncertainty and instability. The narrowness of the margin by which the 1997 referendum endorsed the formation of a National Assembly, the failure of any Party to win an overall majority in the first Assembly elections of 1999 and the volatility that thereafter afflicted almost all political groupings at Cardiff Bay all combined to get devolution off to a very shaky start. It was not until 2000 that the instability was resolved due to two key developments. The first saw the election of a new First Minister, Rhodri Morgan, who used the enormous political capital at his disposal to bring the Liberal Democrats into government, as junior members in a 'partnership' – or coalition – administration. With a secure overall majority, ministers were able to face a series of immediate challenges – widespread flooding, fuel protests, foot and mouth – in a way that combined clear leadership and competent administration. A firmer divide between 'government' on the one hand and 'opposition' on the other also emerged so that, *de facto* if not *de jure*, the Assembly came to turn its back on the 'corporate body', in favour of a more classically parliamentary model. As the Welsh Assembly Government, as it now became known, found its feet, so the second dimension of institutional recovery became apparent. Public opinion, which had been so ambivalent at the Assembly's birth, began to move more positively towards it, as discussed more fully below.

Next moves

One of the specific points included in the 2000 partnership agreement was a commitment to review the experience of the first Assembly, focusing on the legislative powers at its disposal and its form of election. A group was drawn together, combining nominees from all the Assembly's political parties, and experts selected through open competition. The Richard Commission, as it came to be known, was chaired by Lord Ivor Richard of Ammanford and reported early in 2004. It recommended a strengthened Assembly, with full legislative powers and 80 members, elected in multi-member constituencies using the Single Transferable Vote. The Commission emphasised that it had reached these far-reaching and unanimous conclusions because of the *success* of devolution to date, rather than because of any limitations in the Assembly's original design. Not all the Richard recommendations were to be accepted by government, but the report undoubtedly provided the catalyst for a second Government of Wales Act, passed into law in July 2006. Briefly summarised, the Act contained the following provisions:

- it confirmed a 60-member Assembly, and left unchanged its semi-proportional electoral system;
- it reshaped the Assembly in law, so that responsibilities were newly allocated between an 'executive' – or government – and an opposition;

- it provided a new mechanism by which enhanced legislative powers could be drawn down from Westminster to Wales;
- it enshrined in law the process by which the Assembly could, in future, acquire full primary powers, without the need for any further Act of Parliament.

The Government of Wales Act thus provides a further potential staging post on the road to full Welsh devolution, rather than, necessarily, its final destination. The third Assembly, elected in May 2007, inherited the new constitutional arrangements that the Act provides and the prospect of additional powers that it offers. The new administration was able to bring forward a legislative programme in a way that was not previously possible – and as discussed in more detail below. This resulted in a greater and more apparent divergence from that in other parts of the UK: now likely to continue.

Stage three

The result of the 2007 election generated further uncertainty. Labour won 26 seats, while collectively the other parties (and one independent) held 34. The following 10 weeks of negotiations saw a breakdown in the attempt to set up a 'rainbow coalition' (consisting of Plaid Cymru, the Conservative Party and the Liberal Democrats) and the formation of a coalition administration between Labour and Plaid. Their commitment to a joint policy programme was set out in the *One Wales* document (WAG, 2007), which also committed the new government to holding a referendum on full law-making powers for the Assembly, as provided in the Government of Wales Act 2006. This referendum was held on the 3 March 2011. The question before the electorate was whether or not, in future, laws that applied only in Wales should be made only in Wales. In comparison with the highly tentative endorsement provided in the 1997 referendum, the result in March 2011 was far more decisive. Twenty-one of the 22 local authority areas in Wales voted in favour of the proposition, with an overall majority of almost two to one.

The success of the referendum means that Wales now has primary legislative powers within the 20 devolved subject areas. The complex, cumbersome and lengthy process deployed during the third Assembly term has been removed and replaced, from May 2011 onwards, by the new primary legislative arrangements. The delay caused by the previous measures can be best illustrated by the field of public health, where, during the second Assembly term, Wales was the first UK legislature to endorse the principle of a ban on smoking in public places, but the last to be able to implement the policy. Similar delays in housing, the environment and the Welsh language were also characteristic of the third Assembly experience.

As well as creating a quicker and more comprehensible system, the referendum also makes clearer the areas under which the Assembly can legislate. In the field of social welfare, for example, 10 separate areas (some with their own exceptions) are now explicitly listed over which the Assembly has legislative power. These include:

- social welfare, including social services;
- protection and well-being of children (including adoption and fostering of young adults);
- care of children, young adults, vulnerable persons and older persons, including care standards;
- badges for disability on motor vehicles used by disabled persons.

The Assembly and local government

As already noted in this chapter, devolution in Wales was hedged about with ambivalence. One major source of that hesitation was found among the leaders of local government in Wales. In the first place, with the Conservatives lacking democratic legitimacy in Wales during the Thatcher and Major years, leaders of local authorities took on a new importance, as individuals who did, at least, carry the authority of the ballot box. It was easy enough to suspect that 60 new, full-time elected politicians at Cardiff Bay would rival, rather than complement, the importance that Labour local authority leaders (and, by the end of the Conservative period in office, almost all 22 local councils in Wales were Labour led) had come to enjoy. More generally, the limited nature of the Welsh devolution settlement – 'Mid Glamorgan County Council on stilts', to quote one of the disparaging accusations regularly made against it – gave rise to a suspicion among local authorities that the Assembly would attempt to establish itself, not by drawing down power from Westminster, but by sucking up power from local councils.

Against that background, it was perhaps fortunate that so many of those members elected to the Assembly in 1999 (and particularly members of the governing Labour Group) had their background in local government. A majority of the first Labour Cabinet was drawn from individuals who had either worked for local authorities or had been elected to them. They brought with them an understanding of the internal workings of councils and a strong defence of localism.

Why should this be of importance to social workers? In governance terms, the relationship between local and central government remains the key to understanding the administrative shape of the service that employs most social workers and provides many services on which social work users rely. By delivering an approach to local service delivery that emphasises cooperation over competition, and partnership over contestability, this initial concern has not manifested in practice. This has been in sharp contradistinction to England, where the former Seebohm social services departments have been dispersed to Primary Care Trusts and Children's Trusts as part of the 'managed decline' that Blairite ministers have preferred for local authorities. In Wales, social services remain a core function of local councils, with adult, children and mental health workers continuing – in most instances – to operate within unified departments.

This principle was further endorsed in a major policy paper, *Sustainable Social Services for Wales: A framework for action*, published by the Assembly Government in February 2001 (Deputy Minister for Social Services, 2011).

This does not mean that tensions do not exist between local authorities and the Assembly, especially over individual issues, such as delayed transfers of care and the state of children's services. Here the earlier devolution settlement placed weak levers in the Assembly Government's hands for bringing about improvement. However, two specific developments, of a governance variety, have emerged, against that background. First, the Assembly Government and the Welsh Local Government Association have agreed a Protocol, in which Assembly ministers are enabled to intervene in local service delivery, where 'serious concern' has been independently verified. Second, the first legislative programme of the May 2007 administration has used the new powers of the Government of Wales Act 2006 to strengthen its hand in being able to insist on local government implementing particular policies when these are underpinned by the legislative authority of the Assembly, and where funding has been provided to allow them to be put into practice. The changes in post-2011 referendum Wales are likely to see a further strengthening in this regard.

Two further, and more general, policy thrusts have shaped the relationship between the Assembly and local government in Wales, and seem set to do so for the foreseeable future.

The first approach is captured in a key Assembly Government publication, *Making the Connections* (WAG, 2004), which set out the shape and rationale for Welsh public service development and improvement. The document rehearses different models of public service reform, including the marketisation and consumerist agenda pursued at Whitehall. From the perspective of social welfare services it reaches three key conclusions. First, it comes down, unambiguously, in favour of cooperation rather than competition as the best means of securing better performance from public services. In a Welsh context, in particular, the document points to the advantages of scale that a small country possesses, as the basis for working across sectoral and organisational boundaries. Second, it endorses the need to increase the influence of users on the design and delivery of public services, but identifies amplifying the collective *voice* of users rather than individual choice in the marketplace, as the best means of doing so. Third, it models the relationship between providers and users of public services as one based on *reciprocity*, rather than mutual suspicion. In this model, the different qualities that both parties bring to social welfare transactions are equally valued, and grounded in a climate of mutual respect. Finally, it confirms the ongoing need for a mixed economy in the provision of welfare services, emphasising the need for balanced and managed markets in which voluntary sector services complement, rather than replace, those provided in the public sector.

The second approach is derived from a report produced by the Beecham Committee (WAG, 2006), established by the Assembly Government in order to advise on practical ways of securing better performance from public service organisations in Wales. From the point of view of this book, the following conclusions of the Beecham exercise are the most significant. First, the report concluded that structural reform of local government and other public service boundaries did not provide the best route to improved delivery. Rather, the future lay in far greater working across boundaries, both between organisations of the same sort – between local authorities, between Local Health Boards (LHBs) and so on – and across sectors – councils working with their LHBs, LHBs working with Community Safety Partnerships and so on. In the Beecham prescription, such cross-boundary work is to be pursued through new Public Service Boards (PSBs), in which organisations will pool sovereignty and commit resources in pursuit of common goals (this is the approach maintained in the post-2008 recession; see WAG, 2009).

The impact of these developments on social work will be direct. High on the agenda of the new PSBs will be delayed transfers of care, bringing together local councils, LHBs, National Health Service Trusts and the voluntary sector in a renewed attempt to provide the fabled 'seamless service' that governments have pursued without real success for more than half a century. The Welsh recipe for social work (as set out more fully below) envisages the retention of Seebohm-like local authority departments. Beecham developments, however, if successful, may suggest a new model in which formalised joint working may come to predominate.

Ideology

No fully informed understanding of governance can be obtained without some reference to ideology. Few higher education courses now claim to offer 'social administration', as though the wheels of bureaucracy ran on, regardless of the political context in which they turned.

Devolution was, by itself, an intensely political act. It transferred to Wales not simply a set of policy responsibilities, but the political authority to exercise them. Uniquely, in a UK context, Wales has remained a predominantly left-wing country for more than 150 years. The 19th century witnessed the triumph of Liberalism over the Conservative Party. The 20th century saw Liberalism displaced by the Labour Party. In successive General Elections in 1997 and 2001, Wales remained a Tory-free zone, without a single Conservative candidate returned to Westminster.

The upshot is that, within the National Assembly, the essential contest has been between three parties, each of which would self-describe as belonging to the political Left, with Conservative members forming less than a quarter of the institution as a whole. Within its history, the Assembly Government has been variously formed by a majority Labour administration, three minority Labour administrations and two coalitions, one between Labour and the Liberal Democrats (2000–03) and a second between Labour and Plaid Cymru (2007–11). Given the hundreds and thousands of decisions that make up the day-in-day-out activity of any administration, there is something foolhardy in suggesting that there may be some unifying ideological themes that, standing back from the canvas, can be discerned in this mass of activity. Inevitably, there will be examples that could be cited as contradicting any picture that claims to do so. What follows, however, is an attempt to identify a set of underlying principles, which, it will be argued here, are characteristic of Assembly Government policy making and which, together, amount to a particularly distinctive context in which to practise social work.

In the space available here, six core principles will be set out (for a fuller discussion of these ideas, see Drakeford, 2007):

The first of these may be summarised as *good government is good for you.* This may seem like a statement of the entirely obvious, yet there exists a very clearly articulated political position, which concludes exactly the opposite to be the case (see, for example, Butler, 2007; Seldon, 2007). Mrs Thatcher famously advised members of the House of Commons to read the works of von Hayek, a determined advocate of 'small' government for whom government did best when government did least. In the hands of the neo-conservatives, public services, and public servants, were part of the problem faced by the UK – or 'knaves' as Le Grand (2003) famously termed them – rather than part of the solution. Government, in this analysis, was at best a necessary evil, at worst a force for evil, in itself.

That line of argument has never run successfully in Wales. In Wales there is an enduring belief that when competently organised and delivered, government continues to provide the platform for promoting and protecting the best interests of the greatest possible mass of people. That first key principle of Welsh policy making is, of course, one that has long formed the foundation of the case for social work itself, as a function of government.

The second major theme of Welsh policy making has been the adoption of *progressive universalism* as a guiding principle. Thus, wherever possible, the Assembly Government has a preference for universal measures – abolishing charges to museums and galleries for everyone, making prescriptions free for every patient, providing free breakfasts in every participating primary school, providing free swimming for children in school holidays and so on. While at a UK level, behavioural conditionality has become the hallmark of a qualified and restricted approach to social entitlement, the Assembly has sought to make services available to all, based only on residence. Universal services are preferred, because services designed to be a pauper's safety net, reserved for poor people, very quickly become poor services. As previous First Minister, Rhodri Morgan, has said on a number of occasions, universal services help provide the glue that binds together a complex modern society and gives everybody a stake – the articulate, as well as those who find it difficult to make their voices heard, the well informed as well as the less well off – in making those services as good as possible.

This universality is bolstered by a form of targeting, to provide additional help, over and above the universal measure, to those whose needs are greatest. A single example will be provided here in relation to children and young people. In the 2006 Budget, the Chancellor of the Exchequer provided substantial new funding for schools, which, in

England, he directed to be distributed directly to head teachers on a simple formula based on school size. In Wales, the Assembly Cabinet decided to concentrate the same funding exclusively on those schools serving most disadvantaged areas and on the education of looked-after children.

Universal services, with a progressive twist, combine the advantages of the classic welfare state with some of the benefits that can be claimed for targeting. The approach matters to social work because it identifies vulnerable citizens as having a *greater* not lesser call on public services. The sense in which the fate of any one of us affects the fate of us all remains close to the heart of the Welsh approach to social welfare. Progressive universalism is a key to retaining the widespread support on which the survival of that understanding depends.

The third principle can be found in the design, delivery and improvement of public services: *cooperation is better than competition*. This position is well rehearsed in the document, *Making the Connections* (WAG, 2004), in which the First Minister sets out what he calls the 'respectable case' for both models, before concluding that cooperation provides a better fit with the needs and circumstances of Wales. Behind this conclusion lies a very substantial contemporary debate in which the ethic of consumerism has been rejected in favour of an ethic of citizenship.

The fourth major principle, linked to the third, concerns the *ethic of participation*, which is pursued in the Welsh context. Devolution is, of itself, a major experiment in increasing the leverage that people who live in Wales have over the government that serves them. But, if social work is rooted in a commitment to the equal worth of every individual, then the need to draw on the talents of all our citizens applies as much to government itself as to any other aspect of life.

Key to social work is that Assembly Government action in this area is characterised by a unifying preference for improving collective voice rather than relying solely on individual choice. Where public service participation is modelled on the mechanisms of the market, then those who already possess economic and social advantages will, inevitably, do best while others get left further behind. The preference for collective voice, as, for example, in the decision to retain and strengthen Community Health Councils in Wales, is grounded in an understanding that this provides the best way of ensuring that participation produces shared and wider benefits, rather than simply individual advancement. It means that user participation in the design and delivery of social work services is also to be based on capturing and responding to the collective experience of users, not confined to improving mechanisms for dealing with individual complaints or grievance.

The fifth principle relates to establishing a *high-trust, not low-trust, relationship* between the citizen and the Welsh state. Here users of services, and those who provide them, are regarded as essentially engaged in a joint enterprise (see Chapter 11).

Quasi-commercial relationships of marketised services are based, inevitably, on low-trust foundations. The Latin tag *caveat emptor* – 'buyer beware' – reminds us that a self-interested sense of scepticism has underpinned markets for 2,000 years and more. By contrast, collective and cooperative approaches rely on high-trust relationships between those who combine their efforts in the hope of improved outcomes for all. In doing so, they draw on the fundamental recognition that success in public services depends on reciprocity. It seems difficult to imagine a closer alignment with this approach than that which underpins effective social work (see Butler and Drakeford, 2005, for a wider discussion of this point). Trust is, surely, the pivot around which co-production turns, generating qualities of reciprocity and respect and cementing the sense of social solidarity on which the basic premise that one human being may be of assistance to another depends.

The sixth and final principle to be explored here is, perhaps, the most ambitious but the one that provides the most distinguishing feature of Assembly Government policy making. On a series of occasions, the previous First Minister endorsed the notion that, as far as Wales is concerned, greater equality of *outcome* is an ambition that has overtaken the more conventional pursuit of equality of opportunity. Recent figures published by the Chief Medical Officer (2006) show that, in Wales today, a child born in the least well-off part of Wales will live, on average, for five years less than a child born not one hour's travel away. In a lecture at Swansea, and in response to that finding, Rhodri Morgan (2006) reaffirmed the Assembly Government's position in this way:

> *Inequality is the most insidious form of injustice because it prevents individuals from achieving their full potential. And every time inequality prevents any of our fellow citizens from exercising their talents, or accessing the services to which they are entitled, the total stock of freedom available to all of us is diminished.*

The pursuit of greater equality provides the backdrop against which it is possible to retain some optimism about the pursuit of fruitful social work (see Chapter 7, this volume). More equal societies enjoy better health (Wilkinson, 2005), where health is understood as the product of being cared for by others. More equal societies enjoy lower levels of crime and, even more importantly, are marked by lower levels of fear of crime. There is a sense of individual validation and social solidarity, which greater equality brings. Moreover, the sum of freedom in a more equal society will always be greater than in unequal societies, where freedom is unfairly divided.

Taken together, the argument of this chapter is that Wales remains a place where the wider purposes of government and governance remain focused on improving the prospects of the least fortunate, and doing so in a way that reaches out positively to individuals, families and communities where help is most needed. It offers a chance to practise social work in a way that goes with the grain, rather than against the tide, of social policy making.

Consequences of the Assembly

In the earlier edition of this chapter (Drakeford, 2007b), the focus here turned to consider the relationship between the Assembly Government and social work services. A discussion of this important issue can be found in Chapter 11 of this volume. Here, we provide a brief consideration of the wider political context in which devolution, and devolved services in Wales, are now being developed.

As noted earlier, Assembly governments are shaped by both the political preferences of Welsh voters – which cluster around the left of the political spectrum – and the voting system in Wales – which has a demonstrated tendency to produce coalition administrations. Over the UK as a whole, Westminster governments, dominated by the number of Members of Parliament returned in England, have seen a pull to the political Right (Greer, 2005). Even during the period when Labour was in office, both in London and Cardiff divergence in policy (Adams and Schmuecker, 2005) and rhetoric (Lohde, 2005) became apparent. Now, with an explicitly different ideological agenda at play in Westminster, following the formation of a coalition in Westminster between the Conservatives and the Liberal Democrats in the aftermath of the 2010 General Election, this difference is set to emerge more strongly.

In the hands of its advocates, such policy difference is simply an expression of the different preferences of Welsh voters, and likely to see a continuing 'Scandanavianisation' of policy making in the Welsh context. For others, divergence in policy across the UK has been seen as destabilising to the notions of citizenship, which have traditionally underpinned the welfare state (Lodge and Schmuecker, 2010). In such a contention, devolution is viewed as a process of nation building in which entitlements to welfare services, including those used by clients of social workers, vary between different parts of the UK. Citizenship rights may no longer be guaranteed by the state, but at a regional level. This is a debate that will require ongoing attention over the next four years, especially as the Welsh Assembly now has its new legislative ability.

This legislative ability, and the potential for increased divergence in public services, will also be acted out in a sharply different financial context than that which the Assembly enjoyed during the first decade of devolution. The present public spending cuts imposed by Westminster will require any Assembly government, after May 2011, to make decisions that reveal a set of policy priorities. This can already be seen at play in decisions already taken, for example to retain universal benefits of free bus travel for those aged over 60 and for disabled people, and to peg tuition fees for students from Wales at their present real-terms value. In this way, the distinctive approach to welfare services that has been apparent in the early years of devolution seems most likely to lead to even greater policy divergence in the post-2011 period.

Conclusion

This chapter has mapped out a wide canvas, moving through the mechanics of government in a devolved Wales, through the key relationships between different levels of administration, outlining some linking characteristics of post-devolution social policy making and setting out possible challenges in relation to social welfare services.

Other chapters in this book will deal in more detail with other policy dimensions, and contextual factors. The conclusion drawn here is that, in relation to social work, Wales remains a place in which worthwhile practice can be pursued; where the broad policy purposes of greater equality, and reciprocity, provide a solid foundation from which the positive promotion of individual progress can be undertaken. It is also a place where the preference for a unified, publicly provided, critically informed profession allows for some optimism that social workers, as well as social welfare, have a future worth searching out and helping to shape.

References

Adams, J and Schmuecker, K (2005) (eds) *Devolution in Practice 2006: Public policy differences within the UK* London, IPPR

Andrews, L (1999) *Wales Says Yes* Bridgend, Seren Books

Butler, I (2007) 'Children's policy' in Williams, C (ed) *Social Policy for Social Welfare Practice in a Devolved Wales* Birmingham: Venture Press

Butler, I and Drakeford, M (2005) 'Trusting in social work' *British Journal of Social Work* 35(5), pp 639–53

Chief Medical Officer (2006) *Health in local areas: A compendium of maps: Chief Medical Officer's report series 2* Cardiff, Welsh Assembly Government

Deputy Minister for Social Services (2011) *Sustainable Social Services for Wales: A framework for action* Cardiff, Welsh Assembly Government

Drakeford, M (2007a) 'Devolution and social justice in a Welsh context' *Benefits* 19(2), pp 173–80

Drakeford, M (2007b) 'Governance and social policy in a devolved Wales' in Williams, C (ed) *Social Policy for Social Welfare Practice in a Devolved Wales* Birmingham: Venture Press

Greer, S (2005) 'The politics of health–policy divergence' in Adams, J and Schmuecker, K (eds) *Devolution in Practice 2006: Public policy differences within the UK* London, IPPR, pp 98–120

Le Grand, J (2003) *Motivation, Agency and Public Policy: Of knights and knaves, pawns and queens* Oxford, Oxford University Press

Lodge, G and Schmuecker, K (2010) *Devolution in Practice 2010: Public policy difference in the UK* London, IPPR

Lohde, L A (2005) 'Child poverty and devolution' in Adams, J and Schmuecker, K (eds) *Devolution in Practice 2006: Public policy differences within the UK* London, IPPR, pp 172–95

Morgan, R (2006) *Twenty First Century Socialism: A Welsh recipe* London, Compass, accessed on 22 August 2011, from www.compassonline.org.uk/news/item.asp?n=338

Osmond, J (ed) (2003) *Birth of Welsh democracy* Cardiff, Institute of Welsh Affairs

Seldon, A (2007) *Capitalism: A Condensed Version* London, Institute of Economic Affairs accessed on 22 August 2011 from www.iea.org.uk/publications/research/capitalism-a-condensed-version

WAG (Welsh Assembly Government) (2004) *Making the Connections* Cardiff, WAG

WAG (2006) *Beyond Boundaries: Report of the Beecham Commission* Cardiff, WAG

WAG (2007) *One Wales: a programme for government* Cardiff, WAG

WAG (2009) *Better Outcomes for Tougher Times: The next phase of public service improvement* Cardiff, WAG

Wilkinson, R (2005) *Impact of Inequality: How to make sick societies healthier* London, Routledge

Chapter 3

Post-Devolution Health Policy in Wales

Michael Sullivan and Mark Drakeford

Introduction

This chapter charts the development of health policy from pre-devolution to post-devolution Wales and, *en passant*, makes glancing comparisons with the other nations of the United Kingdom (UK). It aims to provide an account of the development of health policy over the first three Assembly terms. In doing so, the chapter suggests that policy differentiation or divergence has sharpened considerably since 1999, considers why this should be so and looks at how policy divergence in social policy has been crafted by an Assembly, which, until June 2007, functioned without primary law-making powers of any sort and which has only operated on the basis of 'full' law-making powers in devolved areas since 2011. It suggests that part of the answer to this latter question is that politicians and officials have worked together to create a 'Welsh way', which places health policy at, or near, the centre of the agenda for health organisations, local government and communities.

Political devolution has led to significant differences in policy between the devolved administrations and between those administrations and successive Westminster governments. This is no surprise: on one reading, at least that was one of the intentions. In Wales, which rejected devolution in the 1979 referendum, one of the main claims for it in 1997 was that it would allow 'Welsh solutions to Welsh problems'. This resonated with an impulse among the Welsh electorate, which had, since 1979, consistently voted for non-Conservative parties only to see the writ of Conservative governments run as far as – and beyond – Cathays Park! What we have observed since 1999 is far more than the policy anomalies claimed by some political pundits. We need therefore to analyse the extent and nature of policy divergence and its relationship to the devolution project.

Asymmetrical devolution

As a glance at the Acts establishing devolved government will indicate, political devolution in the UK is asymmetrical, with distinct differences between the settlements for Wales, Scotland and Northern Ireland.

- The Scottish Parliament and the Northern Ireland Assembly have powers in relation to all matters not specifically reserved to Westminster.

- Scotland has a single list of reserved matters, while in Northern Ireland there is a distinction between reserved matters, which may be devolved in the future, and excepted matters, which are to be reserved permanently for Westminster.
- Both bodies have primary legislative powers over non-reserved matters, as well as executive responsibility for matters where the primary responsibility remains with the centre.
- The Welsh Assembly, on the other hand, had only secondary legislative and executive responsibility for a list of powers devolved from Westminster and was required to get parliamentary approval for any changes in primary legislation. The second Government of Wales Act in 2006 addressed this imbalance and created a situation in which the Assembly was able, gradually and on a case-by-case basis, to acquire primary law-making powers in specific policy areas. Following a successful referendum in March 2001, however, the fourth Assembly, elected in May 2011, has the ability to pass Welsh Acts in all areas of devolved competence.

Policy divergence before devolution

Devolution in the UK builds on an existing and deep-rooted system of administrative devolution in which each of the UK countries had a distinct way of making or adapting policy and delivering services.

While the Scottish Office and its associated agencies acted within the limits of overall UK policy, there were areas in which it was allowed to develop policy and practice (for example in relation to education policy). Government in Northern Ireland, although possessed of devolved powers, tended to imitate British welfare state provision. The Welsh Office, on the other hand, was more extensively integrated into Whitehall networks and tended neither to sponsor legislation nor to initiate policy. However, even in this very restrictive relationship, policy divergence was both possible and, occasionally, actual, as demonstrated in the 1980s All-Wales Mental Handicap Strategy, which led the way in community care arrangements for people with learning disabilities. In the run-up to devolution, clear differences (in emphasis at least) emerged. This is nowhere more evident than in relation to health policy where, perhaps, we see in Wales and Scotland precursors of a new inclusive politics.

In the context of, and run-up to, political devolution to Wales, Scotland and Northern Ireland, three White Papers appeared in 1998 on the refurbishment and modernisation of the National Health Service (NHS) (DH, 1997; Scottish Office, 1997; Welsh Office, 1998). Each of them was informed by a set of values reflecting the key concerns of the UK Labour government. While the foreword to the English White Paper talks of the importance of 'modernisation' (DH, 1997), the Welsh and Scottish versions focus on the need to 'restore' the NHS. In Wales, this was expressed as 'reaffirming its founding principles and devising new responses to the challenges which face it' (Welsh Office, 1998, introduction to section 1) while the foreword to the Scottish document declared its aim as 'to restore the National Health Service as a public service working co-operatively for patients' (Scottish Office, 1997).

In Wales, as Drakeford (2006, p 549) has noted, the Welsh White Paper represented three main policy cleavages with England. First, it heralded the end of general practitioner (GP) fundholding in Wales and established Local Health Groups (LHGs), later transformed into Local Health Boards (LHBs) and made up of GPs, other health care professionals, social services and the voluntary sector, to develop services to meet local needs and priorities The geographical boundaries of both LHGs and the later LHBs were coterminous with those of Welsh unitary authorities. Greer (2001) describes this departure as a 'grudging acceptance' of the purchaser–provider split in which commissioning remained a possible, but minor, feature of the system.

The second cleavage was that a new imperative was placed on the reduction of health inequalities through a renewed obligation to 'protect and improve health as well as respond to illness and disability' (Welsh Office, 1998). Greer (2001) sees this as an intellectually coherent agenda, which recognised that many of the major health challenges in Wales, such as coronary heart disease, were the product of lifestyle and economics. In Drakeford's (2006, p 550) words, it 'positioned the NHS as but one powerful tool in a far wider set of measures needed to address the determinants of health'. Finally, both the Scottish and Welsh White Papers described a model of patient and public involvement, which flew in the face of the consumerist mode that had already begun to emerge in the parallel English system.

Devolution and the emergence of divergence

If some differentiation thus characterised the politics of health policy in the pre-devolution period, this tendency has been sharpened since the formation of the Welsh Assembly and the Scottish Parliament (Sullivan, 2004). During the first term of devolved government, each of the administrations introduced a raft of policies in relation to health. Wales, England and Scotland produced plans for the NHS, setting the trajectory for health policy over the next 10 years.

Improving Health in Wales: A plan for the NHS with its partners (NAW, 2001) sought, *inter alia*, to put policy meat on the rhetorical bones of public involvement. It also aimed to translate the NHS into an agency for the development and implementation of a new health policy trajectory in Wales, which emphasised the primacy of public health and to place public engagement, individually and collectively, at the heart of policy making.

This commitment was given substance in Chapter Three of the document – entitled, echoing Bevan, 'The people's NHS' – where the scope of and mechanisms for involvement were addressed. Put simply, the contract implied in this early Welsh renewal of the NHS is one that stressed the connections between government, service planners and providers and communities of citizens. This was enhanced by the abolition of health authorities and the relocation of power closer to the citizen in LHBs with coterminous boundaries with local authorities. In policy terms, the plan was underpinned by a number of key emphases on participation, partnership, citizenship, health inequalities and the social determinants of health.

All the above were underpinned by an emphasis on population health: turning the NHS from an illness service to one actively involved in promoting health. This sense of a public health-led NHS forms a contrast with both the Scottish Plan (Scottish Government 2000) and the English Plan (DH 2000). The Scottish Plan – while rhetorically committed like its Welsh counterpart to consultation and involvement and to a public health agenda – retained existing structural arrangements intact and saw the NHS, rather than the NHS with its partners, as driving the health policy trajectory. The English Plan was relatively straightforward. It encapsulated a commitment to improving the health service – rather than health or health policy. It implied a contract between government, service and customer (rather than citizen or communities) and its horizons stretched little further than more effective service provision.

The Welsh Plan was also significant in that it indicated that the Welsh way in relation to health policy and improving health was to be rooted in a localist political impulse. To express this sharply, comparatively and succinctly, we might argue the following.

- Scotland tended towards a system based on *professionalism*, in which it tried to align organisation with the existing structure of medicine. This meant reducing layers of management and replacing them with clinical networks, thereby increasing the role of professionals in rationing and resource allocation.
- England's was a *market* model in which independent trusts, similar to private firms, contracted with each other for care.
- The Welsh NHS system, by contrast, entrenched an ethos of *localism*. This meant an emphasis on partnership between health, local government and the voluntary sector in order to coordinate care and focus on the determinants of health rather than simply on treating the sick. It sought to use this localism as the lever to make the NHS into a national health service rather than a national sickness service (see, Greer, 2004, pp 128–58).

To summarise, the Welsh approach rested on an ambition to create a primary care-led preventive and publicly engaged NHS as opposed to the hospital-dominated, treatment-focused and managerially driven emphasis in the NHS Plan for England. To this end, the Welsh Assembly Government, engaged during its first term in policy developments that included the commissioning and introducing of a new evidence-based formula for the allocation of resources to health bodies based on evidence of social, health and economic need (the so-called Townsend formula; see Townsend, 2001; Townsend 2005), alongside the creation of a Health Inequalities Fund to pump-prime initiatives intended to diminish health inequalities.

Developing distinctiveness: opportunities and threats

From the vantage point of over a decade of devolution, a series of themes can be discerned that had their genesis during this early period but which then stretch across the health policy making of the whole period.

Health Minister Jane Hutt's insistence on a service that was to be reoriented from secondary to primary care and from dealing with the consequences of ill-health to addressing its underlying causes remains one of the most coherent and radical statements of Welsh health policy making. As became evident during her terms as Health Minister, however, attempts to concentrate on bringing about long-term shifts in resource allocations and service organisation were always prey to the immediate demands of waiting times, new and expensive drugs and the chronic inability of (parts of) the Welsh NHS to live within its means – even when those means were growing at an unprecedented rate. This was given added focus during the 2005 UK election campaign, with media exploitation of stories focusing on a 'postcode lottery' of services across the country. They also highlighted differences in waiting times between England and Wales.

The result was a new approach to waiting times reduction in Wales (see, for example, *Western Mail*, 2005; Drakeford, 2006), accelerating the issue up the political, policy and professional agendas. Given that, in England, Labour ministers had committed the NHS to an all-in, referral-to-treatment maximum waiting time of 18 weeks, it was inevitable that the Welsh commitment should mirror such an approach, at least in headline appearance. When the final plan was announced by the First Minister in March 2005, it made a commitment that, by December 2009, no patient in Wales would wait more than 26 weeks from GP referral to treatment, including waiting times for any diagnostic tests and therapies required. This headline commitment was followed by a series of detailed documents (see, for example, WAG, 2005a; 2005b; Welsh Health Circular, 2006, 2007) providing the operational detail through which the policy was to be implemented.

Crucially, in terms of health policy making, the plan was based on public investment within the NHS itself, designed to bring about a long-term expansion in capacity to provide treatment within the times laid down. While ministers were always careful to put the principles of the plan positively (rather than to highlight any contrast with Labour policies elsewhere), the absence of any reference to the Private Finance Initiative (PFI) as a means of funding, or initiatives such as Independent Sector Treatment Centres, as a means of providing services, was striking and, in its way, remarkable to any student of health policy making.

The 2009 project proved a conspicuous success. Table 3.1 shows the number of patients waiting for treatment in the Welsh NHS at the end of March 2005, while Table 3.2 provides the same figures for the end of March 2010.

Table 3.1: Waiting times at the end of March 2005

Measures	Number of inpatients and day cases	Number of outpatients
Total waiting	65,538	218,443
Waiting over 3 months	32,370	113,958
Waiting over 6 months	16,363	63,057
Waiting over 12 months	840	13,860
Waiting over 18 months	16	28

Source: This Table has been compiled using data published by the Welsh Government's *Stats Wales* service, available at: www.statswales.wales.gov.uk/ReportFolders/reportFolders.aspx

Table 3.2: Waiting times at end of March 2010

Measures	Number of inpatients and day cases	Number of outpatients
Total waiting	54,309	156,514
Waiting over 3 months	11,233	19,548
Waiting over 5 months	5,247	4,640
Waiting over 12 months	–	–
Waiting over 18 months	–	–

Source: This Table has been compiled using data published by the Welsh Government's *Stats Wales* service, available at: www.statswales.wales.gov.uk/ReportFolders/reportFolders.aspx

The striking reductions over the five-year period in the length of waits, as well as the total number of people waiting for treatment, were dramatic, and continued through the rest of the final year of the project. By March 2011, the basis on which figures were calculated had shifted to reflect the original commitment to an 'all-in' waiting time. At that date, figures showed only one patient waiting more than the target of six months from referral to final inpatient treatment.

Of course, the waiting times project took place within a far wider health policy framework. The 2003 Wanless Review (Wanless, 2003) had been charged with outlining a sustainable future for health and social care services in Wales. The report rehearsed a series of potential futures for the Welsh NHS. Its preferred 'fully engaged' strategy involved a far higher level of involvement by patients (actual and potential) in promoting their own health, together with a reorganised (or 'reconfigured', to use the health service jargon term) set of services. In response, the Assembly Government launched *Health Challenge Wales* as a vehicle for promoting population health improvement (WAG, 2004) and a 10-year programme, *Designed for Life* (WAG, 2005a), as a blueprint for service reform in health and social care.

Wanless contended that the NHS in Wales tried to do too many things, in too many places. It had too many hospital beds, and too many hospitals all trying to provide a full range of District General Hospital services. The result was an expensive way of providing services of less than optimal quality and at a volume that struggled to match demand. The answer was to be 'reconfiguration' so that more specialist services would be concentrated in fewer places (and thus in the hands of clinicians better experienced to provide them), while providing a wider range of point-of-entry services (X-rays, blood tests and so on), and a stronger set of post-operative recovery-and-rehabilitation services closer to patients' homes.

As a result of the different measures set in hand, by 2005, the Welsh NHS was possessed of a substantial degree of policy clarity about the future direction of some key services. In translating that policy into practice, it also possessed one considerable (and new) advantage in doing so, as well as one major difficulty.

On the positive side, with the policy prescription went an opportunity for action provided by the level of capital spending that the Gordon Brown-led investment programme in public services provided. When the National Assembly for Wales came into being, it inherited a public capital programme for the NHS that was almost entirely bare. Now, in his report to the Assembly's Health and Social Services Committee of November 2005, Brian Gibbons, the-then Minister for Health and Social Services, was able to present a draft budget for 2006/07, which included capital funding of £219.8 million, an increase of £73.7 million over 2005–06, as part of the Assembly Government's commitment to increase capital spending in the Welsh NHS from £120 million in 2005/06 to £309 million in 2007/08 (Gibbons, 2005).

The allocation of this substantially increased funding would, the Gibbons (2005, p 12) said, 'enable the first elements of a much longer programme of modernisation to take place over the next 10 years as part of the Designed for Life strategy'. Key elements of the capital programme were to include investment in the reconfiguration of hospital sites and in the diagnostic strategy that would underpin this new pattern of services.

The *Designed for Life* analysis suggested that change was urgent, necessary and unavoidable if the Welsh NHS was to survive. Unfortunately, the political timetable was at least as adverse as the capital programme was helpful. By the time the policy and financial cycles had been aligned, in the way set out above, the political cycle was moving in the opposite direction. By November 2005, the second Assembly term had less than 18 months to run. The difficulty of bringing about service change in the Welsh NHS had already been amply demonstrated when, during 2002 and 2003, the *South Wales Evening Post* persuaded over 105,000 local residents to sign a petition objecting to the movement of a single paediatric neurosurgeon from Swansea to Cardiff. Now, as the 2007 Assembly elections began to loom closer, and the practical implications of the *Designed for Life* prescriptions became clearer, so the pace of objections gathered speed. There is no space here to trace the detail of protests that the *Western Mail* (2006), in its end-of-year review of health matters, said had 'united campaigners from Llandudno to Llanelli, Haverfordwest to Hay-on-Wye'. There is no doubt that, in the early months of 2007, the public focus on the NHS had shifted away from waiting times and had coalesced around fears that 'reconfiguration' was simply a shorthand for removal of services, with 'massive protests' reported in almost every part of Wales where change had been proposed (*Western Mail*, 2007).

In the Assembly elections of 2007, Plaid Cymru, in particular, focused ruthlessly on a campaign which claimed that Labour had a 'secret plan' to close hospitals and services in almost every part of Wales (see Withers, 2011). The claim had no substance, but the events of 2006 and 2007, in which *Designed for Life* had become associated, in the public mind, with removal of services, rather than their reorganisation, provided fertile political ground in which such claims could take root. The extent to which health matters influenced the outcome of the election is impossible to calibrate. Labour was at a low point far beyond Wales, and the campaign was conducted as the dog-days of the Blair premiership drew to their close. Nevertheless, it can be argued that Labour did particularly badly where there had been specific, high-profile health campaigns.

Coalition government and health policy

The 2007 election results produced a hung Assembly. After much to-ing and fro-ing, serious negotiations took place between Labour and Plaid Cymru. When the *One Wales* programme of government was published (WAG, 2007), and agreed, it contained a set of practical proposals, designed to cauterise the differences between the two parties that had emerged during the election campaign, and a set of principles that were to underpin policy development over the next four years. Practically, the document promised a 'new approach' to health service reconfiguration, with a 'moratorium on existing proposals for changes at community hospital level'. In policy terms, *One Wales* committed the administration to eliminating use of the private sector by the Welsh NHS, to using public capital rather than the PFI for investment in the service and to bringing an end to use of the internal market in Wales.

Successful health ministers are as rare as hens' teeth, in any part of the UK. The sheer scale of the task, its complexity and its constant capacity to attract public and political attention for incidents beyond the control of any minister mean that 'events' often drive out any effort to concentrate on strategic intent. The 2007–11 period was by no means insulated from such difficulties. Health Minister Edwina Hart was soon embroiled, for example, in accusations that she had plans to 'force' North Wales patients to travel to South Wales for treatment (see Welsh Affairs Select Committee, 2010, for an account of this), as well as the by-now perennial problems of providing highly specialist services, such as neurosurgery, for a population the size of Wales. Despite these difficulties, however, an overall assessment of the period produces a balance sheet well weighted to the positive side.

The 2003 creation of LHBs and Trusts in Wales had been predicated on a purchaser/provider split in which, it was argued, the power of purchase would allow LHBs to ensure that services provided by Trusts reflected the health needs of their local populations. In practice, this did not occur. Power in the system was largely retained by the large provider organisations, while the 'market' generated huge volumes of transaction costs, to no very visible purpose. The 2007 administration tackled all this by replacing the existing structure with seven combined organisations, bringing together the former LHBs and Trusts into single bodies. The changes very largely moved with the grain of change already gathering within the system and were accomplished with relatively little disruption and an unusual degree of political and professional consensus. The 2007 period also inherited the benefits of the 2009 project, as far as waiting times were concerned. As noted earlier, both waiting times and waiting lists were already falling sharply by the time the *One Wales* administration took office, and the pattern allowed the new Health Minister to make good on the promise to eliminate use of the private sector, at least as far as major District General Hospital services were concerned. And, while the tap on public expenditure was being turned off with a vengeance in the final year of the 2007 Assembly, for most of the period, the NHS continued to benefit from capital expenditure on a hitherto-unprecedented scale.

In focusing her attention on those issues that mattered most to the public – abolishing charges for hospital car parking, free prescriptions, freezing dental charges – and to keeping together the parties within the coalition, Edwina Hart managed not only to neutralise health as an area of political liability but to shift it, modestly, into the assets column. In the final year of the *One Wales* government, of course, the election of a Conservative-led administration in Westminster caused the distinctive approach to health policy in Wales to be highlighted with greater clarity than over the first decade of devolution, as well as allowing Welsh Labour politicians to draw attention to that distinctiveness without the political tensions that differentiation had caused while Labour had been in charge in both Wales and Whitehall.

In the process, inevitably, some issues moved into the background. While primary care and public health, under the formidable leadership of Dr Chris Jones and Sir Mansel Aylward, respectively, continued to receive attention that distinguished Welsh health policy from that in other UK nations (see, for example, Sparer et al, 2011), health inequalities *per se* appeared to recede as a distinct policy focus (see, for example,

Blackman et al., 2006; Smith et al., 2009), while it could be argued that some of the more fundamental reconfigurations for which *Designed for Life* had provided a cogent rationale had been avoided, rather than resolved. Nevertheless, towards the end of the administration, the conclusion offered by the *British Medical Journal* was that the Welsh health system is 'socialised medicine as true as possible to Bevanite principles' (Hawkes and Jewell, 2010, p 12).

Policy divergence and the reform of the welfare state

Having provided an account of some of the main threads in Welsh health policy during the first three Assembly terms, this chapter ends by placing these developments in a wider context of welfare policy making, and contrasting the Welsh approach with that adopted by successive Westminster governments in the post-devolution period.

The first Blair government, which set up the Assembly in Cardiff, introduced a crusade for welfare reform. The Prime Minister argued, in the debate on the government's programme, that the British public were no longer willing to fund an unreformed welfare state and were similarly unimpressed by proposals that suggested raising taxes further and investing more public money in welfare state services. Instead, the New Labour government set its face towards a new contract between government and people, rooted in a concept of social citizenship at some distance from post-war formulations. This much is clear in the social policies of New Labour governments. UK New Labour saw the aims of the welfare state it had created as:

- contributing to economic growth rather than redistributing resources from rich to poor, and providing individual routes out of dependence on state benefits rather than seeing collective provision as a safety net capable of catching those in economic freefall;
- emphasising the *responsibilities* of citizenship as equally, if not more, important than the *rights* that old social democracy had conferred;
- targeting social provision on an identifiably meritorious or deserving section of the population rather than upholding welfare rights as *universal rights*;
- redefining the role of government in addressing the problem of poverty – the effects of poverty (social exclusion – the inability of poor people to share in the opportunities of society) rather than poverty itself is seen as the legitimate concern of government social policy;
- finally, embracing a conception of the legitimate role of the state as a *guarantor of social provision* rather than as always the *provider*. Here the example of diagnostic treatment centres (in England) comes to mind – privately funded, privately owned, privately staffed and privately run, but drawing their entire income stream from the public purse.

In contrast, Labour, or Labour-led, administrations in Cardiff have retained Old Labour's commitment to the welfare state as an engine of equality, social justice and social inclusion based on the political values of universality, social solidarity and free services. To this, they seem to have added a more modern – but also older – set of emphases on collaboration, participation, communities and partnership.

The reality is that the Labour administration in Cardiff has fused an Old Labour tradition with a renewed quasi-syndicalist impulse (Sullivan, 2000, pp 19–20) – a sort of forward-to-the-past rather than back-to-the-future! It highlights the collective nature of the contemporary politics of health policy in Wales and contrasts with an English emphasis on consumerism and individualism.

As such, it opens the door to the development of joined-up or cross-cutting policies to impact on health inequalities: social determinants of health therefore become a legitimate concern of health policy and, more significantly, of NHS policy; the NHS becomes accountable to citizens as members of communities rather than as individuals.

These, then, are the social politics of Old Labour modernised and integrated with new impulses for collaboration, participation and inclusion. They draw succour from a sort of social democracy that characterised post-war Britain. Following the Second World War and the election of a Labour government in 1945, the UK Labour Party set about creating a reasoned and moral case for social democracy.

The values underpinning post-devolution health – and indeed other social – policy in Wales have a reasonably long pedigree. For Labour – or Labour-led – administrations in the Welsh Assembly they are, however, contemporary as well as historical guides. The Welsh way is seen by the Welsh Assembly Government as a further redefinition of Welsh democratic socialism, which began by creating a 'clear red water' (Morgan, 2002) between the administration in Cardiff and some of the principles and many of the policy actions of the UK New Labour project, and which has continued to form an even sharper contrast in the Cameron/Clegg era.

References

Blackman, T, Greene, A, Hunter, D J, McKee, L, Elliott, E, Harrington, B E, Marks, L and Williams, G H (2006) 'Performance Assessment and Wicked Problems: The Case of Health Inequalities', Public Policy and Administration, 21:2, pp 66-80

DH (Department of Health) (1997) The New NHS: Modern, dependable London, DH

DH (2000) The NHS Plan: a plan for investment, a plan for reform London, DH, Cm 4818-I

Drakeford, M (2006) 'Health policy in Wales: Making a difference in conditions of difficulty' Critical Social Policy 26(3), pp 543–61

Gibbons, B (2005) Budget Proposals 2006/07: Paper to the Health and Social Services Committee Cardiff, Welsh Assembly Government

Greer, S (2001) *Divergence and Devolution* London, Nuffield Trust

Greer, S (2004) *Territorial Politics and Health Policy* Manchester, Manchester University Press

Hawkes, N and Jewell, T (2010) 'Back to the future with the Welsh CMO', *British Medical Journal* 341(c3382), pp 12-13

Morgan, R (2002) National Centre for Public Policy Annual Lecture, Swansea, University of Wales

NAW (National Assembly for Wales) (2001) *Improving Health in Wales: A plan for the NHS with its partners* Cardiff, NAW

Scottish Office (1997) *Designed to Care: Renewing the National Health Service in Scotland*, Cm 3811, London, The Stationery Office

Scottish Government (2000) *Our National Health: a plan for action, a plan for change*, Edinburgh, Scottish Executive

Smith, K E, Hunter, D J, Blackman,T, Elliott, E, Greene, A, Barbara, E, Harrington, B E, Marks, L, Mckee, L and Williams, G H (2009) 'Divergence or convergence? Health inequalities and policy in a devolved Britain',*Critical Social Policy* May 2009; 29:2, pp 216-42

Sparer, M.S., France, G. and Clinton, C. (2011) 'Inching toward Incrementalism: Federalism, Devolution, and Health Policy in the United States and the United Kingdom' *Journal of Health Politics Policy and Law*, 36:1, pp 33-57

Sullivan, M (2000) *Labour, Citizenship and Social Policy: A retreat from social democracy?* (inaugural lecture) Swansea, University of Wales

Sullivan, M (2004) 'Wales, devolution and health policy: Policy differentiation and experimentation to improve health', *Contemporary Wales* 17(1), pp 44–65

Townsend, P (2001) *Targeting Poor Health* Cardiff, Welsh Assembly Government

Townsend, P (2005) *Inequalities in Health: The Welsh dimension 2002–2005* Cardiff, Welsh Assembly Government

WAG (2004) *Hutt Welcomes Focus on Preventing Ill Health*, 18 November, Cardiff, WAG

WAG (2005a) *Designed for Life: Creating world-class health and social care for Wales in the 21st century* Cardiff, WAG

WAG (2005b) *Delivering a 26 Week Patient Pathway: Proposed principles and definitions* Cardiff: Welsh Assembly Government

WAG (2007) *One Wales: A progressive agenda for the administration of Wales* Cardiff, WAG

Wanless, D (2003) *Review of Health and Social Care in Wales* Cardiff, WAG

Welsh Affairs Select Committee (2010) *Cross border provision of services in Wales: A follow-up report* London, House of Commons

Welsh Health Circular (2006) *Delivering a 26 Week Patient Pathway* Cardiff, WAG

Welsh Health Circular (2007) *Delivering a 26 Week Target: Operational guidelines* Cardiff, WAG

Welsh Office (1998) *NHS Wales: Putting patients first* Cardiff, Welsh Office

Western Mail (2005) 'Health supremo sets sights on shorter waiting times', 11 January

Western Mail (2006) 'A year of patient power in Wales', 28 December

Western Mail (2007) 'Public demonstrations held throughout Wales', 22 February

Withers, M (2011) 'Plaid Cymru uses old tactics in new election campaign', *Wales on Sunday*, 24 April

Section Two

Key Themes in Service Delivery

Chapter 4

From the Margins to the Centre: Language-sensitive Practice and Social Welfare

Elaine Davies

Introduction

Any attempt to address language-sensitive practice from the standpoint of the Welsh language in Wales relates to three core issues. First, it requires individual practitioners to address the affective or the subjective, an exploration of their personal attitudes, values and perceptions of the language. This links with personal experiences, family histories and group identities and requires an honest exploration of each. Second, it has to do very clearly with the social domain of the Welsh language and an understanding of the complex factors that affect language use in Wales. This helps ensure that social welfare practice and policy is grounded in a firm understanding of factors that relate to the history, status and current use of the language. Third, and most importantly, it has to do with an appreciation of power, disempowerment and empowerment as they affect Welsh speakers.

Language-sensitive practice also requires the adoption of basic principles, inclusivity being foremost. Rather than building barriers and creating fortresses, as has sometimes happened in the past, it is vital to identify common ground and to look at ways of forging alliances and engaging people who would otherwise be on the outside of the issue. This means recognising the role, not only of Welsh-speaking practitioners, but also of non-Welsh-speaking colleagues, in the task of furthering language choice for bilingual users. The vision of 'one Wales' is also central as opposed to the more traditional tendency of seeing Wales as a country divided by its geography and economy, its language and culture. By locating language-sensitive practice firmly in the context of empowerment, it becomes more possible for old misunderstandings to be aired and resolved and for language-sensitive practice to be given a rightful place on the diversity agenda in Wales.

Discussions of power, empowerment and their links with language-sensitive practice raise vital questions about the relationship between the periphery and the core. Fishman (1990) sets this in a sociolinguistic context with reference to 'centralizing the periphery' and working on the 'cultivation of marginality'. Reflecting on this relationship between the periphery and the core, he states that '[t]he periphery magnifies and clarifies. Above all, it refuses to take matters for granted. It refuses to confuse peripherality with unimportance, or weakness in numbers or in power, with weakness vis á vis equity, justice, law and morality' (Fishman, 1990, p 113). It is this tension between the periphery and the core, between marginalising and mainstreaming, that underpins much of the following discussion. To this end, this chapter aims to address why social welfare practitioners in Wales need to engage with the Welsh language and language choice in their work with bilingual service users. It will also discuss what they need to know about the Welsh language and its speakers, that is, the knowledge base needed to inform practice and policy, as well as touching on how social care providers can strengthen the delivery of bilingual services.

The legislative and policy drive

It was the Welsh Language Act 1993 that first set a legislative framework for the language with its aim to 'promote and facilitate the language in Wales, in particular in the conduct of public business and the administration of justice on the basis of equality with English'. As well as introducing the principle of equality, the Act also required public sector providers to prepare statutory Language Schemes, stating the steps they intended taking to implement this principle in their service provision. It also established the Welsh Language Board with the duty of overseeing the implementation of these schemes and promoting the language in a wider sense.

In the context of social care, the guidance provided by the Welsh Language Board to agencies preparing Welsh Language Schemes stated that 'in circumstances where stress, vulnerability, illness or disability are key factors, not being able to communicate in their first language may place those concerned at personal disadvantage. Given the sensitive nature of many of these discussions, it is important to offer language choice wherever possible' (Welsh Language Board, 1996, p 26).

The Act no doubt heightened awareness of the language. For many public sector providers it registered on the radar for the first time, with the production of Welsh Language Schemes setting out changes in the way in which providers intended operating. Many voluntary sector providers also produced similar sets of policies and strategies. But, despite these attempts to afford the language greater equality, there was scant evidence of any real change in the ease and extent of language choice made available to bilingual users across Wales as a whole. There grew a considerable body of anecdotal evidence suggesting that bilingual users continued to face the dual block of low personal expectations and correspondingly low levels of actual bilingual provision. The empirical evidence made available in the Welsh Consumer Council Report prepared by Misell (2000), and Thomas' (1998) research on Welsh-speaking women and bilingual maternity services, has been borne out in more recent work. Jones and Eaves' (2008) review of bilingual service delivery in the criminal justice sector in North Wales and Prys' (2009) work among users of third sector services provide an equally challenging account.

Very often, the onus still appears to be on the assertive service user or carer to ask for Welsh-medium services rather than on the service provider to identify language need and attempt to respond appropriately.

With a growing lobby of opinion in Wales in favour of new and more robust Welsh language legislation to encompass the private sector and, among other things, to strengthen the rights of Welsh speakers, a cursory evaluation of the 1993 Act may conclude that among its successes was the creation of a more positive climate for the language generally. But this was offset by its failure to bring about any real improvement in the bilingual services available to users in Wales as a whole, and especially to social care users, often vulnerable and marginalised and least able to invoke their linguistic rights.

It is against this background that the Welsh Language (Wales) Measure became law in February 2011. It confirms official status for the Welsh language and creates the new post of Welsh Language Commissioner with enforcement powers to protect the rights of Welsh speakers to access services through the medium of Welsh. The current system of Welsh Language Schemes will be replaced by a system of Language Standards and a new Welsh Language Tribunal will offer a right of appeal against decisions made in relation to the provision of services through the medium of Welsh. The Measure also allows for an official investigation by the Welsh Language Commissioner of alleged instances of attempts to curtail the freedom of Welsh speakers wishing to use the language with one another. It also creates a Welsh Language Partnership Council to advise government on its strategy for the language. The Welsh Language Board will be abolished and its functions shared between the office of the Welsh Language Commissioner and a Welsh Language Unit within the Welsh Assembly Government.

Despite affording the language official status, the Measure nevertheless fails to offer speakers an absolute right to receive services in their preferred language. Williams (2011) draws a distinction between Wales and Canada in this respect. In Canada, with its written constitution, language rights are unambiguously affirmed; everyone knows what their rights are; they know what they can expect, and also know that they have legal redress. But in Wales, Williams (2011, p 6–7) argues that while the new legislation may give individuals the right to demand a level of Welsh-medium service delivery, this is not the same, he says, as having 'the right to expect that provision will be made available'. Ultimately, in parts of the country where levels of Welsh-medium provision may be weaker than in others, the onus may still rest with the vociferous user or carer to create demand rather than with the service provider to set in place a sound system to identify and respond to need on a basis of equality and ease of access.

While recognising this inherent limitation, the 2011 Measure nevertheless builds on previous legislation and, coupled with the proposed strategic framework for the Welsh language, it offers a useful and important building block for speakers of a minority language whose language use in the public sphere has traditionally been severely curtailed. The draft Welsh Language Strategy, the subject of consultation during the period December 2010 to February 2011, picks up on several of the themes addressed previously in the *Iaith Pawb* strategy (WAG, 2003). It has as its basis a four-fold vision for:

- an increase in the number of people who both speak and use the language;
- an increase in the opportunities to use Welsh, allied with initiatives aimed at raising people's confidence and fluency in the language;
- an increase in people's awareness of the value of Welsh, both as part of Wales' national heritage and as an important skill in modern life;
- directed initiatives throughout Wales to strengthen the Welsh language at community level (WAG, 2010, p 1).

It builds on the bold affirmation of bilingualism seen in *Iaith Pawb*, that is, of a society in which both languages co-exist with one another and of the need to accommodate this interrelationship in public policy. This theme is significant and helps set the tone for sustaining the development of the inclusive, equality-based, social policies that were touched on in the introduction to this chapter.

Iaith Pawb referred to the rights of the individual to use the Welsh language. Such a reference to the rights agenda as an aspect of public policy in relation to the Welsh language was seen in Wales for the first time with the assertion that '[t]he Welsh Assembly Government aims to safeguard and promote the right of individuals to use the Welsh language' (WAG, 2003, p 47). It identified the importance of language-sensitive provision in health and social care, referring to the specific needs of certain user groups, for example, older people, young children, people with learning difficulties and people with mental health problems, and stated its determination 'to impress the importance of being able to deliver services in the service users' language of choice in key service areas such as health and social care' (WAG, 2003, p 47).

Not surprisingly, this area is revisited in the new consultation strategy, with an emphasis this time on the concept of 'language need', for those priority groups of service users outlined above. The implication therefore is that many of the rights-based service improvements envisaged in 2003 remain as great a challenge as ever. This is how the need for change is articulated:

Strengthening the Welsh language in health and social care is regarded
as a priority since, for many, language in this context is more than just a
matter of choice – it is a matter of need. Language choice refers to the
individual's right to choose language, but language need means
considering language as an integral element of care, for instance, people
with dementia, or people who have had a stroke often lose their second
language. (WAG, 2010, p 16)

It is conceded that 'the provision of Welsh language services remains piecemeal and too often it is a matter of chance whether people receive Welsh language services' (WAG, 2010, p 17). Indeed, qualitative research undertaken on behalf of the Welsh Assembly Government and the Care Council for Wales during the spring of 2011 bears this out. It focused on the same four priority groups of service users – children, older people, people with mental health problems, including dementia, and people with learning disabilities – and found that many suffered double jeopardy as vulnerable, sometimes marginalised service users who also speak a minority language, which is often not reflected or fully considered in the services provided for them (WAG, Department for Health and Social Services, 2011).

To this end, one of the key areas identified in the 2010 consultation strategy refers to 'publishing a Strategic Framework for Health and Social Care aimed at ensuring a more strategic approach to strengthening bilingual services. It will improve the experiences of patients and service users who either choose, or have a need for, services through the medium of Welsh' (WAG, 2010, p 17).

This specific language-related objective coincides with the publication of the new strategic framework for social services in Wales (WAG, 2011). As with other strands of local government and social welfare policy over recent years, the underpinning principle again relates to citizen-focused services that are responsive to the needs of individuals and communities (for example, WAG, 2004, 2006). And as with these previous policy statements, the Welsh language dimension is again addressed explicitly and set firmly in the context of the need to develop services that recognise 'the diversity of Wales and its status as a bilingual nation' (WAG, 2011, p 16). In this respect, it is no different from the assertion made in the 10-year strategy for social services in Wales published in 2007. The thrust there too is to acknowledge that '[t]he Welsh language is an essential part of the Welsh culture and life. It must be reflected in developing effective social care strategies as well as in planning, delivering and improving services for individuals whose language of preference is Welsh' (WAG, 2007, para 3.29).

With the passage of time, the gap between rhetoric and practice grows and the need to take affirmative action through the meaningful application of policy becomes more acute. This is given added weight in the third report of the Committee of Experts of the Council of Europe, published in 2010. (The Committee reports on the situation of minority languages as part of its work monitoring the application of the European Charter for Regional or Minority Languages.) The Committee concluded that in the Welsh context there is more to be done; it urged the United Kingdom (UK), as a signatory to the European Charter with its underpinning principles of respect for diversity, language rights and equality of opportunity, to strengthen its efforts to ensure the provision of health and social care services in Welsh.

Language-sensitive practice: the knowledge base

Language, identity and communication

In the mid-1990s, the Central Council for Education and Training in Social Work (CCETSW) published training materials whose title, *'They all Speak English Anyway'* (Davies, 1994), summed up a not uncommon assessment of language use among bilingual Welsh–English speakers in Wales. Underpinning this assertion that 'they all speak English anyway' is an assumption that language is merely a means of communication.

At the time of publishing the CCETSW materials, and contrary to this popular view, there was a wealth of anecdotal evidence from bilingual speakers themselves and a growing body of international research on bilingualism (Grosjean, 1989, 1994), suggesting that language use among bilingual speakers is complex and multidimensional. Shortly before the publication of *'They All Speak English Anyway'*, the Anglo–Welsh writer, John Barnie, had described his experience of learning a second language, saying: 'I had the common experience that speaking another language alters the "I" that is being expressed. I had not realized before that what you are is partly formed by what you speak' (Barnie, 1992, p 119).

Almost simultaneously with the CCETSW publication in 1994, Aitchison and Carter (1994, p 6) were also affirming the link between language, ethnicity and identity.

> *[L]anguage is much more than a means of communication. Not only does it carry a view of the environment, using that word in its proper inclusive sense, but through its vocabulary and its structure, through the associations generated by its literature, through the symbol which it is and the symbols which it transmits, it creates a distinctive identity which is at once a derivative of tradition and an expression of the present.*

Language was therefore seen as something that powerfully roots speakers in their past, helps them make sense of their present and creates a sense of affinity and shared territory, all themes that were echoed in Fishman's (1972, p 46) work:

> *Language was also the surest way for individuals to safeguard (or recover) the authenticity they had inherited from their ancestors as well as to hand it on to generations yet unborn, and finally, that worldwide diversity in language and in culture was a good and beautiful thing in and of itself...*

Since the mid-1990s, researchers have drawn on evidence to firmly challenge the notion that language is merely a vehicle of communication. Emotion and expression, they argue, are often shaped by the social and cultural context in which they are experienced. Altarriba and Morier (2004), for example, draw on research of language use among bilingual service users in mental health settings; much of this is based on work with Hispanic users and other minority communities in North America. They come to the conclusion that in psychological assessment and diagnosis, 'a bilingual may appear to present him or herself in different ways depending on the language used' (Altarriba and Morier, 2004, p 252). They quote Guttfreund, who had already concluded in 1990 that 'for the Hispanic population the therapeutic process may be far more meaningful in Spanish, because members of this population are likely to feel more comfortable expressing their feelings in Spanish' (Guttfreund, 1990, p 606). Altarriba and Morier (2004, p 274) conclude that 'past experiences are often coded in the language in which they occurred and that the appropriate language can be used successfully as a retrieval cue when engaging in dialogue with a bilingual client'.

Pavlenko (2006) draws together research and analysis from several language communities and addresses more fully these links between language and meaning, expression and emotion, and language and self. The questions raised address whether bilingual and multilingual people experience themselves as different people to some extent when speaking different languages. Do they behave differently in their different languages? And are they perceived differently by those with whom they speak?

Based on several strands of empirical research among bilingual and multilingual speakers, Pavlenko (2006, pp 26–7) concludes that '[r]eflections and explorations by linguists and psychoanalysts show that languages may create different, and sometimes incommensurable, worlds for their speakers who feel that their selves change with the shift in language'. Some bilingual and multilingual people may perceive the world differently, she says, and change perspectives, ways of thinking and verbal and non-verbal behaviours when switching languages.

> *'Yes, when I am using Italian especially. I am more emotional and use my hands more. My husband has also commented that I adopt the Icelandic attitudes when I am using Icelandic especially when speaking to officials. If you pick up the language in the country where it is spoken then you pick up the traits and habits of those people.'*
> (Wendy, 30. Speaks English – French – German – Italian – Icelandic)

> *'I feel much more sophisticated when I speak English probably because I learnt it from sophisticated people in private college in York some time ago. When I speak Dutch I feel like a more precise person. I learned to use it in a very precise and accurate way and for example never to mix up one word with another.'*
> (Clement, 18. Speaks French – Dutch – Italian – English)

'In Welsh I'm more confident and in control. The words flow more easily. In English, I struggle more to express myself. I always think that I sound authoritative in Welsh; in English I sound less intelligent and less in control.
Some things are far easier to discuss in Welsh. I can talk about business matters in English, no problem. In many ways, it's easier to talk about things like this in English. But when it comes to talking about my personal life – ill health, worries about my family, anxieties about the future ... all of these things have to happen in Welsh to have any meaning.'
(Jenny, 45. Speaks Welsh –English)

Source: Pavlenko (2006, p 12)

It could be argued that this body of work helps cast a more favourable light on the previously discredited sociolinguistic work of Sapir and Whorf (1929), often referred to as the Sapir–Whorf hypothesis and based on the view that the language we speak directly influences the way we think. For several years, people argued that if the Whorfian hypothesis were true and if languages created different worlds for people, then bilingual and multilingual people would be doomed to confusion and difficulty in translating meanings and making sense of different language-related experiences. And yet the work of Pavlenko and others suggests that the dismissal of linguistic relativity in the work of Sapir and Whorf may be misplaced, because 'our respondents tell us that their thinking, behaviour, and perception of the self and the world do change with the change in language' (Pavlenko, 2006, p 13). Clearly, in relation to social welfare practice in Wales, this shift away from seeing language merely as a medium of communication is significant. Language use for bilingual speakers is complex; shifts in language use create subtle shifts in the tone, texture and nature of what is being said. To be authentic and meaningful, some experiences and emotions are bound to be related in one language rather than the other.

This is summed up by a bilingual Welsh–English speaker relating her experience of operating a telephone helpline for a large voluntary organisation in Wales.

Welsh speakers often phone for advice. They often start the conversation by asking for factual or practical information and then move on to talk about a far more personal problem which is more difficult to discuss. Although it is difficult to put one's finger on the reason why, I get the impression that they move on to the second subject, often the real reason for phoning, because they are able to speak Welsh. The nature of the service would be different if I was unable to speak Welsh.
(Davies, 1999, p 9)

It is this relationship between language, experience and expression that was described by many of the bilingual service users who took part in research on the experiences of Welsh-speaking users of health and social care services (WAG, 2011). For many respondents, use of their preferred language is powerful in terms of creating affinity and forming closer professional relationships. For others, and especially for users of mental health services, the use of English to access their inner, emotional world does not always enable them to make the best use of the services being provided. And for many, the link between language-appropriate assessment, intervention and sound outcomes is tangible.

Language and power

Issues to do with power are at the core of each and every language. Edwards (1994, pp 1–2) sets this in context:

> While there exist something like 5,000 languages in about 200 countries
> ... only a quarter of all states recognise more than one language. Also,
> even in those countries in which two or more varieties have legal status,
> one language is usually predominant, or has regional limitations, or
> carries with it disproportionate amounts of social, economic and political
> power.

In the relationship between one language and another, the power dimension is a force to be reckoned with. This is especially salient, as Edwards suggests, when one of these languages has recognised status and the other has less status and prestige.

In her analysis, Siencyn (1995) differentiates between perceptions of low-status, low-prestige languages on the one hand, and high-status, high-prestige languages on the other. Box 4.1 presents the common perceptions to which Siencyn refers:

Box 4.1 Perceptions of high- and low-status languages

High-status languages	Low-status languages
easy to learn	difficult to learn
pure, with no borrowed words	full of borrowed words
widely used	of limited use
easy on the ear	full of strange sounds
sophisticated and modern	old-fashioned

Source: Siecyn (1995, p 25)

According to Siencyn, people often reach misplaced conclusions based on perceptions such as these, for example, that:

- some languages are more important than others;
- some languages are more modern and relevant than others;
- some languages are of limited use and of little value.

When perceptions such as these are aired consistently over time, they tend to influence speakers of the language; negative judgements are internalised. And when individuals feel that they are the butt of criticism, insecurities are generated and confidence drained. They are then more likely to change or adapt behaviour in order to reduce anxiety and embarrassment. This helps explain in part why Welsh speakers are often so ready to switch language and why they often play down and denigrate their ability to speak Welsh. All these characteristics are significant for bilingual users of social welfare services in Wales. Added to that, their personal circumstances may mean that they feel particularly fragile and disempowered. In this respect it is worth referring to Dafis' (1996, p 12) distinction between strong and weak linguistic contexts (see Box 4.2):

Box 4.2: Distinction between weak and strong linguistic contexts

Weak linguistic contexts

- when the situation/context are unfamiliar and where there is no training or preparation
- when there is a sense of threat
- when there is anxiety, fear and negative emotions
- when power and authority back up the other speaker

Strong linguistic contexts

- when there is training and preparation
- when there is no threat
- when there are no obvious emotions and when the speaker is relatively neutral
- when the speaker has power and authority

Welsh-speaking social care workers may also share these characteristics and lack confidence in their use of Welsh. And in the Welsh Assembly Government funded research (WAG, 2011) referred to above, respondents speak of a reticence on the part of health and social care staff to use their Welsh language skills. As a result, several respondents suggest the need for employers to acknowledge and value Welsh language skills at all levels within the workforce and to develop support systems to enable staff to further develop and strengthen these skills.

Romaine (2004) summarises this discussion of language and power in a bilingual society with her analysis of what is known as 'diglossia' – a distinct differentiation in the function of both languages. And Wales offers an excellent example of a society in which both languages have occupied very distinct and separate domains:

*Many bilingual communities are characterized by diglossia, a term used
to refer to a kind of functional specialization between languages (referred
to as High and Low) so that the language used within the home and in
other personal domains of interaction between community members is
different from the one used in higher functions such as government,
media, education.* (Romaine, 2004, p 393)

The shadow of history

Bilingual service users in Wales will be influenced unconsciously by several of the factors
discussed above. Deep-seated structural and attitudinal obstacles help explain why, for
many, their language is something to be kept under wraps. The disproportionate power
allocated to the Welsh and English language in Wales was nowhere more acutely
expressed than in the language clauses of the Acts of Union of 1536 and 1542. At this
time, Wales was incorporated within England and it was legislated that English would be
the only official language of Wales; people using the Welsh language were not to hold
any 'manner of office or fees within the Realm of England, Wales or other of the King's
dominions'.

These language clauses had a profound effect on the Welsh language. It was
marginalised and came to occupy the private, unofficial sphere of everyday life. The
historian John Davies (1990, pp 225–6) describes the impact on Welsh speakers in the
following terms: 'Ni allai Cymro uniaith lai na theimlo'n anfreintiedig o dan drefn o'r fath,
a thros y canrifoedd byddai'r ymwybyddiaeth hon o fraint siaradwyr y Saesneg yn
meithrin agweddau at y Gymraeg a fygythiai einioes yr iaith' (A monoglot Welsh speaker
could only feel underprivileged under such a system and over the centuries this
awareness of the privilege of English speakers would nurture attitudes towards the Welsh
language which would endanger the existence of the language).

As the domains of the language shrank, it lost its status and over the centuries, Davies
argues, this had a marked effect on attitudes towards the language and on the use made
of it.

A very cursory exploration of some of the more significant milestones in the history of
the language has to take into account the events of 1847. In that year a report was
published on the condition of education in Wales; it came to be known as *Brad y Llyfrau
Gleision* (The Treachery of the Blue Books). The following quote, lifted from the report
itself, is characteristic of its tone and findings: 'The Welsh language is a vast drawback
to Wales and a manifold barrier to the moral progress and commercial prosperity of the
people. It is not easy to over-estimate its evil effects' (Reports of the Commissioners of
Inquiry into the State of Education in Wales, 1847, p 66). Writing of the significance of
the report, the historian Gwyn A. Williams comments that:

The Education Report of 1847, accurate enough in its exposure of the pitiful inadequacy of school provision, moved on to a partisan, often vicious and often lying attack on Welsh Nonconformity and the Welsh language itself as a vehicle of immorality, backwardness and obscurantism. The London press, led by a racist Morning Chronicle, called for the extinction of Welsh. (Williams, 1985, p 208)

Soon afterwards came the Education Act 1870, which made no provision at all for the teaching of Welsh in elementary schools in Wales. During the last quarter of the 19th century and the first quarter of the 20th century came evidence from several parts of Wales of children being punished for speaking Welsh by having to wear a block of wood around their neck with the letters WN (Welsh Not) carved on it. When a child wearing the Welsh Not heard another speaking Welsh they would eagerly pass it on, keen to be rid of its stigma. This would continue throughout the school day and the child wearing the Welsh Not at the end of the day would be chastised by the teacher before being sent home: 'The Welsh Not slung around a child's neck to accompany his or her punishment for speaking his or her own language has become notorious. It was not very effective but it enormously reinforced the image of Welsh as an inferior and gutter tongue' (Williams, 1985, p 246).

The Welsh Not was not in any way unique. A similar device – a small wooden clog – was used in Brittany to deter Breton-speaking children from using their language in school. And similar techniques were used in several African countries, for example, to stop children from speaking their indigenous languages.

By the end of the 19th century, English was the language for getting on in the world. With the growth of industrialisation, Wales saw an emerging middle class, the owners and managers of the new iron and coal works, who, with the passage of time, were predominantly English speaking. This became a further threat to the Welsh language as working people aped the mores and language of the middle class. Already keenly aware of the message of the 1847 Commissioners' Report, they attached little economic value to the Welsh language and saw little point in transferring the language to their children. What then followed was a period of rapid decline in the number and percentage of Welsh speakers throughout the 20th century.

At the beginning of the 20th century, almost 50% of the population of Wales was Welsh speaking, close on one million people. By the end of the century, the number of Welsh speakers had dropped by almost a half and the loss in proportionate terms was even greater:

- 1901: 929,800 (49.9%)
- 1951: 714,700 (28.9%)
- 1971: 542,400 (20.8%)
- 1991: 508,098 (18.6%)

It is this stark demographic trend which is reflected in the personal and family history of hundreds of thousands of Welsh people for whom the language was lost during the last century. Many, however, are now reclaiming the language and reconnecting with it; this is witnessed in the changing demographics of the 2001 Census.

Implications for service provision today

The 2001 Census showed an upturn in the number and percentage of Welsh speakers, from 508,098 (18.6%) in 1991 to 575,640 (20.5%) in 2001. It also confirmed a trend that was already beginning to emerge in 1991, with boundaries shifting eastwards beyond the traditional heartland of the Welsh language in North and West Wales.

The 2001 Census confirmed that approximately 60% of Welsh speakers now live in urban areas, with very significant numbers living in the urban and old industrial centres of South Wales. Aitchison and Carter (2004) refer to two key areas, the former stretching from Kidwelly, through Pontyberem, Ammanford and Gwaencaegurwen to Ystradgynlais, and the other in Cwm Tawe, the Swansea Valley, spreading from Ystalyfera, through Pontardawe and Clydach to Swansea and westwards to Gorseinon and Llanelli. Jointly these two areas include 100,000 Welsh speakers. Aitchison and Carter also refer to the density of Welsh speakers in Cardiff, with over 30,000 speakers. Just as significant, they say, is a cluster of wards in Newport and parts of the South Wales valleys with substantial numbers of Welsh speakers:

> [While it is customary to identify the Welsh speaking community with rural areas of north and west Wales (Y Fro Gymraeg), the actual heartland of that community in terms of absolute numbers lies in south Wales, embracing longstanding Welsh-speaking communities of the former western coal-field and the burgeoning areas to the east, with Cardiff as a powerful focal point. (Aitchison and Carter, 2004, p 56)

However, '[in these areas] whilst there are some strong clusters where Welsh speakers are locally dominant, these are relatively small in number. The great majority of Welsh speakers are widely scattered and live in areas where percentages are still relatively low' (Aitchison and Carter, 2004, p 53).

Therefore, any consideration of the implications of these demographic trends for service planning has to avoid the temptation to concentrate Welsh-medium service delivery solely on those areas with a substantial percentage of Welsh speakers, the traditional Welsh-speaking areas, such as Ynys Môn (Anglesey, 59.9%), Ceredigion (51.8%) and Gwynedd (68.7%), for example. It is vital to also consider the needs of Welsh speakers in South and North East Wales where percentage rates may be low but where actual numbers are significant; for example, Swansea – 28,581 (13.2%), Rhondda Cynon Taf – 27,505 (12.3%) and Flintshire – 20,277 (14.1%).

In his review of the Welsh language in the health service, Misell (2000, p 15) teases out the service provision implications in the following terms:

> It should be remembered that it is as an individual that patients approach the National Health Service for treatment, rather than as representatives of communities, and the needs and wishes of each individual patient are equally important. From this viewpoint, the linguistic 'Welshness' or otherwise of the region a patient is living in is wholly irrelevant when considering whether provision should be made for him or her through the medium of Welsh.

Misell compares the situation of the Welsh speaker with speakers of other minority languages in Britain and draws on the work of Balarajan and Raleigh (1995) who refer to the risk of concentrating resources wholly on those areas with a density of minority language speakers: 'The issue is important not just for health authorities with large black and minority ethnic communities, but also for authorities where the numbers are smaller and hence there is a risk that their needs will be overlooked' (Balarajan and Raleigh, 1995, quoted in Misell, 2000, p 15). In interviews with health care professionals, Misell hears about the experience of service users – 'the hidden Welsh' as he calls them – in parts of Wales thought of as non-Welsh-speaking areas and where the needs of the Welsh speaker are often overlooked. In an exhortation to those responsible for planning local services, Misell comes to the conclusion that:

> ... there is not, and never has been, such a thing as a 'non-Welsh speaking area' in Wales, and such old-fashioned ideas about the geographical territory of the Welsh language can only stand in the way of any attempts to increase and develop the provision of services through Welsh. Welsh speakers are to be found in all parts of Wales and it is in some of the most Anglicised areas that the greatest growth of the Welsh language is to be found. There is therefore no point attempting to justify restricting Welsh language provision to certain parts of Wales. (Misell, 2000, p 15)

Little has changed during the past 10 years. The 2011 Welsh Assembly Government funded research (WAG, 2011) reaffirmed the distinct needs and aspirations of Welsh-speaking service users in urban Wales and found that they are often confronted with low levels of awareness and service provision on the part of health and social care agencies. Added to this, the 2011 Census is very likely to show continuing increases in the number of Welsh speakers in urban Wales.

The other significant demographic trend to be considered in relation to social care provision is the growth in the number and proportion of young Welsh speakers. In the early 1990s, when analysing the 1991 Census data on Welsh speakers, the *Western Mail* carried the headline, 'The Welsh Language is Getting Younger'. This trend continued, and the 2001 Census witnessed a further increase in the number of young Welsh speakers with 31.2% of 3- to 15-year-olds reported as having an ability to speak Welsh (Aitchison and Carter, 2004, p 87), compared with 22.3% in 1991 (Aitchison and Carter, 1994, p 104).

In parts of South and South East Wales, the percentage of young Welsh speakers, as a proportion of the local Welsh-speaking community as a whole, is striking. For example, in Newport 70.2% of Welsh speakers fall into the 3–15 age group, 69.5% in Torfaen, 68.2% in Blaenau Gwent and 54.5% in Caerphilly.

Each speaker's individual language profile will vary: some will speak Welsh at home, more will be fluent in Welsh through school but may not use the language at home and others may be learning the language without yet being fluent. But from what is known about the complex patterns of language use among bilingual speakers, and the interrelationship between language, expression and emotion, it is argued that issues regarding language choice should always be addressed in any work with bilingual children and young people. Language-sensitive practice is crucial to securing the child's voice, enabling sound assessment and ensuring the best outcome. The challenge of providing appropriate levels of provision is set to continue as 2011 Welsh language Census data are very likely to indicate growing numbers of young Welsh speakers.

Language-sensitive practice – the way forward

Bringing about a shift in the profile of the Welsh language and the availability of services in the user's language of choice – a shift from the margins to the centre – requires social welfare agencies to engage with language as a mainstream issue. In guidance published in 1996, the Welsh Language Board stated that '[t]he key to providing a high quality service through the medium of Welsh is to make the language a natural, integral part of the planning and delivery of that service' (Welsh Language Board, 1996, guideline 2). Since then, the Welsh Assembly Government has firmed up the theme of mainstreaming by embedding language-sensitive provision in many of its policy statements (WAG, 2003, 2004, 2006, 2007, 2010, 2011). The language, rather than being a problematic afterthought, it is suggested, has to become a core consideration in all aspects of policy implementation, planning and monitoring. However, the gap persists between policy rhetoric on the one hand and practical implementation and service improvement on the other.

The use of workforce planning frameworks, with the adoption of Language Skills Strategies, offers one way to bridge the gap between rhetoric and action. This may result in an audit of workforce language skills; the compilation of data on the language profile of users and carers; an identification of the match or mismatch between staff capacity and user need and consequent levels of unmet need. It then becomes possible to identify skills deficits and to consider the adoption of recruitment policies that may include affirmative action in relation to the training and recruitment of a bilingual workforce. Such frameworks may also highlight education and training issues, some of which may be addressed in the short term through continuing professional development opportunities, for example language skills training to top up the language competence of the existing workforce. Other issues, such as the promotion of the social welfare professions among bilingual speakers and the development and support of appropriate educational frameworks, may need to be addressed on a longer-term basis and in collaboration with sector skills councils and higher education institutions.

Another core consideration in terms of mainstreaming and embedding Welsh language-sensitive practice relates to the role of users and carers. By placing language-sensitive practice firmly in the context of empowerment and citizen-centred services as stated in the current Welsh Assembly Government *Framework for action* (WAG, 2011), it follows that the drive for change has to be rooted very much in the perspective of users and carers. Based on the available sociolinguistic evidence of the inter relationship between language, experience and expression, as well as evidence regarding the historical disempowerment of Welsh speakers, the development of language-sensitive practice becomes much more than just a concession or a marginal consideration. It becomes a core practice issue – a matter of hearing the voice of those who are otherwise silenced.

An inclusive approach towards both language communities in Wales, and an accompanying focus on equality and empowerment, also secure a role for all social welfare practitioners, regardless of language. At one end of the continuum will be those who are able to work with users through the medium of Welsh. At the other end will be those practitioners who may not be able to speak the language but whose values are sound and who have a vital role to play in identifying need and advocating on behalf of Welsh-speaking users and carers. Across the continuum will be opportunities for practitioners to acquire different levels of linguistic skill appropriate to their professional capacity, and for all to embrace practice that is informed by principles of equality and empowerment.

Williams (2000, p 377) sets this in the context of devolved government in Wales with an affirmation of the importance of inclusivity and equality:

> *If the National Assembly is to succeed as a political institution people from all over, and from both main linguistic groups, must be able to engage with it and feel a sense of shared ownership. In order for this to occur, the potential sensitivities of the linguistic politics of Wales will need to be recognized and addressed. If, however, the Welsh language is seen in terms of a resource rather than as a problem or, indeed, simply a matter of rights and entitlements, then this will be an important contribution to the development of a common Welsh civic identity – the emergence of which is surely a precondition for the success of the National Assembly and ultimately for the complete rehabilitation of Welsh as co-equal language of everyday life in Wales.*

The Welsh Language (Wales) Measure 2011 and the forthcoming strategy for the Welsh language, together with the specific sector-related commitment to language-sensitive service delivery seen in the 2007 10-year strategy for social services in Wales and the more recent reaffirmation of this in the *Framework for action* (WAG, 2011), create a real platform for change. But the challenge of fusing together both strands of policy over the next few years will call for considerable energy and commitment on a local and regional level and a real conviction that 'the Welsh language is seen in terms of a resource rather than as a problem', with the development of language-sensitive practice being seen as a spur to developing excellence rather than as a minor irritant or a marginal afterthought.

References

Aitchison, J and Carter, H (1994) *A Geography of the Welsh Language* Cardiff, University of Wales Press

Aitchison, J and Carter, H (2004) *Spreading the Word: The Welsh Language 2001* Talybont, Y Lolfa

Altarriba, J and Morier, R G (2004) 'Bilingualism: language, emotion and mental health' in Bhatia, T K and Rithcie, W C (eds) *The Handbook of Bilingualism* Oxford, Blackwell

Balarajan, R and Raleigh, V S (1995) *Ethnicity and Health in England* London, NHS Executive, quoted in Misell, A (2000) *Welsh in the Health Service* Cardiff, Welsh Consumer Council

Barnie, J (1992) 'Foreigners', in Davies, O and Bowie, F (eds) *Discovering Welshness* Llandysul, Gomer

Dafis, Ll (1996) 'The need to be understood: an introduction to language sensitivity', – Barnes, J (ed) *Human Development, Language and Practice* Cardiff, CCETSW

Davies, E (1994) *'They All Speak English Anyway': The Welsh language and anti-oppressive practice* Cardiff, CCETSW

Davies, E (1999) *The Language of a Caring Service* Cardiff, Welsh Language Board

Davies, J (1990) *Hanes Cymru: A History of Wales in Welsh* London, Allen Lane, Penguin

Edwards, J (1994) *Multilingualism* London, Penguin

Fishman, J A (1972), 'Language and Nationalism. Two Integrative Essays,' Rowley, MA: Newbury House, quoted in Garcia, O and Schiffman, H, 'Fishman Sociolinguistics (1949 to the present)' in Garcia, O, Peltz, R, Schiffman, H and Fishman, GS (eds), 2006, *Language Loyalty, Continuity and Change,* Clevedon, Multilingual Matters

Fishman, J A (1990) 'My life through my work: my work through my life' in Koerner, K (ed) *First Person Singular* (vol 2) Amsterdam, Benjamins, John, pp 105–24, quoted in Garcia, O and Schiffman, H, 'Fishman sociolinguistics (1949 to the present)' in

Garcia, O, Peltz, R, Schiffman, H and Fishman, G S (eds) (2006) *Language Loyalty, Continuity and Change* Clevedon, Multilingual Matters

Grosjean, F (1989) 'Neurolinguists, beware! The bilingual is not two monolinguals in one person' *Brain and Language* 36, pp 3–15

Grosjean, F (1994) 'Individual bilingualism' in Archer, R E and Simpson, J M (eds) *The Encyclopaedia of Language and Linguistics* Oxford, Pergamon

Guttfreund, D C (1990) 'Effects of language usage on the emotional experience of Spanish–English and English–Spanish bilinguals' *Journal of Consulting and Clinical Psychology* 58, pp 604–7, quoted in Altarriba, J and Morier, R G (2004) 'Bilingualism: language, emotion and mental health' in Bhatia, T K and Rithcie, W C (eds) *The Handbook of Bilingualism* Oxford, Blackwell

Jones, K and Eaves, S (2008) *The Provision of Welsh Language Choice in the North Wales Criminal Justice Sector* Newcastle Emlyn, Iaith Cyf

Misell, A (2000) *Welsh in the Health Service* Cardiff, Welsh Consumer Council

Pavlenko, A (2006) 'Bilingual selves' in Pavlenko, A (ed) *Bilingual Minds: Emotional experience, expression and representation* Clevedon, Multilingual Matters

Prys, C (2009) 'Defnydd o'r Gymraeg yn y Trydydd Sector yng Nghymru' (Use of Welsh in the third sector in Wales), unpublished PhD thesis, Bangor University

Reports of the Commissioners of Inquiry into the State of Education in Wales (1847) Part II, London

Romaine, S (2004) 'The bilingual and multilingual community' in Bhatia, T K and Ritchie, W C (eds) *The Handbook of Bilingualism* Oxford, Blackwell

Sapir, E and Whorf, B L (1929) 'The status of linguistics as a science' in Mandelbaum, D (ed) (1945) *Selected Writings of Edward Sapir in Language, Culture and Personality* Berkeley, CA, University of California Press, pp 160–6

Siencyn, S W (1995) *A Sound Understanding: An Introduction to language awareness* Cardiff, CCETSW

Thomas, G (1998) 'The experience of Welsh speaking women in a bilingual maternity service', unpublished MSc dissertation, School of Nursing Studies, University of Wales College of Medicine, Cardiff

WAG (Welsh Assembly Government) (2003) *Iaith Pawb: A National action plan for a bilingual Wales* Cardiff, WAG

WAG (2004) *Making the Connections: Delivering better services for Wales* Cardiff, Welsh Assembly Government

WAG (2006) *Beyond Boundaries: Citizen centred local services for Wales* Cardiff, WAG

WAG (2007) *Fulfilled Lives, Supportive Communities: A strategy for social services in Wales over the next decade* Cardiff, WAG/NHS

WAG (2010) *A Living Language: A language for living: A Strategy for the Welsh language: Consultation document* Cardiff, WAG

WAG (2011) *Sustainable Social Services for Wales: A framework for action* Cardiff, WAG

WAG, Department for Health and Social Services (2011) *The Experiences of Welsh*

Speakers in Health and Social Care Services Cardiff, WAG

Welsh Language Board (1996) *Welsh Language Schemes: Their preparation and approval in accordance with the Welsh Language Act, 1993* Cardiff, Welsh Language Board

Williams, C H (2000) 'Conclusion: economic development and political responsibility' in Williams, C H (ed) *Language Revitalization: Policy and planning in Wales* Cardiff, University of Wales Press

Williams, C H (2011) 'Comisiynydd iaith: angen annibyniaeth' (Language commissioner: the need for independence) *Golwg* 23(30)

Williams, G A (1985) *When Was Wales?* London, Penguin

Chapter 5

Child Poverty in Wales – A Failed Promise?

Anne Crowley

The true measure of a nation's standing is how well it attends to its children – their health and safety, their material security, their education and socialisation, and their sense of being loved, valued and included in the families and societies into which they are born. (UNICEF, 2007, p 1)

Introduction

A 'national disgrace' is how Wales' first Children's Commissioner in his first annual report described child poverty and so it is. Child poverty scars the lives of too many children and young people living in Wales. It limits their future life chances for employment; training; enduring, positive family and social relationships; good physical and mental health and longevity (Bradshaw and Mayhew, 2005); and it affects their childhood experiences profoundly.

This chapter will examine the nature and extent of child poverty in Wales and review progress in reducing it since devolution in 1999. The chapter considers the impact of poverty on children with further analysis identifying recurrent themes, lessons learnt and some of the particular obstacles to realising the ambition to end child poverty in Wales and the rest of the United Kingdom (UK). This ambition, first articulated by Tony Blair in 1999, was subsequently adopted by the Welsh Government, six years later in the first Child Poverty Strategy for Wales (WAG, 2005). Respective UK and Welsh Government pledges to end child poverty by 2020 were welcomed and subsequently supported by all of the major political parties but despite a great deal of activity, including new legislation, funding initiatives, programmes and more robust monitoring over the last 10 years, the failure to meet the milestones of reducing child poverty by a quarter by 2005 and by half by 2010 during the 'good times' is not an auspicious start (see Butler, this volume, for additional perspectives on the politics of child poverty in Wales).

The different economic circumstances we encounter in the second decade of the new millennium and the social impacts of the recession, along with the cuts in public services and draconian welfare reforms introduced by the Conservative–Liberal Democrat coalition government in Westminster, look likely to deal a fatal blow to any chance of meeting the pledges to eradicate child poverty by 2020. The Institute for Fiscal Studies has concluded that the distributional consequences of the UK government's Comprehensive Spending Review in 2010 will see average incomes stagnate between

2010–11 and 2013–14 and both absolute and relative poverty among children and working-age adults are expected to rise (Brewer and Joyce, 2010). Child poverty beyond 2013–14 will be affected by the planned introduction of the Universal Credit, which still needs to be assessed.

The second section of the chapter looks forward, outlining the revised policy context in Wales as the National Assembly for Wales commences its fourth term with new powers to legislate as a result of the 2011 referendum (see Chapter 2, this volume). Welfare practitioners in Wales encounter the realities of child poverty and the impact on children's well-being and life chances on a daily basis, with poverty and inequality the all too familiar backdrop to child neglect and social exclusion. As Holman (1987) concluded, while only a minority of all the poor approach statutory social workers, the majority of social workers' clients live in poverty. Still today, the poor are more likely than other sections of the population to become clients of social workers. An understanding of the nature of child poverty in Wales, how it impacts on children and how it affects children's development and their future life chances, along with an understanding of the policy context with reference to both Cardiff Bay and Westminster, will serve social welfare practitioners well in their work both directly with children and families and in the wider approaches they take to challenging the socio-economic inequalities still so evident in Wales today (EHRC, 2011). The chapter concludes with consideration of the key issues for social welfare practitioners and service providers working in Wales.

The reality of child poverty in Wales

Tackling child poverty has become a growing priority for governments across most of the member states of the European Union over recent decades (O'Neill, 2010). The high rates of child poverty in Wales today are a legacy of the 1980s when the gap between rich and poor grew faster in the UK than in almost any other industrialised country (see Figure 5.1).

In 1995, the United Nations Committee on the Rights of the Child expressed concern at the increasing number of children and young people living in poverty in the UK (UNCRC, 1995).

The arrival of a New Labour government for the UK in 1997 brought new expectations and in 1999, the Prime Minister, Tony Blair, set out a commitment to end child poverty forever:

> *'And I will set out our historic aim that ours is the first generation to end child poverty forever, and it will take a generation. It is a 20-year mission but I believe it can be done'* (Blair, 1999)

Figure 5.1: Low income in Britain, 1961–2003

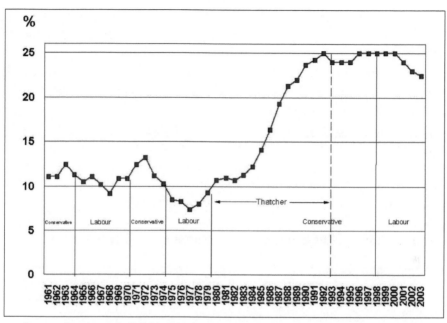

Source: Goodman and Webb (1994) and Households Below Average Income (HBAI)

The UK government's response to missing the target of reducing child poverty by a quarter by 2005 and anticipating a similar shortfall in 2010 (when the target was a reduction of 50% on the 1998/99 figures) was to enshrine the commitment to eradicating child poverty by 2020 in legislation. The Child Poverty Act 2010 received Royal Assent on 25 March 2010 – just weeks before Parliament was dissolved for the General Election of May 2010. The Act established four national income poverty targets, which the Conservative–Liberal Democrat government has now inherited. I return later in the chapter to examine the implications of the Child Poverty Act 2010 and the Welsh legislation that imposes similar responsibilities on the Welsh Government – the Children and Families (Wales) Measure 2010.

Despite both the UK and Welsh governments' commitments to the eradication of child poverty and support for this aim across all political parties and a range of policies and programmes to achieve this goal, statistically child poverty in Wales remains stubbornly high. The most recent estimates suggest that in order to meet the Welsh Government's target of eradicating child poverty by 2020, the rate of child poverty in Wales has to fall four times as fast over the next 10 years as it has over the last 10 (New Policy Institute, 2011).

What do the statistics tell us?

Recent studies of poverty and social exclusion in Wales show that the proportions of children living in poverty went up in the second half of the 2000s, after a fall between 1999 and 2005. The reduction in child poverty in Wales over this earlier period was faster than those in England or Scotland and brought Wales more in line with the UK average (Kenway, 2010). Variations across the UK and trends over time are illustrated in Table 5.1. Poverty is primarily understood as a relative concept across the European Union rather than as an absolute lack of basic necessitates. Income is the principal measurement, with children seen as living in poverty when their household's income is less than 60% of the national median income after deducting housing costs. In 2008/09, this equated to approximately £161 per week for a lone parent with one child under 14 and £288 for a couple household with two children under 14.

Table 5.1: The proportion of children in poverty in the UK

	1996/97–1998/99	2003/04–2005/06	2006/07–2008/09
Wales	36%	28%	32%
Northern Ireland		27%	26%
Scotland	32%	25%	25%
England	34%	29%	31%
UK	34%	29%	31%

Source: Kenway (2010)

The New Policy Institute's analysis highlights that all the improvements in child poverty in Wales in the early 2000s were concentrated on children in workless families. While worklessness is still the single most important reason for poverty in Wales, and economic inactivity levels and incidence of limiting long-term illness in some parts of Wales (notably the South Wales valleys and parts of West Wales) are some of the worst in the UK, there have been growing concerns about the numbers of children in in-work poverty (New Policy Institute, 2009). Parents in low-paid work have undoubtedly been helped and in many cases households lifted above the poverty line by the introduction of Child and Working Tax Credits in the early 2000s, but still across Wales, half of all children living in poverty are living in households where paid work is being done (New Policy Institute, 2011).

Many reports have highlighted the particular problems Wales faces in terms of its weak economy (relative to the other nations of the UK), its low skills base and the proportion of low-paid jobs (see Kenway, 2010; Davies et al., 2011). Compared to the rest of the UK, Wales has an unusually high proportion of its population who are not working. According to the Labour Force Survey in December 2010, more than one third of the working-age population in Wales is not in paid employment.[1] For those who are in work, the average wage in Wales is around 80% lower than the UK average.

One of the most worrying statistics in 2011 is that the unemployment rate among 16- to 24-year-olds at over 20% is the highest in 18 years and three times that for other adults (New Policy Institute, 2010). Fears have been raised about a 'lost' generation and of a 'scarring effect' on young people, which could last for many years to come. The scarring effect refers to the longer-term effects on the psychology of young people, whose self-esteem is dented by their inability to get work in their first year of leaving school or college. The Prince's Trust suggests that the longer a young person is unemployed the more likely they are to experience psychological scarring; 'this means an unhappy and debilitated generation of people who become decreasingly likely to find work in the future' (Prince's Trust, 2010, p 1).

In summary, what the statistics tell us is that using a definition of child poverty focused on relative income, Wales once again has the highest rate of child poverty of all the UK nations. The UK itself has comparatively high levels of child poverty compared to other European Union countries, with only Poland, Italy and Greece having higher rates of child poverty than the UK (O'Neill, 2010). But as welfare practitioners in Wales will be only too well aware, poverty is not solely about income; it is also about exclusion and the impact of income poverty on child well-being. Broader definitions of child poverty include measures of material deprivation and aspects of child well-being such as health, education, housing, participation, financial support and safety. These measures recognise the different and interrelated ways in which poverty impacts on children and families (Bradshaw and Mayhew, 2005). We turn now to consider the outcomes for children associated with poverty in Wales and across the UK.

Outcomes for children

Social welfare practitioners working with children and families see at first hand the effects of income poverty. Much of their work is designed to address the risk factors associated with adverse outcomes for children and promote or strengthen the protective factors. Many of the risk factors have a strong association with poverty, for example low maternal education and low birth weight. Research confirms the negative outcomes for children associated with poverty, including poor health, low self-esteem, poor educational achievement and homelessness (Bradshaw and Mayhew, 2005). Table 5.2 shows the outcomes for children strongly associated with child poverty.

---

[1] 26.3% of the working-age population in Wales are economically inactive while 8.6% are unemployed. 'Economically inactive' is a term used to describe people of working age who are either not available to start work immediately (owing for instance to a caring responsibility or ill-health) or who are not looking for work. 'Unemployed' is a term used to describe those who are available for and actively seeking work (Kenway, 2010).

Table 5.2: Outcomes associated with child poverty

Outcome	Associated with child poverty
Mortality	Yes, strong association with social class
Morbidity	Yes, strong association for most diseases
Accidents	Yes, for fatal accidents (but not accident morbidity)
Mental illness	Yes
Suicide	Yes
Child abuse	Yes, except sexual abuse
Teenage pregnancy	Yes
Environment/housing conditions	Yes
Homelessness	Yes
Low educational attainment	Yes
School exclusions	Don't know
Crime	No
Smoking	Mainly after childhood
Alcohol	No
Drugs	No
Child labour	No

Source: Bradshaw and Mayhew (2005)

UNICEF's report card on the well-being of children in rich countries states that:

> *The evidence from many countries persistently shows that children who grow up in poverty are more vulnerable: specifically, they are more likely to be in poor health, to have learning and behavioural difficulties, to underachieve at school, to become pregnant at too early an age, to have lower skills and aspirations, to be low paid, unemployed and welfare dependent.* (UNICEF, 2007, p 5)

The UNICEF report reveals that children growing up in the UK suffer greater deprivation, have worse relationships with their parents and are exposed to more risks from alcohol, drugs and unsafe sex than those in any other wealthy country in the world. In the latest UNICEF report card on child well-being in rich countries, the UK was in the lowest quintile or fifth of the 24 countries studied. The UK scored 19th on material well-being inequality, 13th on educational inequality and 11th on health inequality (UNICEF, 2010).

In Wales, despite progress in the early 2000s in reducing the numbers of children living in relative poverty, progress on a range of child poverty indicators selected by the Welsh Government has been mixed. The latest report from the Welsh Government in November

2010 on the 32 indicators selected to monitor progress on their first Child Poverty Strategy, suggests that 10 have shown some improvement, 12 have shown little or no change, three have shown a clear deterioration and seven still do not have sufficient data to monitor progress. The baseline for these indicators has recently been changed from 1998/99 to 2006 (WAG, 2010). Table 5.3 provides a summary of progress on the 26 indicators where there are data.

Table 5.3: Summary of progress against the child poverty indicators in Wales

Indicator	Baseline		Most recent		Progress status
	Year	Figure	Year	Figure	
Children living in relative low-income households (HBAI)	2003/04 = 2005/06	28%	2006/07 – 2008/09	32%	=
Children living in workless households	2006	16.9%	2009	19.9%	=
Lone parents in employment	2004/06	54.4%	2007/09	55.7%	=
Children living in in-work poverty	2006/07	25%	2008/09	26.7%	X
Adult learning (working-age adults who have received training in the last four weeks)	2006	15.7%	2009	14.3%	=
Working-age adults with basic skills in literacy	2004	75%			
Working-age adults with basic skills in numeracy	2004	47%			
Adult learning qualifications equivalent to NQF Level 2 or above	2006	67.8%	2009	70.6%	√
Adult learning qualifications equivalent to NQF Level 3 or above	2006	46.2%	2009	49.9%	√

Adult learning qualifications equivalent to NQF Level 4 or above	2006	25.9%	2009	29.6%	√
Credit Union membership *Overall* *Junior*	2006 2006	36,000 5,700	2009 2009	41,000 8,300	√
Infant Mortality *Ratio most: middle* *(deprived fifths)*	2002/06	1.48	2004/08	1.60	=
Child care places	2006	72,894	2009	73,645	√
Pupils achieving Key Stage 2 Core subject indicator *Percentage-point difference between pupils eligible for FSM and those not eligible*	2006	24	2009	21.7	√
Pupils achieving Key Stage 3 Core subject indicator *Percentage-point difference between pupils eligible for FSM and those not eligible*	2006	31.9	2009	32.1	=
Pupils achieving Key Stage 4 Core subject indicator *Percentage-point difference between pupils eligible for FSM and those not eligible*	2006	29.2	2009	31.3	X
Pupils aged 15 achieving Level 2 threshold *Percentage-point difference between pupils eligible for FSM and those not eligible*	2006	29.5	2009	31.9	X
Pupils leaving full full-time education with no approved qualification	2006	2.1	2009	0.9	√
16- to 18- year- olds not in education, employment or training (NEETs)	2006	10%	2009 (provisional)	12%	=

Young people with dental caries experience *Percentage DMFT ratio most: middle (deprived fifths)*	2004/05	1.18	2008/09	1.24	=
Teenage conceptions (under 16s) *Ratio most: middle (deprived fifths)*	2002–06	1.61	2004/08	1.67	=
Pedestrian injuries 5-14 years old (reported to the police) *Ratio most: middle (deprived fifths)*	2002/06	1.58	2004/08	1.50	=
Pedestrian injuries, 5- to 14-year-olds (hospital inpatient) *Ratio most: middle (deprived fifths)*	2002/06	2.06	2004/08	1.71	=
Children who are killed or seriously injured in road accidents	2006	144	2009	136	√
Families living in Bed & Breakfast accommodation	2006	50	2010	12	√
Families living in temporary accommodation	2006	1,774	2010	1,126	√
Families living in overcrowded conditions	2007	19,730	2009/10	22,663	=

Key:
DMFT = Decayed, Missing & Filled Teeth;
FSM = free school meals;
NQF = National Qualifications Framework.
Progress status: √ clear improvement; = little or no change; X clear deterioration.
Notes: Further information on the assessment of the indicators and the awarding of progress status can be found in the source document at
http://wales.gov.uk/topics/statistics/headlines/social2010/101125/?lang=en

Source: WAG (2010)

The progress status is that awarded by the Welsh Government and statisticians have arguably erred on the side of caution to suggest, for example, that the change in the numbers of children living in relative low-income households (indicator 1) from 28% in 2003/04–2005/06 to 32% in 2006/07–2008/09 be awarded an amber status (little or no change) because the indicator is 'subject to large volatility and has only changed a small amount since the baseline year' (WAG, 2010, pp 4–5).

Perhaps of biggest concern to Wales' bid to become a modern and vibrant economy is the relatively low level of basic skills and qualifications of young people from low-income households. With the most recently available figures (2004) indicating that a quarter of adults in Wales lack basic skills in literacy and approximately a half lack basic skills in numeracy (see Table 5.3), this is a serious problem for Wales. Yet efforts to reduce the attainment gap in schools between children from low-income households and their more affluent peers have, as yet, delivered few gains. Using eligibility for free school meals (FSM) as a proxy indicator of poverty, this gap is apparent by the age of seven when FSM pupils are already about 21% behind their more privileged peers. By the age of 15, whereas 62% of students who are not eligible for FSM achieve five or more General Certificates of Secondary Education (GCSEs) at higher grades, the figure for FSM pupils is 28%: a gap of 34% (Egan, 2010). Put another way, pupils eligible for FSM are 2.5 times less likely to get A*–C grades in core subjects than their peers (Davies et al., 2011).

How the association of poverty with poor child outcomes plays out can perhaps be better understood when comparing the varying range of opportunities available to children from low-income and more affluent households. The Households Below Average Income report in 2007 (DWP, 2007) presented for the first time, information on the material deprivation experienced by children living in low-income households. The findings provide a reminder of the stark reality of poverty from a child's perspective. For example, 5% of children in the top quintile are lacking outdoor space/facilities to play safely, in contrast to a quarter of children in the bottom quintile who lack such an item. Just 3% of children in the top income quintile do not have at least one week's holiday away from home but more than half of children in the bottom quintile do not have such a holiday (DWP, 2007).

As social welfare practitioners in Wales are only too well aware, children living in low-income households have the odds stacked against them. Of course, not all poor children do badly in school or go on to develop mental health problems; the point here is that growing up poor increases the risks of adverse outcomes for children (both as children and as future adults). Lead responsibility for tackling child poverty and the structural inequalities in Wales remains firmly in the hands of governments in Cardiff Bay and at Westminster but social welfare practitioners and service providers have a key role to play in highlighting the impact of government policies on children and families and in making good use of the opportunities provided by the divergent policy directions in Wales.

To some extent, referring to my own experience as a social worker in Wales in the 1980s and 1990s and anecdotal conversations with practising social workers since, because poverty is such a feature in the lives of the children and families they work with, social welfare practitioners can at times overlook the more obvious impacts of structural inequalities in favour of more individualised interventions, which at least they have some limited control over (unlike the structural problems). A sound understanding of poverty from the perspective of a child can serve as a reminder of some of the more subtle and pernicious difficulties children growing up in poverty face and also provide pointers to the types of interventions that can contribute to improvements in the lives and circumstances of the children and families who social welfare practitioners work with. The next section of this chapter aims to re-enforce these points by considering the experience of poverty through the eyes of a child.

Through the eyes of a child

In a bold and radical move that steered Welsh policy intentions in a markedly different direction from England's (see Chapter 8, this volume), the Welsh Government of 2004 adopted the United Nations Convention on the Rights of the Child (UNCRC) as underpinning all its policies relating to children (WAG, 2004a). Under the Convention, children have the right to grow up free from poverty and hunger and should not be disadvantaged or prevented from achieving their full potential because of where they live or family circumstances. Article 4 of the UNCRC obliges governments to fulfill children's rights 'to the maximum extent of their available resources' (UNCRC, 2003).

In this context it is especially important to try to understand the effect of poverty on children themselves, not just to focus on income poverty or the impact of childhood poverty on their later life chances. To understand the lived experience of child poverty we need to bring a child's perspective to the analysis of child poverty and social exclusion (Ridge, 2011).

In preparing for its first Child Poverty Strategy published in 2005 (WAG, 2005), the Welsh Government commissioned and reviewed a series of consultations with over 300 children and young people aged 6–25 across Wales. The aim was to ensure that the strategy was informed by children and young people's own understanding of child poverty and what life without money is like for children as well as to feed in children and young people's own ideas and suggestions for how child poverty should be tackled in Wales.

These consultations identified a common set of themes and messages about the effects of poverty on the lives and experiences of children and young people, which were detailed in the report of the Child Poverty Task Group set up by the Welsh Government to advise it on formulating its new strategy (WAG, 2004b). Different emphases are apparent relating to age, for example older young people were more likely than younger children to raise concerns about housing or employment and had a greater understanding and experience of the benefit system. Children and young people of all ages raised issues relating to education, health, crime, drugs, participation, leisure, transport, the unique pressures on families living on a low income and the profound effects of the stigma and shame that poverty brings.

Differences relating to ethnicity and gender were not highlighted in the Welsh Task Group's report but we should be mindful that children's experiences of poverty are not homogeneous and that they reflect a myriad of other factors in the lives of children and families. Ridge (2009), in her review of a number of qualitative studies of children and families' experiences of poverty in the UK, cites Morrow's (2001) research into children and young people's perspectives on their neighbourhoods. This study found that children and young people's experiences differed according to gender and ethnicity (as well as age), with girls more likely than boys to feel unsafe in neighbourhoods, and children from minority ethnic groups reporting unpleasant episodes of racial harassment. As Ridge (2009, p 92) concludes, more research is needed into how 'intersections between different socially and culturally constructed categories such as those based on race and ethnicity, gender, class and disability interact and reinforce conditions of inequality and poverty'.

Returning to the key themes and messages to emerge from the consultations in Wales commissioned by the Welsh Government, children and young people frequently talked about going without clothing and heating because of the lack of money in their household. Some participants mentioned only being able to have one pair of shoes a year or to have a bath once a week and having to keep warm in cold, unheated bedrooms. Other children and young people participating in one of the consultations (Crowley and Vulliamy, 2002) were concerned to point out that most parents in low-income households often went without themselves so that their children could have what they needed and prevent their children from being singled out by their friends as poor:

> 'My mother would give me how much as she could afford. She can't give me all her money ... she won't be able to pay off her gas and electric bills.' (Nia, age seven)

Older young people particularly identified the importance of creating decent jobs and employment opportunities in Wales as a means of tackling child poverty. Some young people who were working in low-paid jobs felt exploited. They wanted to see a minimum wage for the under 18s (which has since been established although at a much lower level than for the over 18s) and more training opportunities and good-quality apprenticeships.

A strong cross-cutting theme relates to the exclusion that children and young people living in poverty, experience. Children and young people living in low-income households repeatedly described how they are made to feel different from other children and young people. The fact that children begin to experience the reality of their 'different-ness' at an early age has been highlighted by other studies (Middleton, 1994; Hogan, 2007).

The clothes young people wear, the place they live, their mode of transport – all set children and young people without much money apart from their peers. The visibility of children's poverty is heightened by the manner in which FSM are administered; by not being able to afford essential learning items or school trips and other activities. Children and young people clearly understand the stigma and shame that living in poverty brings and acutely feel the lack of respect that their 'different-ness' evokes in some of their peers and some of the adults around them:

> 'Poor children can't buy the proper kit and if they didn't have the proper kit some people in the school were meanies and kept saying they haven't got the proper uniform, and they haven't got enough money to get sandwiches either.' (Sean, age seven)

> 'People think you're different and treat you different if you're poor.' (Gemma, age 13)

Some children and young people commented on the unwelcome attention they got from their peers because they were perceived as being 'poor' by dint of where they lived. Some reported being routinely humiliated and bullied because of the clothes that they wear or because of where they live. Some reported feeling that they were seen as undesirable or 'lower class' by peers and by adults. The impact of this on children and young people's sense of worth and self-esteem cannot be underestimated. Projects providing community-based support for young people were seen by young people as helping to ameliorate these feelings – giving them the opportunity to succeed and 'better themselves'. Relationships with trusted and concerned adults who did not judge them or expect certain things because of where they lived were seen as important but changes in the attitude and behaviour of the wider community (adults and peers) were also required.

The accessibility of leisure and social activities was a major issue for young people. The cost and availability of transport were key factors in young people's social exclusion and feelings of isolation. Children and young people complained about how crime and drugs affected their use of public space, by, for example, the proliferation of discarded syringes and the vandalism of play facilities for younger children. One young person illustrated how, on his estate, the vandalism of bored younger people who had no money and had nowhere to go had spoilt facilities for younger children:

> 'Up here now, they don't stick together. Some of the 11- and 12-year-olds are on drugs and things like that, younger than that as well doing it … it's about two years ago now we done that out lovely for the play scheme didn't we, it had a lovely park in there as well, and they wrecked it already, they've coloured all over the walls, they've ripped the stuff up. There was a little house for the little ones to go in, and they burnt that and they're

wrecking it and that's because there's nothing here for the older ones and they've got no money to get a bus or go somewhere else. The older ones are wrecking it because they got nothing.' (Craig, age 15)

In all of the consultations, children and young people identified education as playing a key role in helping children and young people to get out of poverty and to fulfill their hopes and dreams. Education prepares young people for life and can provide the necessary skills and qualifications to get a good job and do well. How well poor children and young people get on in school is affected by many things but young people observed that poor children can experience a lower level of expectation, a lower quality of education and sometimes a lack of understanding or support by teachers and youth workers. This suggests that teachers and youth workers should be better supported to guide and advise young people; to be sensitive to the background and circumstances of children; and above all to show belief in all children and young people.

The key messages from children and young people illustrate how combating child poverty and social exclusion has to be part of mainstream policies and not just the preserve of special initiatives. They also provide a glimpse of the social and human costs of child poverty in the 'here and now' of childhood and in the longer term.

Understanding the reality of child poverty from a child's perspective is important for social welfare practitioners who, working with education, schools, health and other partner agencies, can do much to advocate for improvements in practice, for example in how FSM are administered. Listening to children and young people's perspectives; engaging with them in taking forward their own solutions to the problems they face; supporting them to overcome obstacles; and working with others to widen the range of opportunities available to children and young people – all represent good social work practice. But social welfare practitioners and service providers also need to understand the policy context in which they work in order to make best use of the opportunities available and to engage (with their unique perspective) in the wider debates about how child poverty in Wales can best be tackled.

The next section of this chapter briefly examines the policy responses to child poverty over a decade of devolution, identifying key themes and the lessons learnt before considering what more should be done and the key issues for social welfare practitioners in Wales.

Policy responses

The Welsh Government has power over many of the policy areas associated with the outcomes of child poverty, for example education, health, housing and social care. Following the referendum in 2011, the National Assembly for Wales now has full law-making powers in all of the 20 devolved policy fields. However, the key drivers to reduce income poverty, notably tax and benefits, remain the responsibility of the UK government at Westminster. Throughout the New Labour years (1997–2010), a raft of policies and programmes were put in place by the administrations in Cardiff and in London to boost paid employment as a route out of poverty. The Labour government at Westminster established Working and Child Tax Credits, the Child Trust Fund and the National Minimum Wage, as well as increasing universal Child Benefit while Welsh Governments over this period focused on area-based regeneration, investments in early years provision, facilitating joint working, encouraging greater financial inclusion and on improvements in the uptake of the new regime of tax and benefits support.

Efforts to eradicate child poverty have of course to be understood in the wider context of overcoming poverty and social exclusion. The 'Welsh' approach set out in a think tank piece published by the Joseph Rowntree Foundation (Timmins et al., 2004) has been to look at how the collective condition of disadvantaged communities can be improved in a holistic and participative way and to look for long-term solutions that develop social economies to create a range of social capital. This community approach is, it is argued, more appropriate for the deep-seated structural problems affecting the Welsh economy (particularly in the South Wales valleys but also in rural Wales) featuring relatively high (in relation to most regions of England) levels of economic inactivity fuelled by a low skills base and a high incidence of limiting long-term illness.

Notwithstanding the need to understand the wider context of poverty and disadvantage in Wales, tackling *child* poverty in Wales became a hot political issue in the mid-2000s (see Chapter 8, this volume). For a nation setting its sights on renewed prosperity, children and young people assume particular importance for their future economic value. A focus on children and the development of skills in the next generation are essential to the vision of a vibrant and prosperous Wales as set out in the Welsh Assembly Government's strategic plan *Better Wales* (Thomas and Crowley, 2007). Child poverty is seen as especially wasteful, carrying huge costs both for the children and families involved and also for society.

In 2005, the Welsh Government – stepping up to grasp the gauntlet thrown down by the Children's Commissioner's 'national disgrace' comment (2002) and the challenge of Tony Blair's (1999) historic aim to end child poverty 'in a generation' – published its first strategy to tackle child poverty in Wales (WAG, 2005). The strategy stated the Welsh Government's commitment to the target of eradicating child poverty by 2020 and its contributions to meeting that target. The strategy included an additional £50 million targeted on early years in the most deprived areas of Wales with at least one integrated children's centre in each local authority area.

The proposals on the £50 million spend were subsequently developed into the *Flying Start* programme, a Welsh Government initiative that targets funding on evidence-informed, early years provision for 0- to three-year-olds living in the most disadvantaged communities across the country. Provision includes free, part-time, quality child care for two-year-olds and enhanced health visitor support and parenting programmes (WAG, 2006). *Cymorth*, a larger, more longer-standing Welsh Assembly Government funding programme, was designed to support local authority-led strategic partnerships to deliver targeted support for vulnerable children aged 0–25 and improve the life chances of children, young people and families living in the most disadvantaged areas of Wales (Welsh Assembly Government, WAG, 2007). In 2010, following an evaluation of *Cymorth*, the Welsh Government announced that it would be realigning the fund to a new *Families First* programme from 2012. *Families First* aims to supports the development of new models of service delivery for families with children living in poverty. The programme aims to support the development of 'family centred services delivering effective and efficient support to families living in poverty, thus reducing the inequities that they experience' (WAG, 2011, p 27).

The Labour–Plaid Cymru coalition government of 2007–11 continued efforts to 'proof' all policies for their impact on child poverty and to 'bend' programmes to ensure that resources were targeted on those most in need. Programme bending was lauded whereby mainstream government programmes are 'bent' to favour child poverty. This follows the approach within the Welsh Government's flagship anti-poverty programme *Communities First*. A long-term 'bottom-up' regeneration programme targeting 142 of Wales' most disadvantaged communities, *Communities First*, reflects the principles of the community-focused 'Welsh' approach described on page 85. It aims to improve the living conditions and prospects of people in the most disadvantaged communities in Wales.

The programme of government agreed on by Labour and Plaid in 2007, known as the One Wales Agreement, included a commitment to establish an independent panel of experts to advise the Welsh Government on how to tackle child poverty. The *Child Poverty Expert Group* met quarterly and published its recommendations (and the Welsh Government's responses) on key areas of devolved policy, including health, education, economic inactivity, fuel poverty and housing. There was also a commitment articulated in the One Wales Agreement for the Welsh Government to work more closely with local government on tackling child poverty and to pursue the new law-making powers available to the National Assembly under the Government of Wales Act 2006, to develop legislation that placed a duty on public bodies to make and demonstrate their contribution to tackling child poverty.

Some commentators argue that the Welsh Government's Children and Families (Wales) Measure, which received Royal Assent in February 2010, provides a real opportunity for a joined-up approach to tackling child poverty across all key stakeholders and partners (O'Neill, 2010). In addition to placing a duty on the Welsh Government to produce and publish a Child Poverty Strategy, the Measure[2] also requires local authorities, Local Health Boards and a range of other public bodies in Wales to set out the actions they will take to tackle child poverty. Local authorities and their partners discharge this duty by preparing child poverty strategies as part of their strategic Children

[2] In effect a Welsh law.

and Young People's Plan, which they prepare and publish every three years.

A new Child Poverty Strategy for Wales

The duties imposed on Welsh ministers in the Children and Families (Wales) Measure 2010 reflect the duties placed on UK, Scottish and Northern Irish ministers in the UK's Child Poverty Act 2010, that is, to publish a Child Poverty Strategy as well as articulating government pledges to national poverty targets.[3] In line with this duty, the Welsh Government issued an ambitious Child Poverty Strategy for consultation in May 2010. The strategy focused on three overarching objectives:

- to reduce the number of families in workless households;
- to improve the skill level of parents and young people in low-income families so that they can secure well-paid employment;
- to reduce inequalities that exist in health, education and economic outcomes for children living in poverty, by improving the outcomes of the poorest.

The draft strategy and an accompanying delivery plan were warmly welcomed across the children's sector in Wales – not least because of its focus on cross-departmental working, policy integration, strategic coordination and regular monitoring of the impact of the Welsh Government's policies on child poverty. The lack of a joined-up approach to tackling child poverty by Welsh ministers and by local government has long been seen as a weakness in the Welsh approach (O'Neill, 2010).

However, a few months is a long time in politics and the final strategy when published in February 2011 was a much less comprehensive and less ambitious plan of action. The final strategy, for example, devotes just over one page to the task of raising the educational achievements of children from low-income households, with much of this focused on improving the attainment levels of looked-after children. This seems particularly weak when we note that despite the alleged priority given by successive Welsh governments to tackling child poverty, inequalities in educational outcomes have continued to get worse for children aged 11, 14 and 16 and only marginally better in recent years for children aged seven (Egan, 2010).

Much of the draft strategy had been written (or at least conceived) in kinder economic times and with a Labour government in Westminster. As unemployment increased in Wales and across the UK in 2009 and 2010 and the new Conservative–Liberal Democrat coalition announced public expenditure cuts to deal with the country's burgeoning deficit, it seems that the Welsh government's ambition was scaled back.

---

[3] Although interestingly, the Welsh Government's current target for 2020 is for no more than 5% of children to be living in low-income households, which is more ambitious than the Child Poverty Act 2010, which sets a target of less than 10% by 2020.

The public expenditure cuts announced in 2010 undoubtedly deal a severe blow to the fight against child poverty in Wales. As we enter a new era whereby the government in Wales is of a different ideological persuasion to the one in the UK, the welfare cuts in particular may yet prove just how little power the Welsh government really has to effect the levels of child poverty in its midst.

The UK government's measures to tackle the deficit focus on cutting public expenditure rather than increasing taxation. The welfare bill took a particular hit in the coalition government's emergency Budget of June 2010 and the spending review in October of the same year. A whole host of measures took effect in April 2011, falling heavily on those who are already living in poverty. These include: changes to the inflation measure used to uprate benefits, which will erode their value over time; reductions to Housing Benefit; changes to tax credits; the freezing of Child Benefit payments; and a reduction in help with childcare costs through the tax credit system. The Educational Maintenance Allowance (EMA), which works to support 16- to 18-year-olds from low-income households to continue in education was also scrapped (JRF, 2011).

The Welsh government bravely agreed to continue EMAs for Welsh students – a move that has been widely welcomed but generally it has limited powers to mitigate the worst effects of these welfare reforms on poor children. The Block Grant to the Assembly has been reduced in real terms and it now has less money at its disposal to do what it planned to do to tackle child poverty. Despite the UK government's insistence that its spending review will have no measurable impact on child poverty in the next two years, the welfare cuts (along with cuts to public services) fall disproportionately on children and families and, as noted earlier in this chapter, the Institute for Fiscal Studies is forecasting a rise in absolute and relative poverty among children and working-age adults (Brewer and Joyce, 2010).

Progress towards tackling child poverty in Wales – a failed promise?

The comments of the Children's Commissioner for Wales in 2002 definitely threw an uncomfortable spotlight on the accolade that Wales did not want (CCfW, 2002). Wales was firmly in possession of the award for being the nation of the UK with the worst child poverty record. The UK itself being pretty near the bottom of the European Union's child poverty league table meant that there was not much further for a relatively wealthy country to fall in terms of the inequality in its midst.

The comments did immediately spark individual politicians (of all parties) and the National Assembly as a whole to sit up and think about what more could be done (see Chapter 8, this volume). However, in many ways, things did not move quickly enough during the 'good times'. Successive Welsh governments have somehow failed to translate laudable policy aims into real change on the ground. They have shied away from seriously challenging key delivery partners (in particular local government) to work in true partnership and to target sufficient resources and attention on the poorest children.

The 'policy-rich, implementation-poor' description of Wales since devolution (NAW, 2011) must be one that future Welsh governments reflect seriously on in relation to the 'lessons learnt' and their continuing efforts to tackle child poverty.

It was only in 2005, nearly three years after the Children's Commissioner spoke out about Wales' 'national disgrace' and nearly six years after Tony Blair made his historic pledge to end child poverty in the UK, that a Child Poverty Strategy for Wales was proposed by the Welsh government and adopted by the National Assembly. In truth, responsibility for the progress in tackling child poverty in Wales between 1999 and 2005 must fall more squarely on the actions of the UK government and its reforms to in- and out-of-work benefits. Since 2005, when the Welsh Government had at last caught up with the political imperative – rates of child poverty in Wales have increased.

Of course it is not that simple and the measures that successive Labour-led Welsh Governments have introduced since devolution to tackle child poverty should reap benefits in the longer term. The focus on early years and improving the education for four- to seven-year-olds; on skills development; on financial inclusion; on bottom-up community regeneration; and on support to get parents who are the furthest from the labour market into employment – have the potential over time to reduce child poverty.

But in reality, in this new era of fiscal austerity with cuts to out-of-work benefits and tax credits and cuts to employment in the public sector (on which so many in Wales depend), the answer lies in Wales having a much stronger economy with decent jobs attracted to Wales by a skilled workforce and an economic growth friendly environment and infrastructure. As Kenway (2010, p 24) concludes when considering the future of poverty in Wales, 'a new route will be needed which will surely have to pay as much attention to the quality of jobs and what they are worth as to the mere quantity of them. There is no 'quick fix' here at the Welsh Government's disposal. It should of course continue to do what it can to contribute to reductions in child poverty in the longer term. Improving education and training outcomes for disadvantaged groups, improving the availability of accessible, affordable and good-quality childcare and the promotion of equal pay for women are all key policy aims to realise alongside economic development. As Hirsch (2006, p 5) reminds us, some of the parents of 2020 are still in school today, 'and a decisive effort to improve educational outcomes for disadvantaged groups, and renewed efforts to improve low pay and women's access to child care, would help tomorrow's parents to thrive in the labour market'.

Conclusion and implications for social welfare practice in Wales

Looking forward, it is difficult to be optimistic. We can hope that the UK government – which has signed up to the target of 'eradicating' child poverty by 2020 and is now legally accountable for a broad range of child poverty targets – reconsiders its approach when its current policies fail to deliver. But in Wales, we cannot give up on trying to reduce child poverty and its worst effects. The Welsh Government must review the lessons of the last 12 years and ensure that its renewed efforts to tackle child poverty and improve the outcomes of the poorest children, challenge head on (with strong leadership and all the resources at its disposal) the continuing inequalities in the education and health outcomes for children.

Social welfare practitioners have a key role to play in terms of working directly with children, young people and families to help them improve their circumstances and mitigate the worst excesses of poverty and social exclusion. Practitioners and service providers can use the opportunities provided by Welsh Government funded programmes to implement innovative and evidenced-based interventions that can work to lift families out of poverty. They can work in participative ways to support children, young people, families and communities to pursue their own solutions and challenge the hand they have been dealt. They can work alongside other practitioners in schools, day care settings, hospitals and general practitioner surgeries to enhance opportunities and encourage change.

Perhaps most importantly, they can help to ensure adequate representation of the interests of the poorest in policy development, service planning, delivery and evaluation. Those who spend time among the poorest in our society (including social welfare practitioners) can become inured to the impact of poverty and social exclusion on children and families. But those who do not spend much time in these worlds, such as politicians, policy makers and service planners, need regularly reminding (by those who do) of the real difficulties that poverty brings and the inefficiencies of our current welfare system. Social welfare practitioners can support people themselves to speak out as well as speaking out on their behalf. To use a widely understood metaphor, we still have too many children at the bottom of the cliff requiring the ambulance – we need to invest more in those fences that stop them falling in the first place. In concluding this chapter, a range of other clichéd metaphors, such as 'wake up and smell the coffee' and 'it's the economy stupid', come to mind but investing more (proportionately) in tackling structural inequalities in Wales has to be the key.

References

Blair, A (1999) Beveridge Lecture, Toynbee Hall, 18 March, reproduced in Walker, R (ed) *Ending Child Poverty* Bristol, The Policy Press

Bradshaw, J and Mayhew, E (2005) *The Well-Being of Children in the UK* London, University of York and Save the Children

Brewer, M and Joyce, R (2010) *Child and Working-Age Poverty 2010-2013* London, Institute for Fiscal Studies, www.ifs.org.uk/bns/bn115

Children's Commissioner for Wales (2002) *Annual Report 2001-2002* Swansea.

Crowley, A and Vulliamy, C (2002) *Listen Up! Children and young people talk about: poverty* Cardiff, Save the Children

Davies, R, Drinkwater, S, Joll, C, Jones, M, Lloyd-Williams, H, Makepeace, G, Parhi, M, Parken, A, Robinson, C, Taylor, C and Wass, V (2011) *An Anatomy of Economic Inequality in Wales* Cardiff, WISERD, Cardiff University

DWP (Department for Work and Pensions) (2007) *Households Below Average Income (HBAI), 1994/95 to 2005/06* London, DWP, www.dwp.gov.uk/asd/hbai/hbai2006/contents.asp

Egan, D (2010) 'Educational equity and school performance in Wales' in Bevan Foundation *Poverty and Social Exclusion in Wales* Tredegar, Bevan Foundation

EHRC (Equality and Human Rights Commission) (2011) *How Fair is Wales? Equality, human rights and good relations* Cardiff, EHRC, www.equalityhumanrights.com/wales/publications/how-fair-is-wales/

Goodman A and Webb S (1994) *For Richer, For Poorer: The changing distribution of income in the UK, 1961-1991* London, Institute for Fiscal Studies

Hirsch, D (2006) *What Will It Take to End Child Poverty? Firing on all cylinders* (Findings) York, Joseph Rowntree Foundation

Hogan, G (2007) *Impact of Young Children's School Experience* York, Joseph Rowntree Foundation

Holman, B (1987) 'Research from the underside' *British Journal of Social Work* 17(6), pp 669–83.

Joseph Rowntree Foundation (2011) *Poverty and the 2011 Budget* York, Joseph Rowntree Foundation

Kenway, P (2010) 'Income and wealth in Wales' in Bevan Foundation *Poverty and Social Exclusion in Wales* Tredegar, Bevan Foundation

Middleton, S (1994) *Family Fortunes* London, CPAG

Morrow, V (2001) *Networks and neighbourhoods: children's and young people's perspectives* London: National Institute for Clinical Excellence

National Assembly for Wales, Children and Young People Committee (2011) *Follow Up Inquiry into Child Poverty in Wales: Eradication through education?* Cardiff, National Assembly for Wales, www.assemblywales.org/bus-home/bus-guide-docs-pub/bus-business-documents/bus-business-documents-doc-laid.htm?act=dis&id=209049&ds=3/2011

New Policy Institute (2009) *Monitoring Poverty and Social Exclusion in Wales 2009* York, Joseph Rowntree Foundation

New Policy Institute (2010) *Monitoring Poverty and Social Exclusion 2010* York, Joseph Rowntree Foundation

New Policy Institute (2011) *Monitoring Poverty and Social Exclusion 2011* York, Joseph Rowntree Foundation

O'Neill, S (2010) 'Child poverty in Wales: where there's the will, is there a way?' in Bevan Foundation *Poverty and Social Exclusion in Wales* Tredegar, Bevan Foundation

Prince's Trust (2010) *Yougov Youth Index 2010* London, Prince's Trust

Ridge, T (2009) *Living with Poverty: A review of the literature on children's and families' experience of poverty* (Research Report 594) London, Department for Work and Pensions

Ridge, T (2011) 'The everyday costs of poverty in childhood: a review of qualitative research exploring the lives and experiences of low-income children in the UK' *Children & Society* 25(1), pp 73–84

Thomas, N and Crowley, A (2007) 'The state of children's welfare and rights in Wales in 2006' *Contemporary Wales: An Annual Review of Economic and Social Research* 19, pp 161–79

Timmins, N, Institute for Public Policy Research, Social Market Foundation, Policy Exchange, Scottish Council Foundation and Institute of Welsh Affairs (2004) *Overcoming Disadvantage: An agenda for the next 20 years* York, Joseph Rowntree Foundation

UNCRC (United Nations Committee on the Rights of the Child) (1995) *Concluding Observations of the Committee on the Rights of the Child: United Kingdom of Great Britain and Northern Ireland* Geneva, United Nations

UNCRC 34th Session (2003) *General Comment No 5: General measures of implementation of the Convention on the Rights of the Child* Geneva, United Nations

UNICEF (2007) *An Overview of Child Well-Being in Rich Countries: Innocenti report card 7* Florence, Innocenti Research Centre, UNICEF

WAG (Welsh Assembly Government) (2004a) *Children and Young People: Rights to action* Cardiff, WAG

WAG (2004b) *Report of the Child Poverty Task Group* Cardiff, WAG

WAG (2005) *A Fair Future for our Children* Cardiff, WAG

WAG (2006) *Flying Start Guidance 2006–8* Cardiff, WAG

WAG (2007) *Rights in Action: Implementing children and young people's rights in Wales* Cardiff, WAG

WAG (2010) *Eradicating Child Poverty in Wales: Child poverty indicators progress against the baseline* Cardiff, WAG, http://wales.gov.uk/topics/statistics/headlines/social2010/101125/?lang=en

WAG (2011) *Child Poverty Strategy for Wales* Cardiff, WAG, http://wales.gov.uk/topics/childrenyoungpeople/poverty/newcpstrategy/?lang=en

Chapter 6

Reaching Rural Areas: Social Services in the Welsh Countryside

Richard Pugh

Introduction

Rural areas are typically distinguished from urban areas by population density or settlement size, although for public services other factors affecting access such as travel times and distance may be more important (ONS, 2004; WRO, 2009a). However, there are limitations to mono-dimensional definitions, most notably in their underpinning assumption of the 'sameness' of different rural areas (Pugh and Cheers, 2010). Nonetheless, different definitions are significant because of their impact in decisions about policy and resources. The Welsh Assembly Government has become more aware of the potential implications of different definitions (RDS, 2007a, 2008), and has also considered the notion of 'deep rurality' (NAW, 2008; WRO, 2009b). Nine local authorities in Wales are commonly categorised as being predominantly rural. They are Carmarthenshire, Ceredigion, Conwy, Denbighshire, Gwynedd, Monmouthshire, Pembrokeshire, Powys and Ynys Môn (RDS, 2008).

According to the Office for National Statistics, from 1981 through to 2001 the rural population of Wales increased from 886,200 to 959,700 people (Hartwell et al., 2007). This represents just over a third of the population at 35% (Gartner et al., 2007), the most sparsely populated local authority areas being Powys, Ceredigion, Gwynedd, and Anglesey (White and Tippireddy, 2005). Much of this increase was the result of migration into rural Wales from other parts of Wales and also from England, without which there would have been an overall decline over the period from 1991 to 2001 (Hartwell et al., 2007). There are a number of reasons for population changes in rural areas. Many young people leave the countryside to seek higher education, work or suitable housing, while other people return to rural areas after working elsewhere (Hartwell et al., 2007; WRO, 2008). In rural areas adjacent to larger towns and cities, counter-urbanisation is commonplace as many people have chosen to move to the countryside seeking a better quality of life.

The age structure of the population in Wales shows that rural areas have slightly lower proportions than urban areas in the age bands below 40–44 years, and slightly higher proportions in the older age bands (Gartner et al., 2007; ONS, 2007). Every rural county in Wales has some minority ethnic presence, and although the peak in the numbers of migrant workers from the newer member states of the European Community appears to have passed, their presence continues to add to the diversity of some districts (WRO, 2006a; Hold et al., 2007; Woods and Watkin, 2008). The Trades Union Congress in a report in 2004 (TUC, 2004) found that the patterns of settlement of migrant workers were changing, with many more being recruited to work in industries commonly found in rural areas, such as food processing, hospitality and, of course, agriculture. For various reasons, including non-registration, it is widely acknowledged that official figures underestimate the numbers of migrant workers (Woods and Watkin, 2008).

There is little evidence that rural areas overall in Wales have any higher incidence of poverty as most of the indices continue to show higher levels in urban areas, although, of course, poverty and deprivation do exist. Low wage rates, common in rural areas, are a significant factor in family poverty and evidence indicates that a slightly higher proportion of people in rural Wales receive Working Families' Tax Credit than in urban areas (RDS, 2007b). Wales remains a relatively poor country within the United Kingdom (UK) (Kenway and Palmer, 2007; JRF, 2009) and one study in Gwynedd found that some 50% of households had a gross income of between £7,500 and £10,000 per year (Cyngor Gwynedd Council, 2007, cited in RDS, 2008), while nationally 38% of farming households have an annual turnover of less than £25,000 (WRO, 2010). Furthermore, poor people in the countryside may live in the same areas as relatively comfortable households, which may mask their existence in any statistics that have an averaging effect (Gartner et al., 2007). Housing conditions in some rural areas are poorer (Davidson et al. 2011; NAW, 2005), and there is sound evidence that some people living in rural areas are comparatively disadvantaged in regard to access to affordable housing, welfare services, education, employment, income, and life chances generally (Shucksmith, 2003; Milbourne and Hughes, 2005; Milbourne et al., 2006; RDS, 2007b, 2008; End Child Poverty Network Wales, 2009). As energy prices continue to rise, fuel poverty in terms of both transport and heating costs is becoming a more significant issue, especially given the need for personal transport and the higher proportion of 'hard-to-heat' housing in rural areas (RDS, 2008).

Nevertheless, trying to understand the countryside and the lives of those who live there is not always best done by pursuing a simple urban–rural dichotomy, as this can lead to an oversimplification of the variability and complexity of different rural contexts. For example, the social and economic circumstances of someone living in a depopulated former mining community may be very different from a person living on a hill farm in a more isolated location, or in a small fishing village on the coast. Variability can also be seen in the level and quality of rural social services as the Joint Review reports in Wales reveal, with some areas facing serious problems in management and shortfalls in service delivery (CSSIW, 2006a, 2008).

This chapter draws on earlier published work, especially Pugh (2003, 2007) and Pugh et al. (2007). It begins by setting out some of the general features of rurality and rural context that may influence perceptions of rural problems and impede the development of effective services. The second section reviews some of the specific issues that affect service users, while the third section looks at key issues for workers and service providers. The chapter concludes with recommendations for service development and further reading.

Rurality and the rural context

Historically, the provision of social services in rural areas of the UK has been based on policies that have had an implicit urban perspective (Lloyd and Lloyd, 1984; Francis and Henderson, 1992; Pugh, 2000; Turbett, 2004). This typically ignores the diversity of rural communities and often fails to recognise that personal and social problems may be experienced differently in the countryside and thus may require different approaches and solutions.

In the early years of devolution, political rhetoric often acknowledged the importance of rural places and people but few specific social measures were introduced. Lowe and Ward (2002), in a review of the governance of rural affairs in the UK, noted that although new institutions of administration had been developed since devolution, agriculturally oriented approaches to rural development were still dominant. In contrast, a later review of rural policy across the UK by Woods (2006) suggested that rural politics were changing and that a broader, more social vision of rural affairs was becoming established.

There is little doubt that, in recent years, government agencies and politicians in Wales have devoted more attention to rural issues, particularly in establishing a better research base through the establishment of the Wales Rural Observatory, but substantive policy developments outside of health services (WAG, 2009) remain scarce. In 2008, the Rural Policy Unit within the Department for Rural Affairs was given responsibility for 'rural proofing' the work of the Assembly Government to ensure that rural matters and issues were properly considered in all national policy developments. However, despite the claims made by some ministers, publicly available evidence of its impact is limited. Indeed, in regard to rural social services, with the exception of developments in access to services in Welsh, scrutiny of policy documents and service plans reveals few substantive developments. For example, while *Fulfilled Lives, Supportive Communities* (WAG, 2007), the main strategy document for social services in Wales, acknowledged the importance of services being developed according to the characteristics and needs of particular localities, it made no direct reference to the particularities of rural communities. Similarly, a summary of Joint Reviews undertaken by the Care and Social Services Inspectorate for Wales and the Wales Audit Office made no reference to rural proofing or identified any differential experiences between urban and rural areas (CSSIW, 2009).

In addition to this neglect and the general tendency to superimpose urbanist assumptions upon rural situations, there are two other broad reasons why people in rural areas may be poorly served by public services; idealisations of rurality and inadequate funding for rural services

Idealisation and assumptions

In the UK there is a tendency to idealise the countryside and see it as a place without problems (Cloke and Little, 1997), and in Wales, the common perception of the rural interior as the heartland of Welsh identity and Welsh language may hinder the recognition of social problems and lead to a reluctance to accept that difficulties exist. Thus, issues such as alcohol and drug misuse, domestic violence or homelessness may be seen as being predominantly 'urban' problems or ones brought in by 'outsiders', and as such are thought not to require any local response (Collins and Billingham, 2001; Milbourne et al., 2006). Similarly, the apparent lack of diversity in rural areas compared with many urban areas can contribute to a lack of awareness of racism and discrimination and the deleterious consequences for some rural dwellers (Chakraborti and Garland, 2004; Robinson and Gardner, 2004; Williams, 2007; Woods and Watkin, 2008). The presumption that there are problems but 'not around here', bedevils many efforts to initiate appropriate developments in service provision, and as a result other groups such as those in poverty, people with mental health problems, and gay men and lesbians, who may be relatively 'invisible' among the more dispersed population of rural areas, may also find that their presence is not recognised either.

The idealisation of the countryside may be evident in simplistic assumptions about the readiness of family and friendship networks to provide informal care and support. The notion that there are invariably strong networks that will support those who need help can undermine the impetus to provide supportive services (Craig and Manthorpe, 2000). Research in older women's experiences and expectations of friendship and family in rural Wales reveals more variable and complex patterns of dependence and interdependence (Wenger, 2001). Similarly, the tendency to idealise rural Wales as a 'community of communities' ignores the changes that have taken place (Day, 2006), and in part, is based on some uncritical assumptions about what constitutes a community in the first place (Charles and Davies, 2005). More recent research indicates that people in rural Wales do feel a strong sense of community, with 82% of respondents to a household survey considering themselves to be members of their local community (WRO, 2008). Interestingly, a strong sense of community was most evident among fluent Welsh speakers.

Many writers have noted that inaccurate and idealised views of the countryside can play an important symbolic and political role in society (Cloke and Little, 1997) and may influence local responses to particular problems. Sibley (1997) notes that 'discrepant minorities' such as Gypsies, Travellers and people from minorities ethnic groups are often seen as transgressors, as people who don't belong, especially when the countryside is seen as a symbolic heartland in terms of identity. Thus, the local political and cultural context in which decisions about service policies and priorities are made, may be influenced by much broader ideas of rurality and belonging. Day (2002) has noted that both Welsh language and rurality are linked in some conceptions of national identity in

Wales. Surprisingly, a survey in 2004 found that only half of the people living in rural areas defined themselves as Welsh, although younger respondents were more likely to do so (WRO, 2004). Nonetheless, the in-migration of non-Welsh speakers into rural areas may well lead to some tensions in the community (Griffiths, 1992; Cloke et al., 1997; Hartwell, et al., 2007). Specifically, Charles (1995) has noted that women's refuges in some rural areas of Wales such as Gwynedd and Powys tend to take a higher proportion of women from outside of the immediate area largely because of the difficulty of ensuring safe accommodation within their own home area, and that this was perceived by some local authority officers as encouraging an influx of outsiders.

Inadequate funding and lack of recognition of rural costs

Typically, it costs more to provide public services in rural areas because of the geography of rural areas and the dispersed populations within them, which lead to longer journeys and more staff time spent travelling (Asthana et al., 2003; Hindle et al., 2004). These costs are further intensified by the lack of suitable facilities in some areas and by poorer public transport networks, which lead to more home visits by workers. For example, a survey of car mileage and time spent travelling in a mental health team on the Scottish Borders found that rural staff spent about 25–33% of their work time travelling compared to 7–10% among their urban staff (Wilson, 2003). Yet funding for rural services in Wales rarely meets the full costs of provision and the result is a trade-off between the extent of provision, service quality and costs (White et al., 2007; WAG, 2009).

Local government across the UK has struggled for years to persuade central government of the need for fairer funding for rural areas (Hayle, 1996). While the Assembly has explicitly recognised that service provision in rural areas is more costly and that levels of service are problematic (White et al., 2007), there is continuing dissatisfaction with arrangements in Wales from local government bodies (RDS, 2008). Nevertheless, putting aside the question of what would be appropriate levels of provision in different areas, the ratios of social workers to local authority populations in the most rural parts of Wales have been no better than in many more urban areas (ADSS, 2005), and the levels of expenditure per head of local population have shown that some rural councils spent around £100 less than some urban districts (CSSIW, 2006b).

Across the UK, there have been many attempts to find a fair solution to this issue, but most of these do not adequately address the funding shortfall, because they use a simple urban–rural distinction that does not adequately reflect the real differences in costs between different areas (Pugh, 2007b). For example, costs are likely to be lower in a compact rural area surrounding a town with good transport networks, than in a more remote upland area. A further difficulty is that attempts to base funding on existing service provision are constrained by the fact that they will be based on *what is* provided rather than *what ought* to be, and so, tend to fossilise existing inadequacies in service provision (Cheers, 1998).

Issues for service users

Many of the problems facing users of rural services are the same as those facing people in urban areas, but the geography of the countryside, the weaker infrastructure of public services, the absence of alternative provision and the social dynamics of small communities result in rural dwellers facing some further difficulties in accessing and using services. For some potential service users, the degree of social visibility within their small communities poses particular difficulties in regard to confidentiality, risk and recognition of their needs.

Transport and access to services

Poor public transport networks in rural areas results in higher levels of car ownership. Consequently, poorer households are likely to spend a higher proportion of their income on transport than their urban counterparts, and access to private transport remains a problem for many people. One study in Wales found that 22% of rural households reported an adult who lacked access to transport and relied on lifts from other people (White et al., 2007). Access remains stratified in other ways too, with many women having difficulty because the family's car is being used by a male partner to travel to work, or by age, as the young and the old, as well as the unemployed, are less likely to have access to private transport. White and his colleagues noted that 16% of those over 65 years reported difficulty in accessing their general practitioner surgery. Unfortunately, surveys into access to public services do not specifically include access to social care services, but research into health services reveals a phenomenon of 'distance decay'. That is, the use of health services diminishes the further away people live from them (Deaville, 2001; Gibbon et al., 2006). It is likely that the same phenomenon might be found in regard to the use of social services.

The Wales Spatial Plan has identified the need to improve access to health services and improve community transport provision (WAG, 2004) and there have been useful developments such as the Bwcabus scheme in North Carmarthenshire, the Teifi Valley and South Ceredigion. However, poor transport infrastructure remains a significant problem in accessing health and social care provision (WAG, 2009). Public transport may be too infrequent, perhaps requiring users to spend too long at their destination, or may not be available at convenient times. People with disabilities may have difficulty boarding buses, and many people may be reluctant to wait for long in exposed places or may fear being stranded if services are delayed or cancelled (Scharf and Bartlam, 2006). While access to some services in rural areas of Wales, like child care and community transport schemes, has improved in recent years (White et al., 2007), poor transport still impedes access to a wide range of social services, with long journey times being a common feature. For example, one man attending a treatment programme for sex offenders spent nearly five hours travelling to and from the venue. Thus, offenders in rural areas may be disadvantaged compared to urban offenders in terms of the time taken to comply with court orders. They may also be less likely to complete their programmes, and so find their difficulties exacerbated (Pugh, 2007b).

Finally, access to services in Welsh (as noted in Chapter 4, this volume) remains a problem in many rural areas (WAG, 2009). Despite the rural upland areas of Mid- and North Wales being areas with relatively high proportions of Welsh-speaking households, the chances of them receiving linguistically appropriate services remains patchy (Pugh and Jones, 1999; Madoc-Jones and Buchanan, 2003; Pugh and Williams, 2006).

Confidentiality, risk and stigma

In urban areas, confidentiality is supported by the relative anonymity of individuals within the larger population that surrounds them. Conversely, in smaller communities in rural areas, where people are more likely to notice the comings and goings of other people, or to notice a stranger's car, simply to be seen entering a particular building or driving to a house may compromise confidentiality. This can be especially difficult for those whose problems do not elicit a sympathetic response, or who feel ashamed or are at risk in some way. For example, a woman wishing to escape domestic violence may be deterred from seeking help at a family centre or Women's Aid office if she fears that her visit might come to the attention of her abuser (MacKay, 2000). In more remote areas, violence towards women and children may be less likely to be observed by others or be deterred by their presence, and those who are victims may find it more difficult to escape their situation (Stalford et al., 2003) .Violent men may restrict their capacity to contact others by removing the telephone, or restricting their access to transport, and threats of violence may be lent added credibility by isolation of location, as well as by the higher levels of gun ownership in rural areas (MacKay, 2000).

Stigmatisation and isolation are widely reported in studies of people with mental health problems in rural areas. The lack of anonymity may deter people from seeking help and fears of local reactions may inhibit the use of even the limited services available (Pugh and Richards, 1996; Philo et al., 2003). Some groups may also experience isolation because of negative ideas held about them. This has been particularly true of travelling peoples such as Gypsies whose lifestyles may be stigmatised by providers and the local community (Cemlyn, 2000). The National Assembly ((NAW, 2003) has reported that the community care needs of travelling people are being neglected, and both Cemlyn (2000) and Roberts (2005) stress the importance of multi-agency approaches to developing service provision for Travellers. Interestingly, Roberts (2005) noted that the use of a caravan as a mobile advice centre was perceived by Traveller communities as 'private space' in which people would talk about sexual health, domestic violence and mental health problems.

Social isolation by virtue of difference is also experienced by other groups and individuals. For example, informal networks for gay men and lesbians may be sparse in some rural areas. This can create difficulties in establishing contact with other gay men and lesbians (NWREN and Stonewall Cymru, 2010). There may be few places where it is possible to meet and talk with others, to try out different identities or to experience different degrees of 'coming out', and Australian research has noted that such isolation may have significant implications for HIV prevention strategies in rural areas (Roberts, 2003).

Neglect of minorities

While it was noted earlier that racism is widely reported in rural areas, the social and political position of people from minority ethnic groups in rural Wales is complex. For example, in North Wales they are more likely to have better than average employment, housing and income (Williams, 2006). Thus, any simple assumption that they are necessarily a deprived and marginalised group is likely to be mistaken, or at least to be an over-generalisation, as there is some evidence of a more variable experience (Pugh, 2004a; Williams, 2007). It should be noted that for many minority ethnic individuals, the decision to live in a rural area is an intentional choice, made with the knowledge that the perceived advantages in terms of the comparative safety and security for their children and overall quality of life are offset by some degree of social marginalisation or isolation.

While the demographic presence of some minority ethnic groups in rural areas is well established, relatively little is known about their experience of social services, but it is clear from reports from other areas and from in Wales that, generally, provision for them is poor and that their expectations are often correspondingly low (SSI, 1998; de Lima, 2001; DH, 2001a, 2001b, 2002; NAW, 2003; Pugh, 2004b; CSCI, 2004, 2006). Because of the absence of larger minority ethnic communities and the consequent lack of voluntary organisations, minority ethnic individuals and families who need help are unlikely to have anyone else to advocate for their needs and will have few alternative options for service provision. Elsewhere in the UK, research into rural child care services found that minority ethnic people were less likely to use them, partly because of the costs, but also because of the perception that these were aimed at a white clientele (ACRE, 2002).

Recently arrived migrant workers tend to be relatively young adults without dependants (Gilpin et al., 2006; Woods and Watkin, 2008) who are unlikely to need much help from health or social services, although low wages and precarious housing may make them more vulnerable to homelessness and problems of isolation (Radcliffe and Aneen Campbell, 2010. Nevertheless, a study in Flintshire found that about a quarter of migrant workers were married or in civil partnerships (Hold et al., 2007), and most of these had children (81%). About two-thirds of them also had at least one of their own parents living with them to help with child care. This study found that while nearly all respondents knew how to get access to health care, less than half were registered with a local doctor. Only seven people knew about local authority or housing association provision, and less than half of the overall sample of 60 respondents (26) knew how to get access to translation, although most thought that this was the service that would improve their quality of life. Evidence of increasing linguistic variation was also noted as 96 pupils in local schools were speaking one of 23 languages other than English or Welsh. The researchers estimated that, in total, there were around 44 different languages being spoken in the district. A study undertaken in Powys found that the number of children in local schools who did not have English or Welsh as their first language had risen from 80 to 143 in the previous 18 months (WRO, 2006a).

Many of those in rural areas who suffer racism, or other forms of oppression, and who would benefit from services, may be reluctant to seek help or 'make a fuss' because they fear that in drawing attention to their problems and needs, they may be blamed for their own situation, or even worse, become subject to further discrimination, perhaps even violence. As de Lima (1999, p 37), writing in a Scottish context, observed, 'there is often a reluctance to become involved in any initiative which they feel would focus attention upon them as individuals, and they are often not keen to discuss their experiences of living in communities'. Workers seeking to develop better services need to be sensitive to these concerns and recognise just how inhibiting this reluctance may be.

User expectations and satisfaction with services

It is sometimes assumed that rural dwellers are more stoical about their circumstances and consequently have lower expectations of public services, although there is little direct evidence of this. However, it is the case that the rural poor do not always recognise themselves as such (Milbourne and Hughes, 2005; Scharf and Bartlam, 2006) and this may well influence their perceptions of their needs and any subsequent responses to them. User surveys in England have generally found relatively high levels of satisfaction (Defra, 2004), but caution should be noted in the interpretation of such results. For example, some studies ask users what they think about particular aspects of a service, such as its accessibility, while others enquire about overall satisfaction with a service. Bowden and Moseley (2006) also noted that the averaging of results across rural populations means that the views of the most disadvantaged rural dwellers may be collapsed with the perceptions of those who have higher incomes, better access to personal transport and better information about services. They also noted that in regard to access to services, users were willing to trade off some factors against others, depending on the nature of the problem and the service concerned. For example, they were prepared to travel for 30 minutes for primary health care if this meant that they could have a full-time service, rather than accept shorter journey times to a more local, part-time service.

Issues for workers and agencies

The current context of policy, practice and training in social work takes little account of the demands of rural settings. The urbanist assumptions implicit in much policy and guidance often presents social workers as individuals who float free of their local social context. Furthermore, little attention is paid to questions about the training, supervision, support and professional development of rural staff, yet these things may have a considerable bearing on who comes to work in rural areas, whether they stay in post and how they practise.

Placing and personalisation

The more personalised basis of formal relationships in many rural areas makes it difficult for workers to maintain professional neutrality, and attempts to maintain professional distance may be rejected by local people. Social workers in rural areas often find that clients wish to 'place' them, that is, to establish who they are and where they come from. This may serve several purposes: to establish some 'safe ground' on which to base the working relationship; to allow the service user to show that despite the current difficulties they are nonetheless a competent and functioning member of the community; or perhaps to allow the service user to redress the power imbalance that inevitably exists between helper and helped. Most significantly, information about the worker can be used to check out what other people think of the worker and to decide to what extent the worker can be trusted. Professional credibility in small communities often rests upon a broader appreciation of the behaviour of workers outside of their work. Their behaviour, as well as that of other family members, may play a part in how the wider community and service users view the service and the worker (Pugh, 2000).

Dual relationships

Rural workers who live in the area in which they work face some interesting challenges in managing personal and professional boundaries in their relationships within the community, as 'out-of-hours' contacts are often unavoidable (Gripton and Valentich, 2003 Galbreath, 2005; Pugh, 2007a). Dual relationships have received very little attention in the UK generally and professional codes of practice provide no guidance other than to prohibit exploitative relationships between workers and clients. However, there are risks to workers too. When they carry out statutory duties in child protection and mental health work, or become involved in domestic violence work, their social visibility can leave them vulnerable to social pressure, isolation or even threats and violence. One of the most difficult aspects of rural practice is the question of how social workers should engage with the local community and yet still exercise their formal powers. Experience in Scotland has shown that there are considerable difficulties in carrying out child protection tasks with intimidating adults in small communities (Social Work Inspection Agency, 2005).

Tensions between organisational and local expectations

Many social workers in rural areas will have developed ways of working that enable them to operate effectively in their communities and which help them maintain the cooperation of service users, but the 'space' for such local adaptations may be becoming squeezed as practice becomes ever-more proceduralised. Thus, tensions may emerge between organisational imperatives and local expectations. Turbett (2007, cited in Pugh, 2007a) provides an interesting example of how workers in a remote Scottish location used local knowledge to inform community care assessments, which nevertheless seemed problematic to a temporary worker from the mainland.

Rural social workers may face considerable pressures to share information within their community, especially when it concerns issues of safety and risk. Writing in an Australian context, Green (2003) has noted that a worker undertaking work with a released child sex offender, although bound by professional expectations of confidentiality, could be subject to criticism if the person were to re-offend, as local people might well think that the worker was able to provide some protection for their own children while they remained unaware of the potential risk. These sorts of pressures are likely to increase as Multi-Agency Public Protection Arrangements to manage the risks of more dangerous offenders in the community become more widely used.

Recruitment, support and supervision

Rural services often experience difficulty in recruiting suitable staff simply because of the smaller local pool of potential employees. While it may seem to be less problematic when seeking professionally qualified staff, who might be expected to seek jobs over a much wider geographical area, recruitment remains problematic across a wide range of public services. Many people who move to rural areas do so to improve their quality of life, but higher living costs, shortages of suitable housing and limited career prospects may deter potential employees. It can also be difficult to recruit local ancillary and part-time workers, as people may be reluctant to undertake work that places them in authority over people whom they know or whose reputation gives them cause for concern.

In rural areas there is often less opportunity for specialism and workers may have to undertake many different roles, with the result that they may not develop their expertise to the same degree as those working in larger urban teams. Rural workers may be professionally isolated and not get the informal support and advice of colleagues that is common in larger teams, nor receive the levels of in-service training and supervision available to their urban counterparts. These factors can affect the quality of service provision and can also make it more difficult for workers to gain promotion, partly because they find it harder to develop the expertise and experience required for advancement, and partly because of fewer opportunities for promotion. These pressures on workers may be exacerbated by a lack of support from other services, which may also be operating under similar constraints. Staff from minority ethnic groups who come to work in rural areas may feel more isolated within the workplace and, lacking local connections, may be excluded from informal networks.

Generally, social workers in rural areas often comment that they are never off-duty, as they report working longer hours and having to field more out-of-hours calls. These demands may arise from the lack of other workers and other services, but also result from local expectations of informality and approachability (Pugh and Cheers, 2010). Rural services, because of the smaller staff numbers, are particularly vulnerable to staff illness, absence and departure, and rural agencies often face a dilemma in deciding how best to organise their services. If they centralise them to maintain efficiency and preserve service capability, they incur higher travel costs and run the risk of becoming isolated and distant from the communities they serve. On the other hand, if they localise them, they can find it difficult to respond satisfactorily to specialist needs.

Service development

Several writers have noted that it can take longer to establish new developments in service in rural areas (Francis and Henderson, 1992; Edwards et al., 1999). There may be difficulty in gaining local support for initiatives, especially when people are unwilling to acknowledge that there is a problem, or when the proposed initiative is aimed at an unpopular group. This has been evident in anti-racism strategies, in many drug initiatives and in proposed developments for Gypsies and Travellers (Cemlyn, 2000; Chakraborti and Garland, 2004; McKeganey et al., 2004). The scarcity of local groups who can act as advocates for unpopular and minority interests may require that social workers take a more political role in advocating for their needs. New initiatives also remain more vulnerable to failure in the early stages, either because of continuing opposition or simply because of staff change as project workers move on to other jobs.

It is clear that social workers need to use some of the methods adopted by community development workers. They may need to identify significant local people who wield power and influence within the area and seek their views and suggestions. They may need to undertake an educational role in helping people and organisations such as parish councils, farming organisations and Women's Institutes to understand what is needed and what is being proposed, and use these bodies to canvass opinion and to disseminate information. Initiatives that resonate with local sentiments and perceptions or that are promoted by local people are more likely to succeed.

The weaker infrastructure of other public services and the relative paucity of voluntary and independent sector provision in rural areas that was noted earlier means that there are fewer alternative sources of service and fewer opportunities for collaborative development with other agencies. Nevertheless, given the problems of inadequate resources and the need for community support for new developments, cooperation and joint work between agencies are desirable. In North Wales, an outreach initiative aimed at the health needs of Gypsies/Travellers successfully adopted a multi-agency approach (Roberts, 2005), and evidence from elsewhere in the UK shows that multi-agency approaches to racism or domestic violence can also be effective, although small voluntary organisations can find their scarce resources overstretched by the demands of cooperation with statutory agencies (Edwards et al., 1999; Dhalech, 1999 ; Hague, 2000; Blyth, 2005). Williams (2006, p 200) has noted how the North Wales Race Equality Network experienced 'consultation overload' and how its work became largely 'pitched towards servicing the consultative needs of "white" organisations' (2006, p 196).

Conclusion

In recent years, the rhetoric of recognition of rurality in Wales has become more evident and there is certainly more research into different problems and issues, although much still remains to be done. But, in social services and social care, substantive changes have so far been limited, while the key issue of how best to allocate funding for rural areas has not been settled. For service planners and providers, the challenge is to transform the rhetoric of recognition into practical initiatives to meet the needs of Wales' poorly served rural population, for whom access to suitable services remains problematic, especially for the poorest households in the most sparsely populated areas.

This chapter has focused on some of the key issues in service delivery in rural areas of Wales, but we should recognise that the broader question of whether rural social work is different from or requires different approaches than social work in urban areas has not received much consideration in a UK context (Pugh, 2003; Turbett, 2004). Indeed, most British social work literature makes little or no mention of rural settings. While there have been many small-scale studies of some features of rural provision, many aspects of rural practice have not been researched at all and there is a tendency for uninformed or unproductive repetition of existing work (Craig and Manthorpe, 2000). However, there is much to be learned from the experience of other countries such as Australia, Canada and the United States, as rural social work raises crucial issues about how we conceptualise the social work role in small communities.

My view is that working in rural areas re-emphasises the importance of local context in practice, something that also tends to be neglected in urban contexts. It is easy to see why the temporary worker in the earlier cited example of community care practice in rural Scotland might have thought that the use of local knowledge in the assessment process was unprofessional. Yet such local adaptations may be justifiable if we draw on the conceptual frameworks developed by writers overseas. Martinez-Brawley (2000, p 221) explicitly addressed this sort of issue when she described the role of rural-based workers as 'translating the vertically generated policies and programs into specific action geared to the civic and sociocultural style of the community'.

Rural practice also challenges notions of professional neutrality and detachment as the separation of workers from the communities in which they live and work is often impractical. The assumption that objectivity follows from detachment is also open to challenge; emancipatory perspectives have challenged assumptions of expertise and power, and as Miller (1998) has noted, have undermined the assumption of formal distance between clients and workers and have legitimated self-disclosure and integration into communities.

While this chapter has focused on many problematic aspects of rural practice, we should not assume that the daily experience of rural practitioners is a negative one. Most writers on rural social work have noted the high levels of satisfaction expressed by rural workers, who seem to relish the variety of the work and the opportunity to play a bigger role in service development. Research from other countries shows that they value the sense of engagement and achievement that is possible in smaller communities (Martinez-Brawley, 2000; Lonne and Cheers, 2004; Pugh and Cheers, 2010).

References

ACRE (Action for Rural Communities) (2002) *Challenging Inclusion: Childcare: The way forward* Ipswich, ACRE

ADSS (Association of Directors of Social Services) (2005) *Social Work in Wales: A profession to value* Cardiff, ADSS (Cymru)

Asthana, S, Gibson, A, Monn, G and Brigham, P (2003) 'Allocating resources for health and social care: The significance of rurality' *Health and Social Care in the Community* 11(6), pp 486–93

Blyth, L (2005) 'Not behind closed doors: working in partnership against domestic violence' in Carnwell, R and Buchanan, J (eds) *Effective Practice in Health and Social Care: A partnership approach* Maidenhead, Open University Press/ McGraw-Hill, pp 112–25

Bowden, C and Moseley, M (2006) *The Quality and Accessibility of Services in Rural England: A survey of the perspectives of disadvantaged residents* www.defra.gov.uk

Cemlyn, S (2000) 'Assimilation, control, mediation or advocacy? Social work dilemmas in providing anti-oppressive services for Traveller children and families' *Child and Family Social Work* 5(4), pp 327–41

Chakraborti, N and Garland, J (2004) *Rural Racism* Cullompton, Willan Publishing

Charles, N (1995) 'Feminist politics, domestic violence and the state' *The Sociological Review* 43(4), pp 617–40

Charles, N and Davies, C A (2005) 'Studying the particular, illuminating the general: Community studies and community in Wales' *The Sociological Review* 53(4), pp 672–90

Cheers, B (1998) *Welfare Bushed: Social care in rural Australia* Aldershot, Ashgate

Cloke, P and Little, J (1997) *Contested Countryside Cultures: Otherness, marginalisation and rurality* London, Routledge

Cloke, P, Goodwin, M and Milbourne, P (1997) *Rural Wales: Community and marginalisation* Cardiff, University of Wales Press

Collins, S and Billingham, J (2001) 'Alcohol services in Wales' *Journal of Substance Abuse* 6, pp 114–22

Craig, G and Manthorpe, J (2000) *Fresh Fields: Rural social care: research, policy and practice agenda*s York, Joseph Rowntree Foundation

CSCI (Commission for Social Care Inspection) (2004) *Inspection of Social Care Services for Older People: Herefordshire County Council*, www.csci.gov.uk

CSCI (2006) *Inspection of Social Care Services for Older People: Cumbria County Council*, www.csci.gov.uk

CSSIW (Care and Social Services Inspectorate Wales) (2006a) *Joint Review of Powys County Council Social Services* Cardiff, CSSIW, www.joint-reviews.gov.uk

CSSIW (2006b) *Social Services in Wales 2004–2005: The Report of the Chief Inspector* Cardiff, CSSIW, http://new.wales.gov.uk/social_services/?lang=en

CSSIW (2008) *Joint Review of Gywnedd Council Social Services*, Cardiff, CSSIW and the Wales Audit Office

CSSIW (2009) *Reviewing Social Services in Wales 1998–2008: Learning from the journey,* Cardiff, CSSIW and the Wales Audit Office

Cyngor Gwynedd Council (2007) *Living in Gwynedd: An examination of the costs and issues arising from living on the periphery*, Caernarfon, Cyngor Gwynedd Council

Day, G (2002) *Making Sense of Wales: Politics and society in Wales* Cardiff, University of Wales Press

Day, G (2006) 'A community of communities? Civil society and rural Wales' in Day, G, Dunkerley, D and Thompson, A (eds) *Civil Society in Wales: Policy, politics and people* Cardiff, University of Wales Press, pp 227–48

de Lima, P (1999) 'Research and action in the Scottish Highlands' in Henderson, P and Kaur, R (eds) *Rural Racism in the UK* London, The Community Development Foundation, pp 33–43

de Lima, P (2001) *Needs Not Numbers: An exploration of minority ethnic communities in Scotland* London, Commission for Racial Equality and the Community Development Foundation

Deaville, J (2001) *The Nature of Rural General Practice in the UK: Preliminary research* Newtown, Powys, Gregynog British Medical Association and Institute for Rural Health

Defra (Department for Environment, Food and Rural Affairs) (2004) *Survey of Rural Customers' Satisfaction with Services*, London, Defra, www.defra.gov.uk

DH (Department of Health) (2001a) *Responding to Diversity*, London, DH

DH (2001b) *From Lip Service to Real Service*, London, DH

DH (2002) *Developing Services for Minority Ethnic Older People*, London, DH

Dhalech, M (1999) *Challenging Racism in the Rural Idyll* Exeter, The Rural Race Equality Project

Edwards, B, Goodwin, M, Pemberton, S and Woods, M (1999) *Partnership Working in Rural Regeneration*, Rowntree Research Findings 039, York, Joseph Rowntree Foundation, www.jrf.org.uk

End Child Poverty Network Wales (2009) *Child Poverty and Social Exclusion in Rural Wales* Cardiff, End Child Poverty Network Wales (also available online at www.endchildpovertycymru.org.uk)

Francis, D and Henderson, P (1992) *Working with Rural Communities* London, Macmillan

Galbreath, W (2005) 'Dual relationships in rural communities', in Lohmann, N and Lohmann, R (eds) *Rural Social Work Practice* New York, NY, Columbia University Press, pp 105–23

Gartner, A, Gibbon, R and Riley, N (2007) *Rural Health: A profile of rural health in Wales* Cardiff, Wales Centre for Health

Gibbon, R, Riley, N and Meyrick, J (2006) *Pictures of Health in Wales: A technical supplement* Cardiff, Wales Centre for Health

Gilpin, N, Henty, M, Lemos, S, Portes, J and Bullen, C (2006) *The Impact of Free Movement of Workers from Central and Eastern Europe on the UK Labour Market*, DWP Working Paper 26, London, Department for Work and Pensions, www.dwp.gov.uk/asd/asd5/wp2006.asp

Green, R (2003) 'Social work in rural areas: A personal and professional challenge' *Australian Social Work* 56(3), pp 209–19

Griffiths, D (1992) 'The political consequences of migration into Wales' *Contemporary Wales* 5, pp 65–80

Gripton, J and Valentich, M (2003) 'Dealing with non-sexual professional–client dual relationships in rural communities', paper presented at the International Conference on Human Services in Rural Communities, 29–30 May, Halifax, Canada.

Hague, G (2000) *Reducing Domestic Violence: What works – multi-agency fora* London, Home Office

Hartwell, S, Kitchen, L, Milbourne, P and Morgan, S (2007) *Population Change in Rural Wales: Social and cultural impacts*, Research Report. 12, Cardiff, Wales Rural Observatory

Hayle, R (1996) *Fair Shares for Rural Areas? An assessment of public resource allocation systems* London, Rural Development Commission

Hindle, T, Spollen, M and Dixon, P (2004) *Review of the Evidence on Additional Costs of Delivering Services to Rural Communities* London, SECTA, www.defra.gov.uk

Hold, M, Korszon, S, Kotchekova, E and Grzesiak, F (2007) *Migrant Workers in Flintshire* Wales, North East Wales Race Equality Network

JRF (Joseph Rowntree Foundation) (2009) *Monitoring Poverty and Social Exclusion in Wales 2009* York, JRF, www.poverty.org.uk/reports/wales%202009%20findings.pdf

Kenway, P and Palmer, G (2007) *Monitoring Poverty and Social Exclusion in Wales 2007* York, Joseph Rowntree Foundation, www.jrf.org.uk/publications/monitoring-poverty-and-social-exclusion-wales-2007

Lehmann, J (2005) 'Human services management in rural contexts' *British Journal of Social Work* 35(3), pp 355–71

Lloyd, G and Lloyd, S (1984) 'The changing context of rural social work and service delivery' *Social Work in Rural and Urban Areas*, Research Highlights Number 9, Aberdeen, University of Aberdeen

Lonne, B and Cheers, B (2004) 'Practitioners speak – balanced account of rural practice recruitment and retention' *Rural Social Work*, 9, pp 244–54

Lowe, P and Ward, N (2002) 'Devolution and the governance of rural affairs in the UK' in Adams, J and Robinson, P (eds) *Devolution in Practice* London, Institute for Public Policy Research, pp 117–39

MacKay, A. (2000) *Reaching Out: Women's Aid in a rural area* St Andrews, East Fife Women's Aid

Madoc-Jones, I and Buchanan, J (2003) 'Welsh language, identity and probation practice: The context for change' *Probation Journal* 50, pp 225–38

Martinez-Brawley, E (2000) *Close to Home: Human services and the small community* Washington, DC, NASW Press

McKeganey, N, Neale, J, Parkin, S and Mills, C (2004) 'Communities and drugs: Beyond the rhetoric of community action' *Probation Journal* 51(4), pp 343–61

Milbourne, P and Hughes, R (2005) *Poverty and Social Exclusion in Rural Wales* Cardiff, Wales Rural Observatory, www.walesruralobservatory.org.uk

Milbourne, P, Hughes, R and Hartwell, S (2006) *Homelessness in Rural Wales*, Cardiff, Wales Rural Observatory, www.walesruralobservatory.org.uk

Miller, P J (1998) 'Dual relationships in rural practice: a dilemma of ethics and culture' in Ginsberg, L H (ed) *Social Work in Rural Communities* (third edition) Alexandria, VA, CSWE, pp 55–62

NAW (National Assembly Government) (2003) *Review of Service Provision for Gypsy Travellers* Cardiff, NAW

NAW (2005) *Welsh Index of Multiple Deprivation* Cardiff, LGDU, National Statistics

NAW (2008) *One Wales* Cardiff, NAW

NWREN (North Wales Race Equality Network) and Stonewall Cymru (2010) *Toe in the Water*, Conway, NWREN, www.nwren.org.uk/TiW-E.htm

One Wales (2007) *One Wales: A Progressive agenda*, Labour and Paid Cymru groups in the National Assembly, Cardiff, NAG

ONS (Office for National Statistics) (2004) *Rural and Urban Area Classification: An introductory guide* London, ONS, www.statistics.gov

ONS (2007) *Mid-Year Estimates of the Population* London, ONS, www.statistics.gov

Philo, C, Parr, H and Burns, N (2003) *Social Geographies of Rural Mental Health: Experiencing inclusion and exclusion*, http://web.ges.gla.ac.uk/projects/website/main.htm

Pugh, R (2000) *Rural Social Work* Lyme Regis, Russell House Publishing

Pugh, R (2003) 'Considering the countryside: Is there a case for rural social work?' *British Journal of Social Work* 33(1), pp 67–85

Pugh, R (2004a) 'Difference and discrimination in rural areas' *Rural Social Work* 9(1), pp 255–64

Pugh, R (2004b) 'Responding to racism: delivering local services' in Chackraborti, N and Garland, J (eds) *Rural Racism* Cullompton, Willan Publishing, pp 176–203

Pugh, R (2007a) 'Dual relationships: professional and personal boundaries in rural communities', *British Journal of Social Work* 37(8), pp 1405–23

Pugh, R (2007b) 'Rurality and the Probation Service' *Probation Service Journal* 54(2), pp 145–59

Pugh, R and Cheers, B (2010) *Rural Social Work: An international perspective* Bristol, The Policy Press

Pugh, R and Jones, E (1999) 'Language and social work practice: minority language provision within the Guardian ad Litem service' *British Journal of Social Work* 29(4), pp 529–45

Pugh, R and Richards, M (1996) 'Speaking out: A practical approach to empowerment' *Practice* 8(2), pp 35–44

Pugh, R and Williams, D (2006) 'Language policy and provision in social service organisations' *British Journal of Social Work* 36(7), pp 1227–44

Pugh, R, Scharf, T and Williams, C (2007) *Obstacles to Using and Providing Rural Social Care*, SCIE Research Briefing 22, London, Social Care Institute for Excellence, www.scie.org.uk/publications/briefings/briefing22/index.asp

Radcliffe, J. And Aneen Campbell, J. (2010) *Living in Wales – The Housing and Homelessness Experiences of Central and Eastern European Migrant Workers* Swansea, Shelter Cymru.

RDS (Rural Development Sub-Committee) (2007a) *Scoping Paper for the Committee's Rural Service Delivery Inquiry* Cardiff, RDS, National Assembly for Wales

RDS (2007b) *Rural Poverty and Deprivation Scoping Paper: Annex 1* Cardiff, RDS National Assembly for Wales

RDS (2008) *Report on Poverty and Deprivation in Rural Wales* Cardiff, RDS, National Assembly for Wales

Roberts, A (2005) 'Working with Gypsy Travellers: A partnership approach' in Carnwell, R and Buchanan, J (eds) *Effective Practice in Health and Social Care: A partnership approach* Maidenhead, Open University Press, pp 97–111

Roberts, R (2003) *Men who have Sex with Men in the Bush: Impediments to the Formation of Gay Communities in Some Rural Areas* Chicago, IL, Chicago State University, www.csu.edu/research/crsr/ruralsoc/v2n3p13.htm

Robinson, V and Gardner, H (2004) 'Unravelling a stereotype: the lived experience of black and minority ethnic people in rural Wales' in Chakraborti, N and Garland, J (eds) *Rural Racism* Cullompton, Willan Publishing

Scharf, T and Bartlam, B (2006) *Rural Disadvantage: Quality of life and disadvantage amongst older people: A pilot study* Cheltenham, Commission for Rural Communities

Davidson, M, Nicol, S, Roys, M and Beaumont, A (2011) *The Cost of Poor Housing in Wales* Watford, Shelter and the Building Research Establishment.

Shucksmith, M (2003) *Social Exclusion in Rural Areas: A review of recent research* Aberdeen, Arkleton Centre, www.defra.gov.uk

Sibley, D (1997) 'Endangering the sacred: nomads, youth cultures and the countryside' in Cloke, P and Little, J (eds) *Contested Countryside Cultures: Otherness, marginalisation and rurality* London, Routledge, pp 218–31

Social Work Inspection Agency (2005) *An Inspection into the Care and Protection of Children in Eilean Siar* Edinburgh, Scottish Executive

SSI (Social Services Inspectorate) (1998) *They Look After Their Own, Don't They?* London, Department of Health

Stalford, H, Baker, H and Beveridge, F (2003) *Children and Domestic Violence in Rural Areas: A child-focused assessment of service provision* London, Save the Children

TUC (Trades Union Congress) (2004) *Propping Up Rural and Small Town Britain: Migrant workers in Britain* London, TUC

Turbett, C (2004) 'A decade after Orkney: Towards a practice model for social work in the remoter areas of Scotland' *British Journal of Social Work* 34(7), pp 981–95

Turbett, C (2006) cited in Pugh, R (2006) 'Dual relationships: professional and personal boundaries in rural communities' *British Journal of Social Work*, Advance Access, 8 September.

WAG (Welsh Assembly Government) (2004) *Wales Spatial Plan* Cardiff, WAG

WAG (2007) *Fulfilled Lives, Supportive Communities: A strategy for social services over the next decade* Cardiff, WAG

WAG (2009) *Rural Health Plan* Cardiff, WAG

Wenger, C (2001) 'Myths and realities of ageing in rural Britain' *Ageing and Society* 21(1), pp 117–30

White, S and Tippireddy, H (2005) *Statistical Report on Rural Wales: Volume 1* Cardiff, Wales Rural Observatory, www.walesruralobservatory.org.uk

White, S, Walkley, C, Radcliffe, J and Edwards, B (2007) *Coping with Access to Services* Cardiff, Wales Rural Observatory, www.walesruralobservatory.org.uk

Williams, C (2006) 'Black and ethnic minority associations in Wales' in Day, G, Dunkerley, M and Thompson, A (eds) *Civil Society in Wales: Policy, politics and people* Cardiff, University of Wales Press, pp 183–205

Williams, C (2007) 'Revisiting the rural/race debates: A view from the Welsh countryside' *Journal of Ethnic and Racial Studies* 30(5), pp 741–65

Wilson, F (2003) *Key Issues for Rural Areas in Northumberland* (first draft) Newcastle, North Tyneside and Northumberland Mental Health Trust

Woods, M (2006) 'Redefining the "rural question": The new "politics of rural" and social policy' *Social Policy and Administration*, 40(6), pp 579–95

Woods, M and Watkin, S (2008) *Central and Eastern European Migrant Workers in Rural Wales*, Report 20, Cardiff, Wales Rural Observatory

WRO (Wales Rural Observatory) (2004) *An Overview of Life in Wales*, Key Findings Paper 2, Cardiff, WRO, www.walesruralobservatory.org.uk

WRO (2006a) *Scoping Study on Eastern and Central European Migrant Workers in Rural Wales* Cardiff, WRO, www.walesruralobservatory.org.uk

WRO (2006b) *A Survey of Rural Services in Wales* Cardiff, WRO, www.walesruralobservatory.org.uk

WRO (2008) *Report on the Household Survey in Rural Wales* Cardiff, WRO, www.walesruralobservatory.org.uk

WRO (2009a) *The Impacts of the Current Recession in Rural Wales* Cardiff, WRO, www.walesruralobservatory.org.uk

WRO (2009b) *Deep Rural Localities* Cardiff, WRO, www.walesruralobservatory.org.uk

WRO (2010) *A Survey of Farming Households in Wales* Cardiff, WRO, www.walesruralobservatory.org.uk

Chapter 7

Equalities and Social Justice in a Devolved Wales

Charlotte Williams

Introduction

The last decade has witnessed widespread change in the equalities field. The 2000s opened with groundbreaking reforms to equality law under the Race Relations (Amendment) Act 2000 and closed with the introduction of a major piece of legislation – the Equality Act 2010 – which established a new approach to equalities. A new enforcement body had been set up – the Equality and Human Rights Commission (EHRC) – and a new infrastructure for delivering on equality duties at the local level had been created. United Kingdom (UK) equality law now leads the way in Europe as the framework for the 'single equality approach' now in place. These developments were put in place alongside the existing architecture for promoting equality established under devolution and the Government of Wales Act 1998. It is not too difficult therefore to assert that the climate for taking forward issues of anti-discrimination and equality of opportunity has never been better. This chapter will outline these major changes initiated by the UK government on equalities. It will explore the legal framework for advancing equalities within Wales and review aspects of the approach taken by the Welsh Government in implementing its equality duties. The chapter concludes by discussing these developments within the wider context of the social justice ambitions of the Welsh Government and raising issues for consideration by social welfare and equalities practitioners.

New Labour and a new equalities era

Bagihole's (2009, p 58) analysis of the development of equal opportunities policies in the UK identifies five distinct eras where particular drivers for change have come to the fore. She charts what she calls the 'moral era' between the 1940s and 1950s, the 'liberal legislative era', which covers the 1960s and 1970s, the 'politically hostile era' of the 1980s followed in the 1990s by the 'public relations and professional era' when, she argues, equal opportunities became an integral part of the jargon of bureau professionals (2009, p 68). She outlines an era from the 2000s of 'fairness tempered by economic efficiency' (2009, p 73), outlining an approach that extended the equalities mandate but within the context of a keen sense of not undermining economic growth. In this respect, the 1997 Labour government significantly advanced regulation around equality in public services, broadened family-friendly policies and extended the equality protection to include a number of new groups beyond race, gender and disability. The decade of the 2000s saw a significant tranche of reforms and equality of opportunity established as a fundamental part of the New Labour modernising agenda in public services. The single equality framework adopted signals a generic approach to legislation, policy and institutions relating to inequality and discrimination rather than treating each minority status as distinct. The EHRC, established under the Equality Act 2006 as the major enforcement body, replaced the existing Commission for Racial Equality, the Equal Opportunities Commission and the Disability Rights Commission. The EHRC brought together the expertise and resources to promote equality and tackle discrimination in relation to nine protected characteristics: age, disability, sex, gender reassignment, pregnancy and maternity, race, sexual orientation, religion and belief, and marriage and civil partnership; and to promote human rights. Alongside this development, the Labour government published a comprehensive report on its independent review into the persistence of discrimination and inequality in British society: *Fairness and Freedom* (Equalities Review, 2007). *Fairness and Freedom* proclaimed Britain as having the most advanced and effective equality legislation, 'unrivalled in Europe' (2007, p 1). It signalled a new methodology for measuring inequalities and established the principle of National Equality Panel Reports on inequality, the first of which appeared in 2010 (Hills et al., 2010).

This era witnessed a fundamental shift within discrimination law from '*negative* equality duties' to '*positive* equality duties', a development first introduced under the Race Relations (Amendment) Act 2000. This measure required public authorities to *promote* good race relations as well as provide protection against discrimination. These duties have now been incorporated into the Equality Act 2010 and place a requirement on all employers to take anticipatory actions to prevent and pre-empt inequality by taking positive steps to promote equality within the workplace and in service delivery. With regard to race, for example, positive duties oblige public authorities to take steps to promote integration and social cohesion in their communities, to consult with minority groups and to conduct ethnic monitoring (for a good discussion of negative and positive equality duties, see McLaughlin, 2007). The establishment of positive duties considerably strengthens the potential for real and effective change as authorities must now not merely react to issues to discrimination, but have a duty to be *proactive* in working towards equality.

There can be little doubting that the Labour government's forthright approach to equalities was unprecedented. The explicit acknowledgement of the concept of 'institutional discrimination' following the MacPherson Report (1999) and the systematic approach to requiring public bodies to be responsive and to be held to account for their actions mean that there can be nowhere in the country where issues of equality are not ringing in the ears of public servants. However, the broader approach of 1997–2010

Labour government was not without criticism. This approach to equality, largely adopted by the current coalition government, is based on a concept of equality of *opportunity* that emphasises the removal of barriers that hinder people's potential rather than a more radical ambition of producing equality of *outcomes* through redistributing resources in society. *Fairness and Freedom* (Equalities Review, 2007, p 6) described the more equal society as one that 'protects and promotes equality, real freedom and substantive opportunity to live in the ways people value and would choose, so that everyone can flourish. An equal society recognises people's different needs, situations and goals and removes the barriers that limit what people can do and can be'.

This approach embraces the myth of an open and meritocratic society in which removing 'barriers' that limit opportunity allows people to realise their potential. This type of approach denies or at best seeks to shift attention away from systemised structural inequalities in society towards a focus on the individual and their capabilities (Ellison and Ellison, 2006). Equalities are viewed as addressing the personal characteristics of individuals (see Equalities Review, 2007). Yet people's choices and agency, and especially for the most vulnerable, are constrained in a constellation of ways that limit their ability to take up opportunities even when they may be offered to them. Benefiting from opportunities is not wholly in the control of individual propensities or idiosyncrasies, but deeply reflective of unequal societal arrangements. This individualised approach leads to the twin policy strategy of opening access to the labour market and prompting greater participation in policy-making as the formula for redressing inequality. Such a strategy itself obscures the fact of limited opportunities in some territorial areas and limited opportunities for some groups of people and proffers a rather simplistic view of the exercise of choice.

The approach flagged in *Fairness and Freedom* (Equalities Review, 2007) suggests a strategy for measuring equality that serves to fragment issues of inequality. The analysis it adopts disaggregates the impacts of unequal chances into different policy fields such as education, housing or health in order to prioritise for action the most pressing and thus target effort and resources. This is referred to as the '*Equalities Scorecard*'. So, for example, it prioritises early years education, employment, health and crime for targeted action, while housing and income support fall quietly off the equalities agenda. This disaggregation has two effects. First, it blurs the complex interrelationship between dimensions of inequality in individual's lives. Second, it powerfully shifts attention away from systemised and persistent inequalities as they are experienced collectively by certain status groups across the spectrum of policy areas. This targeted, as opposed to universalistic, approach to policy necessarily hampers the government's ability to deliver on equality and social justice (Ellison and Ellison, 2006). Thus, McLaughlin and Baker (2007, p 60) argue that the Labour Party's approach 'has been strong in discourses of well-being and need but weak in terms of discourses of rights and social solidarity'.

The underpinning philosophy of the Welsh Government differs markedly from this approach. The Welsh Assembly Government agenda has been driven by an equalities mandate embedded within its constitutional arrangements that is comprehensive in its coverage and one that supports the redistributive approach of 'progressive universalism' in public services (see Chapter 1, this volume).

The equalities challenge in Wales

The principle of equality is fundamental to the work of the Welsh Government and has far-reaching implications for those working within or in association with public services in Wales. Prior to devolution, no coherent approach to issues of inequality in Wales existed. Indeed, a widespread lethargy on the part of government bodies prior to the establishment of the National Assembly casts a long shadow forward. The vision set out in *Wales: A better country* (WAG, 2003, p 12) stated:

> *We will promote gender equality, good race relations and race equality and tackle discrimination on grounds of age and disability. We want to see people in public life reflecting the diversity in the population as a whole. We will comply with our Welsh Language Scheme, thus ensuring that Welsh and English are treated on a basis of equality in the conduct of public business.*

Wales is a profoundly unequal society. Overarching economic disparities affect people from a range of status backgrounds producing widespread poverty for older people, women, disabled people, black and minority ethnic people, lone parents and children, among others (Davies et al., 2011). Fundamental inequalities of income and wealth cannot be disassociated from life chances and for some groups of individuals, deep and persistent discriminations reduce their freedoms, well-being and ability to participate in society. The systemised patterning of these discriminations is revealed in the available statistical evidence (Winkler, 2009; Davies et al., 2011).

Approximately one-fifth of the Welsh population live in poverty. Nearly 400,000 working-age adults, 200,000 children and 100,000 pensioners in Wales are in poverty as measured by low income after housing costs have been deducted (JRF, 2011). While overall the levels of inequality are not as wide as for the rest of the UK, this is attributable to the fact that Wales has few people who earn the highest salaries or who can be counted amongst the very rich of the UK (Davies et al., 2011). At the same time, there is evidence to suggest that those groups protected by anti-discrimination legislation face more disadvantage in Wales than in the UK as a whole. Disadvantage in education, employment and earnings attaches particularly to young people, disabled people and those of Bangladeshi and Pakistani ethnicities, with women in each of these groups being more disadvantaged (Davies et al., 2011).

Women in Wales are by and large concentrated in low-pay, low-skilled sectors of the economy and a lifetime of disadvantage results in poverty in older age. The incidence of low weekly pay for women in full-time employment in Wales is 38% and there is a gender pay gap in weekly earnings of 22%. Single-parent households in Wales are largely headed by women and are the most susceptible group to be living in poverty. Even single women without children appear to be vulnerable to living in poverty (Davies et al., 2011). Women's access to work is hampered by a lack of child care in Wales. There is only one child care place to every seven children in Wales and in some areas, such as Blaenau Gwent, there is only one place for every 20 children (EOC, 2006). Of the 340,000 people providing unpaid care in Wales, the majority are women (EOC, 2006). Lack of support for caring responsibilities seriously disadvantages their employment prospects. The EHRC's (2011) most recent *Who Runs Wales* report indicates women's representation in key decision-making roles in Wales to be consistently poor. Despite strong representation as members of the Assembly (42%), women are largely absent from the committee rooms and council chambers of Wales. Only 5% of council leaders in Wales are women (just one woman leader of the 22 councils) and only 25% of councillors in Wales are women. Most startlingly, only 23% of local authority chief executives are women, despite 68% of all local authority staff being women.

Some of the most profound inequalities in terms of race and ethnicity in Wales relate to employment. The *Anatomy of Economic Inequality in Wales* report (Davies et al., 2011) graphically illustrates the particular disadvantage faced by Bangladeshi and Pakistani groups in Wales. They are, for example, more likely than their white counterparts to have no educational qualifications, have an above-average incidence of non-employment (47%) and even when in work to be among those with the lowest earnings. Employment and unemployment are, however, just one indicator of the ways in which black and minority ethnic groups experience inequalities in Wales. The Bevan Foundation report on equality issues in Wales (Winkler et al., 2009) notes, for example, that access to health and social care appears to be poorer for minority ethnic groups than within the population as a whole, that the health status of minority ethnic groups is poorer and that they experience poorer housing and high levels of poverty and social exclusion. The report suggests that there is evidence of substantial inequality in Wales and that minority ethnic groups are among those who consistently experience disadvantage and discrimination in almost all areas of life (Winkler et al., 2009). The Welsh Government's approach to minority communities historically has been criticised as laisser faire with devolution seeing the government now taking a more proactive role in addressing minority concerns (Williams and De Lima, 2006).

In terms of disability, the evidence is equally stark. Wales has the highest proportion of disabled people in the whole of Great Britain, with 22% of the working-age population having a work-limiting disability, four percentage points higher than the UK average. The Disability Rights Commission's report *Disability in Wales: Impact report 2005–6* (DRC, 2006a) indicates that Wales has a higher proportion of young people not in education, employment or training by the age of 16 and by the age of 19 they are still twice as likely as their peers to be in this predicament. People defined as both Disability Discrimination

Act 1995 disabled and as having a work-limiting condition have by far the lowest educational achievements of all equality categories, being roughly three times more likely to have no qualifications than those non-disabled. In employment, 74% of those so defined are not employed, more than three times the overall UK percentage, and they are among those living on the lowest incomes (Davies et al., 2011).

While the pattern and persistence of gender, race and disability disadvantage are amenable to monitoring, new fields of discrimination such as age, sexuality and religion are more difficult to demonstrate in quantitative terms due to lack of available data. This is not to suggest that they are any the less trenchant in Wales. For example, Stonewall Cymru continues to document its concerns about hate crimes and workplace discriminations against gay, lesbian and bisexual people. A survey undertaken by Stonewall Cymru (2003) showed that one in three respondents had been the victim of physical violence or bullying and 25% of respondents had been dismissed from a job because of their sexuality. It is only since 1999 that the Sex Discrimination (Gender Reassignment) Regulations has provided for the recognition of transgender people for the first time in UK legislation but their voiced experiences of discrimination have been known for sometime.

The relationship between religion and disadvantage is more difficult to establish. The emergence of British Muslims as a group widely recognised as being systematically disadvantaged, can be extrapolated from the high number of Bangladeshi and Pakistani among this group. For example, women of Muslim faith in Wales are twice as likely as those of Christian faith to have no qualifications (Davies et al., 2011).

While the Welsh language has not traditionally been viewed as an equal opportunities issue it is nevertheless clearly associated with discriminations and disadvantage (see Chapter 4, this volume) and forms an important – and at times complex – interface with other equality issues such as disability and age.

The difficulty of demonstrating the interplay between major sources of inequality should be noted when reading these bare facts of inequality. To isolate, for example, education and skills disadvantage of young disabled people in Wales from facts relating to their health chances is to miss the profound impact of inequality across people's life experiences. Or to disassociate workplace discrimination of women from the facts of poverty across the lifecourse is to oversimplify the nature and effects of inequality. It is also very clear that people may be disadvantaged on a number of levels relating to their multiple statuses and identities. They may not simply be women but older women, black and minority ethnic women and/or disabled women. This multidimensional nature of inequality demands approaches that tackle change across a range of social policy spheres in an integrated way and that utilise a range of methods. It is also worth reiterating the much-noted point that all kinds of disadvantage are bad for those who experience them but they are also bad for society (Wilkinson and Pickett, 2010). The first Welsh national equality report accordingly concludes that the detailed statistical overview it outlines on the extent and nature of economic inequality in Wales provides an opportunity to 'revisit and reinvigorate the redistributive principles of the unique Welsh mainstreaming equality duty – equality of opportunity for all' (Davies et al., 2011, p 157). It is to those principles that we now turn.

The Welsh government's equality duties and powers

The Welsh Assembly Government has a panoply of duties and powers at its disposal in pursuing equality objectives. The range of legal, constitutional, governance and structural arrangements unique to Wales indicates that Welsh policy in respect of equalities has a significant degree of divergence from practices elsewhere in Great Britain. The National Assembly for Wales' unique statutory duty (under sections 120 and 48 of the Government of Wales Act 1998 and section 77 of the Government of Wales Act 2006) provides that the Assembly 'make appropriate arrangements with a view to securing that its functions are exercised with due regard to the principle that there should be equality of opportunity for all people'. And section 48 of the 2006 Act provides that '[t]he Assembly shall make appropriate arrangements with a view to securing that its business is conducted with due regard to the principle that there should be equality of opportunity for all people'. The Government of Wales Act 2006 placed this duty specifically on the Welsh Assembly Government as opposed to the earlier statute, which placed the duty on the National Assembly for Wales as a whole. This legislation separated the legislative and executive branches of the Assembly and section 77 of the 2006 Act lays a clear equality duty on the executive to 'make appropriate arrangements' to exercise its functions 'with due regard to the principle of equality of opportunity for all people'. This twin arrangement, wherein the government is duty-bound to plan and deliver action and report on it on an annual basis to the Assembly and the Assembly ministers scrutinise the government's actions, provides a powerful platform for driving through equality achievements in Wales. To this end, the Assembly has adopted a mainstreaming approach to the development of its equalities strategy. The mainstreaming approach, now the dominant methodology in use by governments across Europe, has attracted considerable applications and, in its wake, critical debate (Williams, 2001). It is described as follows:

> *Mainstreaming equality is about the integration of respect for diversity and equality of opportunity principles, strategies and practices into the everyday work of the Assembly and other public bodies. It means that equality issues should be included from the outset as an integral part of the policy-making and service delivery process and the achievement of equality should inform all aspects of the work of every individual within an organisation. The success of mainstreaming should be measured by evaluating whether inequalities have been reduced.* (NAW, 2004, p 6)

It represents a shift away from seeing equality of opportunity as a special measure to seeing it as an approach fully integrated into the functioning of all policy areas of an institution. The approach implies a proactive and comprehensive commitment to equalities, taking the long view as a change strategy rather than quick-fix measures.

The nature of this mainstreaming equality duty in Wales goes well beyond the legal equalities framework applying to the governments in Scotland and England (Chaney and Fevre, 2002). Such is the reach of these powers that they apply to all people in Wales, irrespective of status, and to all of the Assembly's functions, including those carried out on behalf of the Assembly. All public services are bound by this duty. This in itself is an extensive application of equality law, but in addition, as Chaney (2004, p 67) has rightly pointed out, the duty implies *distributive* as well as rights-based actions. This foregrounds public service provision as a key instrument in producing fairer outcomes for individual citizens, by redistributing opportunities and resources between those who have and those who have not. McLaughlin (2007, p 111) has used the concept of '*equality regime*' to describe the combination of a country's equality law together with the total redistributive or equalising impact of its social welfare system. She suggests that the equality regimes apparent in the various UK countries differ from each other in significant respects, both in terms of their legislative mandate and in terms of their approach to equality issues. This combination of strong legal duties and the specific remit of the Assembly over core social policy areas is therefore conducive to making significant inroads on issues of inequality.

A number of other aspects of the constitutional settlement favour equalities work. The Assembly is not the only actor in delivering on equalities and work with a range of public and private bodies is important in achieving change. The Government of Wales Acts of 1998 and 2006 place unique statutory duties on the Assembly to implement formal partnership schemes with local government and the voluntary sector, and schemes of co-working with police authorities, fire authorities and national parks in Wales, and to carry out consultations and legislative impact assessments relating to future legal enactments with organisations representative of business. These arrangements have no direct parallel in Scotland or England. Thus, the statutory framework itself promotes partnership and collaboration across sectors that can be used as a powerful lever for change. An example of this in action is the Assembly's efforts to engage private businesses in Wales in its equality ambitions using the mechanism of 'contract compliance'. The Assembly has £3 billion to spend in the procurement of services (NAW, 2004) and requiring those tendering to offer services to comply with equality standards is an important mechanism in effecting change. The Assembly has developed a voluntary code of equality practice, encouraging its suppliers to subscribe to these good practice guidelines. It has also used its relationship with local government to drive forward change, with instruments such as the Welsh Local Government Association's *Equality Standard*, which sets the benchmark for local authority equality practices (WLGA, 2002).

Wales also has an extensive state regulatory framework. These unique, statutory Wales-only regulatory bodies are required to include equality assessments in their inspection reports. They include bodies such as the Wales Audit Office, the Welsh Public Services Ombudsman, the Care Standards Inspectorate for Wales, the National Assembly for Wales Ombudsman, the Welsh Schools Inspectorate (ESTYN), General Teaching Council Wales, Social Services Inspectorate for Wales and the Health Service Ombudsman for Wales – as well as the offices of the Welsh Commissioners for Children and Older People. These bodies are charged with monitoring and reviewing performance on equality issues.

Finally, the Assembly can use concordats and a Memorandum of Understanding (MOU) in its relationships with public bodies, which provide protocols of how they will work together. These concordats establish a framework for working arrangements between central government and the devolved administrations and operate within the overarching MOU, which sets out the common principles and practices that will underlie relations. The UK legislation Equality Act 2010 public sector duty, however, takes precedence over the Welsh mainstreaming duty in the day-to-day practices of public sector providers. Welsh ministers are shortly to be empowered to enact two Welsh-specific equality duties: the Equal Pay Duty and the Procurement Duty. These may yield significant influence over the operation of the labour market in Wales, for example in respect of minimum wage rates and the levelling out of pay inequalities, first in respect of gender but gradually extending to all the protected characteristics. This could be poised to have a significant impact on areas such as social care work and domiciliary services.

Perhaps most importantly for the progress towards equality is that Wales has a single minister covering the social justice and equalities portfolios. This means that all elements of 'the equality regime' – the *recognition* of groups, the protection of *rights* and *redistribution* – can be more easily integrated in Wales, enabling the analysis of inequalities to influence impact assessments and underpin policy making to promote equality.

The EHRC in Wales

The EHRC in Wales became fully operative from October 2007. Recognising the unique nature and duties of the devolved governance was explicit in the development of the Commission, affording Wales its own EHRC Committee and its own EHRC Commissioner with the mandate to set priorities for work in the devolved nation. The EHRC Great Britain Board delegates functions and allows for procedural and governance practices applying in Wales that are complementary to the elected body. While the Equality Act 2006 does not give the EHRC enforcement powers in Wales, the operation and the actions of the EHRC in Wales take into account its distinct legal context. A measure of continuity with the outgoing Commissions was assured by the fact that many employees in the incoming EHRC and people appointed to the board were drawn from existing equalities practitioners and activists across Wales. Wales has a strong tradition of collaborative working on equalities issues. As a small nation, equalities practitioners, advice workers and social welfare workers have been able to work to build informal networks and establish close working relationships (Williams, 2004). Chaney (2009), for example, provides evidence to illustrate coordination of government, private sector bodies and the unions in the 'Close the Pay Gap Campaign' led by the former Equal Opportunities Commission (EOC, 2005). This close and cooperative working may have contributed to the ability of the EHRC in Wales to progress with a number of high-profile projects very quickly following its establishment, by contrast with the infighting that became apparent in the London-based centre of the EHRC.

The EHRC's programme of work has focused on the development of the statistical evidence in Wales (Davies et al., 2011), funding research that has monitored progress against the mainstreaming duty of the Welsh Government (Chaney, 2009), a major publicity campaign to highlight awareness of and tolerance of diversity – Who Do You See? – plus a number of other initiatives.

The generic approach heralded by the EHRC has undoubtedly had an impact on the ways in which the Assembly has approached and funded its equality agenda. The institution of the Welsh Assembly Government, like any other public body in Wales, has had to make the shift from a 'strand' approach focusing on issues of race, gender and disability as discrete mandates, to working with equality issues in the round. The EHRC's potential to influence has perhaps best been seen by its commissioning of a report aimed at monitoring the progress of the Welsh Government on equalities after a decade of devolution (Chaney, 2009). Progress on implementing and delivering on the gamut of powers at the disposal of the Welsh Government in promoting equality reveals a picture whereby aspirations far outstrip outcomes.

Implementing equality

Equality of opportunity was established at the outset of the Welsh Assembly as one of three cross-cutting themes that would shape all policy making, the other two being sustainable development and social inclusion/justice. The evolution of the equality duty and evidence of its implementation have indicated a political culture willing to embrace a much broader concept of equality than the more narrow definition of equality of opportunity used in England. The working definition of equality highlighted by the Welsh Assembly in its 2004 review of progress stands in contrast to that adopted by the UK government in the report *Fairness and Freedom* (Equalities Review, 2007) with its emphasis on achieving equality of outcome rather than removing barriers: 'Equality, in the context of this report, is about treating people equally in status, rights and opportunities through a set of policies and actions, with the aim of securing equality of outcome for all' (WAG, 2004, p7).

In his 2002 *Clear Red Water* speech, hailing the second term of office of the Assembly, the First Minister Rhodri Morgan endorsed this view, stating: 'Equality of provision must be underpinned by equality of access, and equality of opportunity. But most importantly of all, we match the emphasis on opportunity with what has been described as the fundamentally socialist aim of equality of outcome' (Morgan, 2002, unpaginated). This more radical approach to equality is firmly linked to the wider social justice ambitions of the Welsh Government, which have determined a broad range of initiatives and reforms across most of the policy areas within the remit of the Welsh Assembly.

Chaney's most recent overview (2009) notes a number of developments flagging the Welsh Government as actively pursuing its intention to 'mainstream' equality. He charts a very distinctive approach across the first decade of devolution, mapping out a number of measures that demonstrate policy divergence with England. Notable among a plethora of policies are the establishment of an infrastructure to engage the voice and participation of children in decision making (Funky Dragon and the Children and Young Person's Parliament); successive strategy documents and curriculum orders that have required equality issues to be embedded in educational policy and practice; and the steady broadening of the agenda on equalities beyond a focus on race, gender and disability to include a number of strategies aimed at asylum seekers, Gypsies and Travellers, older people, lesbian, gay, bisexual and transgender people, faith groups and carers. Chaney provides evidence to show that the Welsh Government has developed a more sophisticated approach to the development of equalities, for example in its use of Equality Impact Assessments, and been bold in policy innovations, including the establishment of a Children's Commissioner and a Commissioner for Older People, and in national strategies on issues such as domestic violence and forced marriage where none previously existed. In addition, successive governments have increased funding to equalities-related organisations and projects such as the All Wales Saheli Association aimed at enriching the lives of Asian and Muslim children and shown themselves to be committed to participatory and consultative policy making through the funding of bodies such as the All Wales Ethnic Minority Association. This consultative rights-based principle underpins the Welsh Government's approach and is evident in its adherence to the social model of disability based on rights, choice and equality for disabled people and to its broad approach to public service delivery. Making the Connections (WAG, 2006) sets out the Welsh Assembly Government's vision of a prosperous, sustainable, bilingual, healthier and better-educated Wales. This package of public sector reform has equality and social justice as one of its four key pillars in the delivery of better public services.

It is clear that the Welsh Government's statutory duty and its actions on equality indicate a clear break from the past. A systematic attempt is being made to tackle inequalities using a broad range of measures. There are, however, a number of reservations to be noted. The Assembly's own early assessment of its progress revealed considerable frustrations. In 2004, its review Mainstreaming equality in the work of the National Assembly (NAW, 2004) found the Assembly lacking in a coherent strategy towards equality, with ad hoc gains, but with a lack of leadership. It stated: 'We are left with a sense that people generally regard equality as important and know that they need to be proactive, but that they are not always sure how to apply mainstreaming principles in their particular policy area' (NAW, 2004, p 31).

By 2009 Chaney's overview lists a number of issues suggesting that the government has taken a 'declaratory approach' to equalities rather than focusing on tangible outcomes and targets. He notes variability between government departments and policy areas in taking forward and promoting equality issues, with good practice vulnerable to going into attrition with changes of personnel. He raises questions about seniority, resources and the level of influence of a devolved bureaucracy in terms of the full realisation of the mainstreaming agenda and points to continuation of a fundamental implementation gap as a major concern. Above all, both Chaney (2009) and the *Anatomy of Economic Inequality in Wales* report (Davies et al., 2011) point to the persistence of major inequalities in Welsh society.

Establishing rights is one thing, exercising and realising them another. Studies undertaken across Wales on rights awareness indicate a largely ill-informed public across a range of rights issues (Williams et al., 2002; Williams, 2004; DRC, 2006c). The Disability Rights Commission document, *Our Rights our Choice* (DRC, 2006c), highlights the widespread lack of awareness about black disabled people's rights. In 2002, a collaboration between the Disability Rights Commission, the Equal Opportunities Commission and the Commission for Racial Equality commissioned research on advice and support in cases of workplace discrimination for women, disabled people and people from black and minority ethnic groups. The report *Snakes and Ladders: Advice and support in employment discrimination cases in Wales* (Williams et al., 2002) assessed the available evidence on advice provision across the three equality strands and found:

- a lack of accessible information about rights and sources of advice;
- a weak infrastructure for delivering advice, support and representation, revealing significant 'advice deserts' across Wales;
- a lack of training and quality accreditation among major advice providers;
- a poor system of referral and coordination between agencies, including a failure to transfer expertise between agencies such that people in need were passed from pillar to post;
- ineffective systems of client support with no formalised protocols on pathways to advice and support;
- a lack of bilingual provision for advice giving;
- a lack of accurate statistical information disaggregated for Wales.

Snakes and Ladders provided important baseline information on the nature and extent of the delivery system for rights-based work in Wales. While the report did not cover the new equality strands or human rights provision, nor offer any discussion of non-employment discrimination, it was important in signalling the huge gulf between the establishment of positive rights for all citizens in Wales and their ability to realise them (Williams, 2004).

Social welfare practitioners and equality issues in Wales

The philosophy and approach of the Welsh Assembly to issues of equality, and the more prominent profile that has been given to these issues over the last eight years, will be instrumental in reshaping the opportunities for anti-discriminatory/anti-oppressive practice by social work and social welfare professionals. This new enabling context for proactive work on equalities is matched at the local level. In each local authority in Wales there is a designated individual with responsibility for equality issues and clear standards are available to guide performance on equalities issues. All local authorities are obliged to produce an Equality Code of Practice. The broad philosophy of the Welsh Government that values 'voice' over 'choice' in its approach to the user of services (see Chapter 2, this volume) provides a bolster to the push towards greater user participation and user involvement in social work, health and social care. Wales has a relatively large public sector, which provides greater opportunity to implement good practice. The challenge will be to establish appropriate and effective user engagement that delivers on these intentions and to bolster civil society in such a way as to make the grassroots effective partners in leading change. In addition, as the equalities infrastructure for delivering on equality at the local level emerges or reconfigures, there will be additional resources and support for social welfare workers in signposting users to appropriate help and advice and in offering support to practitioners. Existing and future progress cannot rely on government statute alone but also on the engagement of the expertise within organisations in civil society and with the private sector.

Despite this framework, there are concerns at the local level that local authorities and Local Health Boards (now reorganised) fail to meet their statutory duties (see, for example, CRE Annual Report, 2006/7). Developments are patchy and uneven and there is still a long way to go. There are a number of explanations put forward for the implementation gulf, ranging from 'initiative overload' to lack of political will and leadership. It is clear that there are a number of countervailing forces undermining bureaucratic equality strategies that will impinge on the goodwill and efforts of frontline practitioners. The tension between the neoliberal managerialist aims of recent governments and delivering on equality and fairness for all, strikes at the heart of contemporary social welfare practice. It is professionals at the interface of service delivery who have to engage with and navigate these tensions to work in the interests of service users. Early social policy academics such as Titmuss (1958) recognised the discretion in the hands of public service professionals that could promote or restrict equality aims. He saw professionals as key arbiters of welfare, determining the pattern, nature and extent of welfare services. The equalities responsibilities have never been greater as social welfare practice manages the tension between the demands of the bureaucracy and the social justice concerns of the professions. Policy makers cannot achieve change alone. Legislation will always be weak without wider cultural and social change and without the goodwill and commitment of frontline workers to assert the value base of the professions.

Opportunities for social welfare practitioners in Wales to take a more proactive stance in relation to equalities and social justice issues are being opened up within a wider culture of welfare that is resistant to the neoliberal mandate (see Chapter 11, this volume). Practitioners will need to move beyond minimalist, bureaucratic requirements in their interventions in order to ensure that equality and social justice principles are realised in practice. In the context of Welsh public service delivery, the government's stance is steering a path towards greater recognition of social solidarity and citizenship rights, underpinned by the principle of 'progressive universalism' (see Chapter 2, this volume). It is the attempt to provide a coherent framework for tackling equality that is embedded in the wider social justice ambitions that marks the distinctiveness of the Welsh approach.

References

Bagihole, B (2009) *Understanding Equal Opportunities and Diversity* Bristol, The Policy Press

Chaney, P (2009) *Equalities and Human Rights, the First Decade of Devolution in Wales* London: Equality and Human Rights Commission, www.equalityandhumanrights.org.uk

Chaney, P (2004) 'The post-devolution equality agenda: the case of the Welsh Assembly's statutory duty to promote equality of opportunity' *Policy & Politics* 32(1), pp 63–77

Chaney, P and Fevre, R (2002) *An Absolute Duty: The equality policies of the government of the National Assembly for Wales and their implementation: July 1999– 2002*, Report for the Equal Opportunities Commission, the Disability Rights Commission and the Commission for Racial Equality, Cardiff, Institute of Welsh Affairs

CRE (Commission for Racial Equality) (2006/7) Annual Report and Accounts 2006/7, www.official-documents.gov.uk/document/hc0809/hc03/0347/0347.pdf

Davies, R, Drinkwater, S, Joll, C, Jones, M, Lloyd-Williams, H, Makepeace, G, Parhi, M, Parken, A, Robinson, C, Taylor, C and Wass, V (2011) *An Anatomy of Economic Inequality in Wales* Cardiff, WISERD, Cardiff University, www.equalityhumanrights.com/wales/publications/

DRC (Disability Rights Commission) (2006a) *Disability in Wales: Impact report 2005–6*, www.drc.org.uk

DRC (2006b) *Are you Taking the Dis? Campaign*, www.drc.org.uk

DRC (2006c) *Our Rights Our Choice*, www.drc.org.uk

Ellison, N and Ellison, S (2006) 'Creating opportunity for all? New Labour, the new localism and the opportunity society' *Social Policy and Society* 5(3), pp 337–48

EHRC Equality and Human Rights Commission (2011) Who Runs Wales? www.equalityhumanrights.com/wales/publications/who-runs-wales-2011/

EOC (Equal Opportunities Commission) (2005) *Close the Pay Gap Campaign* www.eoc.org.uk

Equalities Review (2007) *Fairness and Freedom: The final report of the Equalities Review* London, HMSO

EOC (2006) *Facts about Women and Men in Wales 2006* www.eoc.org.uk

Hills J (Chair), Brewer M, Jenkins S, Lister R, Lupton R, Machin S, Mills C, Modood T, Rees T and Riddel S (2010) *An Anatomy of Economic Inequality in the UK: Report of the National Equality Panel* http://eprints.lse.ac.uk/28344/1/CASEreport60.pdf

Joseph Rowntree Foundation (2011) Monitoring Poverty and Social Exclusion in Wales 2011, JRF Findings: www.jrf.org.uk/sites/files/jrf/poverty-social-exclusion-Wales-summary.pdf

MacPherson, W (1999) *The Stephen Lawrence Inquiry: Report of an inquiry by Sir William MacPherson of Cluny* London, HMSO

McLaughlin, E (2007) 'From negative to positive equality duties: the development and constitutionalisation of equality provisions in the UK' *Social Policy and Society* 6(1), pp 111–21

McLaughlin, E and Baker, J (2007) 'Equality, social justice and social welfare: a road map to the new egalitarians' *Social Policy and Society* 6(1), pp 53–66

Morgan, R (2002) Speech to the University of Wales, Swansea, National Centre for Public Policy Third Anniversary Lecture, 11 December

NAW (National Assembly for Wales) (2004) *Equality of Opportunity Committee: Report on mainstreaming equality in the work of the National Assembly*, Cardiff, Welsh Assembly Government

Stonewall Cymru (2003) *Counted Out* www.stonewall.org.uk/cymru

Titmuss, R (1958) *Essays on the Welfare State* (second edition) (1963), London, Unwin University Books

WAG (Welsh Assembly Government) (2003) *Wales: A better country* Cardiff, WAG

WAG (2004) *Report of the Equal Opportunities Committee: Asylum Issues*, 15 July 2004 EOC(2)06-04(p4), Cardiff, WAG

WAG (2006) *Making the Connections* Cardiff, WAG

WAG (2007) *Review of Service Provision for Gypsy and Travellers*, Report LD2070, Cardiff, WAG

Williams, C (2001) 'Can mainstreaming deliver? The equal opportunities agenda and the National Assembly for Wales' *Contemporary Wales* 14, pp 57–79

Williams, C (2004) 'Access to justice and social inclusion: The policy challenges in Wales' *Journal of Social Welfare and Family Law* 26(1), pp 53–68

Williams, C and De Lima, P (2006) 'Devolution, multicultural citizenship and race equality: From laissez-faire to nationally responsible policies' *Critical Social Policy* 26(3), pp 498–522

Wilkinson R and Pickett K. (2010) The Spirit Level: Why Equality is Better for Everyone. London, Penguin Books

Williams, C, Borland, J, Griffiths, A, Roberts, G and Morris, E (2002) *Snakes and Ladders: Advice and support in employment discrimination cases in Wales* London, Disability Rights Commission, Commission for Racial Equality, Equal Opportunities Commission and Legal Services Commission

Winkler, V (ed) (2009) *Equality Issues in Wales: A research review* Research Report 11, Cardiff, The Bevan Foundation

WLGA (Welsh Local Government Association) (2002) *Equalities Standard* Cardiff, WLGA, www.wlga.gov.uk

Section Three

Service Delivery Areas

Chapter 8

Children's Policy in Wales

Ian Butler

Introduction

The first Government of Wales Act 1998, perhaps inadvertently, settled legislative competence in relation to almost all of those 'traditional' policy areas that bear directly on children – namely education, social care and health – on the Welsh Assembly and subsequently the Welsh Assembly Government (now more commonly referred to simply as the 'Welsh Government'). There are some notable areas where the policy lead remains with the United Kingdom (UK) government (for example youth justice and immigration) and some of these are discussed in detail elsewhere in this volume but, to all intents and purposes, almost all public policy explicitly directed towards Welsh children and young people that has emerged since the 1998 Act, is 'made in Wales'. This point is just as often missed in Wales as it is elsewhere in the UK.

It is with frustrating regularity that major policy initiatives that had their origin in Westminster or Whitehall but which did not extend to Wales are assumed to apply on both sides of Offa's Dyke. Notable among these over recent years was the now extinct *Every Child Matters* framework, a collection of policies and programmes that was developed, largely in the Department for Education and Skills (DfES), after the Laming inquiry into the Climbié case (Laming, 2003). *Every Child Matters* (HM Treasury, 2003) was England specific, as was its precursor ('*Quality Protects*'). Neither had effect in Wales. Similarly, the Children Act of 2004 and the Children and Young Person's Act 2008 carefully distinguish between those provisions that relate to Wales and those that do not.

There remain some important similarities with arrangements in England and elsewhere in the UK and, of course, there is a substantial common heritage in terms of service delivery structures and the knowledge base of professional practice with children and families but it is the differences between children's policies and programmes in Wales and those operating elsewhere in the UK (in England specifically) that this chapter will address.

It remains a moot point as to how far children and young people have come to occupy a *distinctive* Welsh 'policy space'. Changes in the politics and structures of welfare that have taken place in the more economically developed countries (MEDC), especially the commodification of welfare and 'new public management' approaches to service delivery, provide the same broad policy context for Wales as they do for everywhere else in the MEDC.

Similarly, childhood in Wales, understood as a social artefact and as a set of lived experiences, cannot be isolated from the constructions and experiences of childhood and of children more generally. (For a detailed account of the 'new sociology of childhood' and an exploration of childhood as a social construction, see Foley et al., 2001; James and James, 2004; Prout, 2004.) The dynamics of social change, especially the changing balance of inter-generational relations and of developing trends in household formation, structure and dissolution have run through Wales as surely as they have run through the rest of the Britain and Europe.

For example, the proportion of children in the population of Wales is projected to remain at around 18% between 2010 and 2023, having fallen from around 25% in 1971 (WAG, 2006a). In contrast, the proportion of people aged 65 and over is expected to increase from 18% to 23% over the same period (WAG, 2010). Arguably, given their declining literal and demographic visibility and the shift of political 'weight' in favour of the older citizen, children may be thought to have lost the vanguard status that they once possessed in public policy terms across the developed world (see Phillips et al., 2010, for an introduction to social gerontology and the intersection of ageing and public policy).

To a considerable degree, the post-war welfare state in the UK was constructed out of a deep national concern for the well-being of children (usually thought of as the primary beneficiaries of collective investment in welfare and, as such, an investment in the future). Earlier visions of the active part played by the state in the lives of the nation's children encompassed an ambitious set of policy objectives to enrich the lives of the present generation and of future generations, from free school milk to playing fields (see Hendrick, 1994; Butler and Drakeford, 2005). Other than in relation to educational attainment, as measured in public examination passes, and their perennial potential to jeopardise the social order, it might be argued that children and young people have slipped down the list of political priorities over recent years. This is especially true if one does not include episodic yet fevered interest in child protection as reflecting a strong political interest in children and young people. Here, arguably, the overriding political concern has been with the management of governmental risk, the regulation of the professions and the governance of the family rather than with the welfare of children *per se* (see Butler and Drakeford, 2011).

A long historical perspective is beyond the scope of this chapter, however. The chapter will focus on the policy processes and outcomes directed at children and young people that have been produced in Wales, for Wales, since 1998. In passing, one might note that this process of gradual divergence and nuancing of children's policy is observable across all four of the devolved administrations of the UK. For present purposes, it is the differences that are emerging between England and Wales that will occupy our attention. For, although a continuous process, these differences are already substantial and significant. They turn on the question of citizenship and the civil status of children but they relate also to the politically dominant conception of what constitutes a 'welfare state' at each end of the M4.

The issue of child poverty is a specific but illustrative instance of the developing character of children's policy in Wales (see also Crowley, this volume).

The politics of child poverty

In March 1999, at Toynbee Hall, the previous residents of which include Clement Attlee and William Beveridge and which was the birthplace of the Child Poverty Action Group some 30 years previously, the Prime Minister of the day, Tony Blair, committed the government of New Labour to an ambitious programme to tackle child poverty. He declared his government's 'historic aim that ours is the first generation to end child poverty for ever' (Blair, 1999). (Further quotations from the Prime Minister in this section are taken from the same Beveridge Lecture, 18 March 1999.) He cast his vision in terms of his wider ambitions to 'make the welfare state popular again', based on a particular vision of 'social justice', which is 'about ... decency ... merit ... mutual responsibility ... fairness ... values'. The New Labour vision for the welfare state would be quite different from that with which the electorate was in danger of loosing faith; one that was associated with 'fraud, abuse, laziness, a dependency culture, social irresponsibility'. By reconnecting 'social justice to economic vision', the New Labour welfare state would tackle the root causes of social exclusion, poverty and community decay and offer a 'hand-up not a hand-out'. This would be achieved through a mixture of targeted and universal services delivered through an expanded range of service providers, including a 'modernised' public sector.

Approvingly quoting his Chancellor's (Gordon Brown) recent Budget speech, Blair repeated the conventional political rhetoric that while children may be 'only 20% of the population ... they are 100% of the future'. He identified key targets, including 'lifting 700,000 children out of poverty by the end of the Parliament'. This would help 'sow the seeds of ambition in the young' in the belief that 'the role of the welfare state is to help people to help themselves, to give people the means to be independent. We are creating an active welfare state focussed on giving people the opportunities they need to support themselves, principally through work'.

There is little to distinguish this rhetoric from that of the UK coalition government that took office in May 2010, although that was a government of an entirely different political complexion. In a remarkably familiar 'new approach' (DWP and DfE, 2011), the Conservative–Liberal Democrat government appears equally committed to eradicating child poverty in a 'co-ordinated effort to achieve social justice and increase social mobility' through a 'strong focus' (2011, p 11) on work as the means to end poverty. The commitment to the provision of public services to help support people out of poverty is much weaker and more localist and the personal pathology of poverty is much nearer the surface (2011, p 21 ff) but the policy baton of child poverty has been handed on relatively smoothly between successive UK governments.

There may, of course, be room to differentiate between the degree of sincerity with which the commitment to end child poverty is held by the various political parties. Taken with the increasing authoritarianism, instrumentalism and conditionality that had come to characterise welfare policy towards children and young people in England, starting with Thatcherism in the 1980s and continued under New Labour to the present day (see Butler and Drakeford, 2001), even this may be doubted. Of primary interest to us, however, is the difference in form, style and content with which the anti-poverty agenda for children has been developed in Wales against the blueprint offered by Blair and his various heirs and successors over the border.

In 2003, the Welsh Government commissioned an independently chaired Task Group to map out its contribution to the UK child poverty strategy. The Task Group's report resulted in the publication in February 2005 of *A Fair Future for Our Children: The strategy of the Welsh Assembly Government for tackling child poverty* (WAG, 2005). The specifics of *A Fair Future* are considered elsewhere in this volume. What is important for our present purposes is to understand the different rhetorics around poverty employed in England and Wales and how these speak to a distinctive approach to children's policy in Wales.

A Fair Future is unambiguously 'built on a set of core values in line with the UN Convention on the Rights of the Child' (WAG, 2005, p 9). While this reflects the position taken by the Task Group, in introducing the Plenary Debate on *A Fair Future*, the Minister for Children, Jane Hutt (Labour; Vale of Glamorgan), emphasised that, as far as the Welsh Government was concerned, 'Our duty as a Government is to use our powers to their maximum potential and effect on behalf of those children who face poverty in their daily lives in Wales. It is a matter of both entitlement and social justice. Freedom from poverty is a basic human right' (The Official Record of the National Assembly for Wales, 9 February 2005, p 34).

In responding on behalf of the Conservative Party, its spokesman expressed himself as 'pleased' at the reference to the United Nations Convention on the Rights of the Child (UNCRC) made in the Strategy (The Official Record of the National Assembly for Wales, 9 February 2005, p 48) and tabled an amendment to the substantive motion under debate to 'commend the Welsh Assembly Government on basing its strategy on the core principles of the UNCRC' (The Official Record of the National Assembly for Wales, 9 February 2005, p 42). The amendment was subsequently agreed by every Assembly Member present.

He demurs (unsurprisingly!) from endorsing a commitment to redistributive socialism advocated by other speakers in the debate. On the other hand, perhaps more surprisingly to those less familiar with Welsh Labour than New Labour or even the Labour Party led by Ed Milliband, in winding up for the Government, the Minister for Social Justice, Edwina Hart (Labour; Gower) is happy to make clear that she has 'always stood as a socialist and ha[s] always believed in the redistribution of wealth' and that she does 'not care about upsetting the UK Government if there are policy issues in Wales that we want to take forward' (The Official Record of the National Assembly for Wales, 9 February 2005, p 53 ff). Even from this position, the Minister for Social Justice was quick to point out her willingness to work in partnership with those in Wales who had a genuine interest in the subject: 'we must get the partnerships right. This is about creating a strategy for all, involving everybody and getting everything signposted and integrated' (The Official Record of the National Assembly for Wales, 9 February 2005, p 4252 ff).

Earlier, the Minister for Children in her opening speech had gone on to 'reaffirm' the Welsh Government's 'commitment to listen and respond to children and young people' (The Official Record of the National Assembly for Wales, 9 February 2005, p 35) and stated that the Government 'will continue our dialogue with children and young people and seek their views on how we deliver this strategy' (The Official Record of the National Assembly for Wales, 9 February 2005, p 36). The Minister for Children had also made reference to the close attention with which the Children's Commissioner for Wales would keep the Welsh Government's progress under review. She emphasised that the Cabinet Sub-Committee on Children and Young People, which she chaired, would focus on delivering the strategy. There is a commitment to tackling poverty through improving universal services but with a greater commitment to 'Assembly programmes to direct additional resources to areas facing multiple deprivation' (The Official Record of the National Assembly for Wales, 9 February 2005, p 34). A Fair Future itself emphasises the view of the Welsh Government that '[w]ithin a framework of universal services the most disadvantaged and vulnerable groups will need positive action to promote equality' (WAG, 2005, p 11). In the debate, the Minister for Children emphasised that '[t]he Assembly Government has many powers that can ensure that children and families in poverty get the services they need' (The Official Record of the National Assembly for Wales, 9 February 2005, p 36).

In this one debate on a particular strategy one can see the outlines of what has become distinctive about the National Assembly/Welsh Government's approach to children and young people's policy:

- an unambiguous and explicit commitment to a rights-based agenda that crosses conventional party political lines;
- a determination to provide Wales-relevant solutions to Wales-specific problems even if this requires a break with Westminster and Whitehall;
- a commitment to work in partnership rather than in competition with all of those who have a contribution to make and to actively engage with young people as part of that process;
- a commitment to transparency and external scrutiny of the Government's record, including by the first children's independent rights institution to be established in the UK (the Children's Commissioner for Wales);
- a commitment to ensure continuity and coherence in children's policy making through maintaining a high-profile presence in Cabinet discussions and structures;

- a continuing confidence in the capacity of the institutions and instruments of government to shape the lives of individuals and communities, including those of children and young people.

Although dealt with more extensively elsewhere in this book, it should be noted that Welsh Government's response to child poverty continues to reflect this approach. In his *Written Statement* launching the Delivery Plan for Wales' own Child Poverty Strategy on 2 February 2011, the Minister for Children (Huw Lewis, Labour; Merthyr) reiterated that 'reducing child poverty is a fundamental element of [the Welsh Government's] social justice agenda and also part of its key priorities to implement the United Nations Convention on the Rights of the Child' (Written Statement by the Welsh Assembly Government: 'Child Poverty Strategy and Delivery Plan for Wales', 2 February 2011).

In his *Statement*, Lewis also announced significant additional investments in early years provision and family support, both of which were carried over into Labour Party Manifesto commitments for the May 2011 National Assembly elections (Welsh Labour Party, 2011, p 32 ff).

All of this is consistent with previous Welsh Governments' public policy ambitions for Wales (see Drakeford, this volume). Welsh Labour's commitments to promoting 'openness, partnership and participation' had been set out in *Wales: A better country* (WAG, 2003, p 11), repeating the commitment to:

> ... *work across boundaries, communicate consistently and give responsibility to those who are best placed to take decisions. We will be clear about what we want to achieve and how we will measure success. We will continue to develop a distinctively Welsh approach to improving the delivery of public services.* (WAG, 2003, p 12)

These key themes of more citizen-focused public services that are more responsive to the needs of communities, more focused on equality and social justice, and more efficient and effective, were taken up and developed in *Making the Connections: Delivering better services for Wales: The Welsh Assembly Government vision for public services*, published in October 2004 (WAG, 2004a) and have been developed subsequently in the review of local service delivery, *Beyond Boundaries: Citizen centred local services for Wales* published in June 2006 (WAG, 2006b – 'The Beecham Report').

After the National Assembly elections in May 2007 and the advent of a new and previously unimagined coalition between Welsh Labour and Plaid Cymru (The Party of Wales), the same broad principles were reflected, albeit in perhaps more rhetorically muted terms, in *One Wales; A progressive agenda for the government of Wales*, the formal agreement that set out the two parties' programme for government for the period of the Third Assembly (2007–11):

Shared values, common goals and joint aspirations for the people of
Wales will drive this four-year programme for government. It offers a
progressive agenda for improving the quality of life of people in all of
Wales's communities, from all walks of life, and especially the most
vulnerable and disadvantaged. (WAG, 2007, p 5)

One Wales captures what has come to be called the 'progressive universalism' of the Welsh welfare state no less accurately (see Drakeford, 2007; Marquand, 2008; Stead 2008) than earlier statements of strategic intent. The *One Wales* coalition continued previous policies on free prescriptions for everyone resident in Wales, free public transport for older people and those with disabilities, free school breakfasts and free swimming in the holidays for young people and took forward, despite some difficulties within Plaid Cymru, a very different funding structure for higher education that means students ordinarily resident in Wales will, in most cases, be paying less than half in tuition fees than their counterparts in England, no matter where they choose to study.

The central role played by public services in delivering this 'progressive universalism' as far as services to children and their families were concerned, was captured particularly sharply in the Welsh Government's *Sustainable Social Services for Wales: A framework for action* (WAG, 2011, § 2.3):

Public services are a critical part of that community and it is good news
that they are there to support us. They are not an unfortunate necessity for
a small group of people who for some reason are not able to resolve
matters for themselves. We all need them, sometimes in significant
measure, and sometimes in the background. They may be universal in
nature or there to underpin us at times of significant difficulty. They are our
right as citizens.

Similarly, in the Welsh Labour Party's Manifesto for the 2011 elections to the National Assembly, the rhetoric was equally unambiguous and even more red-blooded (Welsh Labour Party, 2011, p 21):

Welsh Labour believes in accessible, quality citizen-centred services for
all, not choice for the few. Whilst the Tory-led Coalition aims to reduce the
state, Welsh Labour believes in a Welsh Public Service with a strong
public service ethos: in delivering quality citizen-centred services where
service users are engaged with providers, including the third sector, in the
design, delivery and improvement of those services; in placing public
interest above private profit; in fostering collaboration not competition and
in building fairer communities, not the Tories' 'Big Society'.

One should note that the commitment to free prescriptions, travel concessions, free breakfasts and student support constituted four of the '5 to keep' pledges in the Labour Party Manifesto for the 2011 Assembly elections.

The task of delivering all of these commitments will fall to the Fourth Assembly, which commenced on 11 May 2011. Carwyn Jones (Labour; Bridgend), as leader of the largest political party elected to the Assembly, will head a Labour Party only government, without an outright majority, for what he would hope to be a five-year term of office.

While further detailed consideration of such overarching strategic considerations is beyond the scope of this chapter, it is important to understand that any specific policy initiatives towards children that have been developed by the Welsh Government must be located in this very particular political and policy context; a policy context that owes a great deal to the political ideology of Welsh Labour and that this looks likely to continue for the foreseeable future. This reflects, in turn, an historical legacy of collectivism and a cultural antipathy to the politics of 'choice', consumerism and self-enrichment (see Jordan, 2008) that is to be found in Wales. It may also be due to the fact that the voters of Wales feel closer to the 'traditions of Titmuss, Tawney, Beveridge and Bevan rather than those of Hayek and Friedman' (Morgan, 2002) as part of a political culture that has tended to be left of centre for the last 150 years.

Hence, the fundamental distinguishing characteristic of children and young people's policy in Wales since 1999 is its strong foundations in a commitment to children's rights. This in turn is of a piece with Welsh Labour's broader political traditions and understanding of what constitutes a modern welfare state and its proper relationship to its citizens. (For a more detailed account of the conceptual and political origins of children's rights, see Franklin, 2001; Archard, 2004.)

Rights to action

Arguably the first major statement of children's policy made by the Welsh Government was published in November 2000 as *Children and Young People: A framework for partnership* (NAW, 2000). Intended primarily to bring coherence and focus to the planning and funding of services for children at the local level, the *Framework* establishes early the Welsh Government's commitment to children's rights and, in particular, its endorsement of the UNCRC:

> *Over the past 10 years [the UNCRC] has helped to establish an internationally accepted framework for the treatment of all children, encouraged a positive and optimistic image of children and young people as active holders of rights and stimulated a greater global commitment to safeguarding those rights. The Assembly believes that the Convention should provide a foundation of principle for dealings with children.* (WAG, 2000, p 10)

This commitment was given real substance when on 14 January 2004, the National Assembly, in plenary, formally, and again with no votes cast against the motion:

> [r]eaffirm[ed] the priority which it attaches to safeguarding and promoting the rights and welfare of children and young people in Wales, particularly those who are vulnerable; [and] [f]ormally adopt[ed] the United Nations convention on the rights of the child as the basis of policy making in this area ... (The Official Record of the National Assembly for Wales, 14 January 2004, p 44)

The subsequent debate contained some discordant notes, along predictable party lines, on the Welsh Government's record in office, especially in relation to its capacity to ensure delivery of its aims and objectives by local authority 'partners'. Arguably however, this was fuelled by a continuing and sincere commitment, on all sides of the Senedd, to improve services for children, particularly vulnerable children. It should be remembered that this debate was taking place in the context of the post-Climbié period of high anxiety that had provided the momentum for the *Every Child Matters* programme in England and the Children Act of 2004. The Minister for Children chose to make reference to the Welsh Government's own 'Safeguarding Vulnerable Children Review' that it had commissioned some weeks earlier, in December 2003. This Review would publish its report, *Keeping us Safe*, in June 2006 (WAG, 2006c). In the debate, the situation of looked-after children in particular drew critical attention from Assembly Members (AMs), over which another significant inquiry report, that of Sir Ronald Waterhouse (2000), still casts a long shadow.

The cross-party consensus on a rights-based approach might be considered remarkable enough by itself but this plenary debate was remarkable also for an amendment that was made to the substantive motion. Welsh Liberal Democrat AM Kirsty Williams (Brecon and Radnorshire) proposed that the Assembly 'regrets that the UK Government continues to retain the defence of reasonable chastisement and has taken no significant action towards prohibiting the physical punishment of children in the family'. The Assembly had already established its opposition to corporal punishment during a short debate introduced by a Labour AM, Christine Chapman (Cynon Valley), some two years previously. What is interesting to note is that AMs from Plaid Cymru, the Welsh Liberal Democrats as well as the Labour government located the issue squarely in the context of the protection of vulnerable children, frequently citing the Climbié case. Even Welsh Conservative AMs who voted against the amendment itself, voted for the amended substantive motion. This is indicative once again, not only of the Welsh Government's preparedness to put 'clear red water' between itself and Westminster but also of a progressive, largely consensual approach to policy making on behalf of children and young people.

By the time of the debate, progress had been made in giving the UNCRC a distinctively Welsh cast. This found expression in the publication, later in the same year, of *Children and Young People: Rights to action* (WAG, 2004b). Here the Convention was translated into what the Welsh Government was to call its Seven Core Aims, which would, in turn, form the basis for all of the Welsh Government's policies and programmes for children and young people throughout its second term. The Seven Core Aims are designed to ensure that all children and young people:

- have a flying start in life;
- have a comprehensive range of education and learning opportunities;
- enjoy the best possible health and are free from abuse, victimisation and exploitation;
- have access to play, leisure, sporting and cultural activities;
- are listened to, treated with respect and have their race and cultural identity recognised;
- have a safe home and a community that supports physical and emotional well-being;
- are not disadvantaged by poverty.

A comprehensive and detailed account of the Assembly's progress towards delivering its programme during this period was set out two years later in *Rights in Action: Implementing children and young people's rights in Wales* (WAG, 2006d). In many ways, *Rights in Action* was a landmark document in that its publication had to be negotiated by the Welsh Government as its contribution to the periodic reporting required of signatories to the UNCRC. In law, it is the 'state party' that is the signatory to the Convention rather than any constituent countries, dependencies or territories. With Whitehall officials initially reluctant, the UK Children's Minister agreed to a request by the Welsh Government's Minister for Children to publish, in effect, a separate 'country report'. Scotland and Northern Ireland also subsequently published 'country reports'.

In *Righting the Wrongs: The reality of children's rights in Wales* (Croke and Crowley, 2006), the Wales UNCRC Monitoring Group, an alliance of non-governmental agencies, academics and others, founded in 2002, set out a competing account to that contained in *Rights in Action*. The Monitoring Group also submitted a report to the Committee of the UNCRC (UNCRCC) as part of the periodic reporting process (Croke and Crowley, 2007) as did the Children's Commissioner for Wales, along with representatives of young people's organisations.

I have written elsewhere (Butler and Drakeford, 2010) of the experience of attending the UNCRCC in September 2008 and of the positive experience that it proved to be, at least for the Wales members of the UK delegation. In Wales, the immediate policy consequences of this appearance were set out in *Getting it Right 2009* (WAG, 2009). This put in place a five-year rolling Action Plan that would both address the challenges that the Welsh Government had identified for itself in its report to the UNCRCC and provide a response to the Committee's Concluding Observations (published in October

2008; UNCRCC, 2008).

The Action Plan identified 16 priorities, related to specific Articles of the Convention and directly to the Concluding Observations. It also identified those policies and programmes of the Welsh Government that would contribute to meeting the targets set by the Action Plan and where the policy lead would lie. The 16 priorities (and associated Articles) are reproduced below:

- Tackling poverty for children and young people in Wales (Articles 22, 24, 26 and 27).
- Delivering positive outcomes for the most vulnerable children and families (Articles 9, 19, 20, 21, 23, 25 and 29).
- Raising awareness of the UNCRC and the Concluding Observations (Article 42).
- Reducing the gap between policy and outcomes for children and young people (Articles 2, 3 and 4).
- Improving learning achievements for all children and young people (Articles 13, 28, 29 and 30).
- Supporting emotional well-being for all children and young people (Articles 6, 24, 27 and 39).
- Improving opportunities for all children and young people to play in safety (Articles 15 and 31).
- Increasing opportunities for all children and young people in Wales to participate in decision making on issues which affect them (Article 12).
- Working to eliminate discrimination against children and young people with disabilities; improving their access to services and support (Articles 23, 26, 27 and 31).
- Working to make physical punishment of children and young people illegal in all situations (Article 19).
- Working to eliminate bullying, including homophobic bullying (Articles 2, 3, 14, 28 and 29).
- Working to ensure that refugee and asylum-seeking children and young people in Wales can claim their UNCRC and human rights (Articles 22 and 37 generally and 22, 30, 32–36, 39 and 40 with specific reference to asylum seekers).
- Working to eliminate discrimination/inequality against children and young people (Articles 2, 14, 22 and 30).
- Working to ensure that children and young people in the most deprived areas of Wales can enjoy all of their UNCRC and human rights (Article 27).
- Improving the transparency of budgeting for children and young people at Welsh Assembly Government level (Articles 4 and 12).

- Working to ensure that children and young people from Wales in the criminal justice system can claim their UNCRC rights (Articles 37 and 40).

In this way, the political and administrative context for children and young people's policy was set for the greater part of the Third Assembly and, potentially, into the Fourth Assembly. (The Welsh Labour Manifesto [Welsh Labour Party, 2011, p 56] promised to 'continue to use the Seven Core Aims as the national framework for developing policy for children and young people'.) In intent at least, the approach of the Third Assembly was of a piece with the broad strategic outline of previous Welsh Governments and in a direct line of descent from the commitment made by the National Assembly in 2004 to base its children and young people's policy firmly on the requirements of the Convention.

It is beyond the scope of this chapter to enumerate all of the various policies and programmes that were intended to achieve the Actions set out in *Getting it Right* and, in any case, this remains a work in progress. However, an important commentary on the achievements of the Welsh Government in delivering on its commitments more generally during the Third Assembly has been provided by the National Assembly for Wales Children and Young People's Committee (NAW, 2011) chaired by the Plaid Cymru AM, Helen Mary Jones (Plaid Cymru; Llanelli).

One might note that the Committee, established on 16 October 2007 by a motion in plenary, was the first such scrutiny committee of its kind in Europe and itself has made some considerable efforts to make its own working practices model the participatory principles of the UNCRC. In the words of the Committee in its Legacy Report (NAW, 2011, p i), '[o]ften adults do not take the views of children and young people seriously. As politicians, we have a responsibility to encourage children and young people to voice their opinions and to listen to them. The Children and Young People Committee was established to help do that'.

The Committee adopted several innovative ways of gathering evidence from young people as part of its various inquiries. These included surveys, visits, play and drama sessions at the Assembly, a newsletter as well as formal oral and written evidence sessions. The scope of the Committee's work is equally impressive and in its list of 'issues facing children and young people at the end of the Third Assembly' it illustrates how extensive the children and young people's 'policy space' had become in Wales by this time (May 2011). Included in the list of issues that it hopes a future incarnation of the Committee might address are matters relating to young people and access to transport; healthy eating; environmental issues such as waste management and energy supply; housing in rural communities; as well as the more conventional areas such as school, health, community safety and misrepresentation of young people in the popular news media.

Representation and participation

While it may be beyond the scope of a single chapter to provide an exhaustive account of how policy over three Assembly terms has been substantiated in practice, especially since children and young people's interests are no longer so narrowly defined in Wales as they might be in other jurisdictions, it is important to record how two of the most fundamental principles of Wales' children's rights framework have been given practical expression. Central to any human rights agenda are the issues of representation and participation. In Wales, arguably the most distinctive contributions to ensuring something more than a rhetorical commitment to children's rights have been the appointment of a Commissioner for Children and the establishment of *Funky Dragon*, the Children and Young People's Assembly for Wales.

Although often traced back to a specific recommendation of the Waterhouse (2000) inquiry into child abuse in North Wales, the idea of a Commissioner for Children had been gathering momentum since the Staffordshire 'pindown inquiry' almost 10 years earlier (Staffordshire County Council, 1991). Rather than provide the *case* for a Commissioner, 'Waterhouse' provided the *opportunity* for the Welsh Government to establish the UK's first independent human rights institution specifically for children. In other words, the choice to make such an appointment had been available to the UK government for some time. This appointment was a conscious act of the National Assembly in Wales that might easily have been deferred, as it was in England, for several more years. The post was established by the Care Standards Act 2000 and extended by the Children's Commissioner for Wales Act 2001.

The Commissioner's primary duties are to safeguard and promote the rights and welfare of children in Wales and, in so doing, to have regard to the UNCRC. His functions include reviewing the effect on children and young people of the activities of the National Assembly/Welsh Government or of those public bodies for which it has responsibility. The Commissioner also has the power to examine particular cases if this involves an issue that could have a wider application to the lives of children in Wales. He can also make representations to the Welsh Government about any matter affecting the rights and welfare of children in Wales, including in relation to non-devolved matters.

The Commissioner is required to publish an *Annual Report* that is subject to a plenary debate by the National Assembly. The Assembly must prepare and publish a *Response to the Children's Commissioner's Annual Report* by 31 March each year.

The seriousness with which the Assembly and the Government regard the Office of the Commissioner is indicated by the considerable support from government, not least financially; his budget for 2006–07 was established at over £1.6 million rising to £1.8 million during the course of the Third Assembly. The formal and informal means he has had at his disposal to access government are unsurpassed by those of his fellow commissioners now established in Scotland, Northern Ireland and England. As such, the Welsh Government's commitment to establishing an effective, independent champion of children's rights who is well resourced to carry out his functions, including holding the government to account, gains some substance.

The standing and influence of the Children's Commissioner for Wales contrasts strongly with the experiences of the Commissioner for England (OCC), if one is to judge by the response of the UK government to the findings of the Dunford report into the work of the Commissioner (DfE, 2010). Dunford took the view that:

> *The OCC has had some significant achievements on specific issues.*
> *However, the impact on the vast majority of children and young people*
> *has been negligible. Most stakeholders are disappointed by the OCC's*
> *overall performance, which was perhaps inevitable in view of the limited*
> *remit, lack of respect and commitment on the part of the Government and*
> *restrictive legislation.* (DfE, 2010, p 15)

While accepting 'in principle' (Written Ministerial Statement, 6 December 2010, p 2) Dunford's recommendations aimed at strengthening the independence of the OCC, the UK government's attention was also drawn to other considerations:

> *Whilst accepting that the Commissioner needs to be adequately*
> *resourced to fulfill the role, I believe that all public funding should be used*
> *in accordance with the Cabinet Office's efficiency guidelines for Arm's*
> *Length Bodies, and that this need not compromise independence or*
> *statutory powers and duties. Dr Dunford recommends merging the*
> *functions of the Office of the Children's Commissioner with the Children's*
> *Rights Director in Ofsted, providing the opportunity for greater coherence*
> *and impact, and scope for savings. I believe that this is a sensible way*
> *forward … Dr Dunford has also identified that the salary of the Children's*
> *Commissioner is excessive in comparison to others in similar roles and I*
> *will address this in setting up the new arrangements.*

At the time of writing (June 2011), it is far from clear what the fate of the OCC will be, whereas Welsh Labour's 2011 Manifesto was clear. Welsh Labour will '[w]ork with the Children's Commissioner for Wales, children's organisations and the third sector to promote wider understanding and appreciation of rights-based policy making and service delivery' (Welsh Labour Party, 2011, p 58).

Representation is an important safeguard for children and young people but central to achieving unconditional status as a rights-holding citizen, especially where suffrage is not a likelihood, is the question of participation.

Article 12 of the UNCRC states: "States Parties shall assure to the child who is capable of forming his or her own views the right to express those views freely in all matters affecting the child, the views of the child being given due weight in accordance with the age and maturity of the child'. As already indicated, from the outset, the Welsh Government demonstrated a positive interest in listening to children and to securing their active participation in the process of policy formation, notably supported by the Children and Young People's Committee of the National Assembly.

The 2000 key policy statement, *Framework for Partnership* (NAW, 2000), devoted a whole chapter to 'Listening to Children'. It noted the 'strongly held view' (2000, p 26) across Wales of 'listening more closely to the voices of children and young people' and continued: 'The Assembly believes that the framework should ensure that children and young people are listened to and enabled to play an active part in decision making and in determining the services they receive' (2000, p 26).

The Welsh Government had previously launched an ambitious project, *Llais Ifanc/Young Voice* to find ways of engaging with young people on a sustainable long-term basis and there already existed in Wales a relatively small number of local 'youth forums' as well as a number of *ad hoc* and 'single issue' groups of young people that were consulted from time to time. Beginning at a conference ('Bite Back') in July 1999, organised by members of local youth forums, and continued later that year at a residential, the outlines of a national organisation that could represent the views of young people across Wales began to take shape. In July 2000, following another conference ('Breaking Barriers'), this embryonic organisation joined with *Llais Ifanc/Young Voice* and subsequently, after a process of consultation with children and young people across Wales, the Children and Young People's Assembly for Wales (known as *Funky Dragon*) was established with funding from the Welsh Government.

Both in its origins and in its operation, Funky Dragon is a peer-led organisation, of young people and by young people. Its stated aims are:

> ... to give 0 – 25 year olds the opportunity to get their voices heard on issues that affect them. The opportunity to participate and be listened to is a fundamental right under the United Nations Convention Rights of the Child. Funky Dragon will try to represent as wide a range as possible and work with decision-makers to achieve change. Funky Dragon's main tasks are to make sure that the views of children and young people are heard, particularly by the Welsh Assembly Government, and to support participation in decision-making at national level.
> (Funky Dragon, 2003, p 2)

The Welsh Government has fostered the participation of children and young people in other ways too. Wales is the first country to have introduced a statutory requirement for all primary, secondary and special schools to have a school council. In secondary schools, two students can be nominated to serve as associate governors on the school's governing body; the governing body being required to accept such nominations. Also, in 2002, the Welsh Government commissioned a national voluntary organisation to establish a Children and Young People's Participation Consortium for Wales. The Consortium has subsequently received European Structural Fund support to accelerate its work. As a result of the Consortium's work, in January 2007, the Welsh Government published national standards for involving children and young people in decision making (WAG, 2007).

There are numerous other examples of how participation is shaping the children's agenda in Wales. The Education (Wales) Measure 2009 (with Royal Approval on 9 December 2009) gave young people a statutory right, in their own name, to make special educational needs appeals and claims of disability discrimination to the Special Educational Needs Tribunal for Wales (note: prior to full implementation of Part Four of the Government of Wales Act 2006, a Welsh law, in simple terms, was referred to as a 'Measure').

In May 2010, the Welsh Government launched Meic, a national information and advice line for those aged under 25 as part of its national advocacy service. At its launch, the Deputy Minister for Children, Huw Lewis (Labour; Merthyr), again made the explicit connection with children and young people's participation rights: 'Meic is a significant step forward for children and young people's advocacy in Wales. Not only are we leading the way – we are making sure children and young people are getting support to have their voices and opinions heard in decisions that affect them' (Welsh Assembly Government Press Release, 14 May 2010, launch of Meic).

Even beyond government, the 2009 Economic and Social Research Council Festival of Social Science included, in Cardiff, an event, '"By Us, For Us, About Us": A Children and Young People's Festival of Participation in Research', in which some 200 young people were able to 'learn about and participate in research and to express their views about research methods and findings'.

As part of the 2008 Periodic Reporting process to the UNCRCC, Funky Dragon prepared and submitted two reports describing 'the experience of young people living in Wales, in order to determine how well they are able to access their rights under the UNCRC' (Funky Dragon, 2007a, p 13; see also Funky Dragon, 2007b) based on extensive research with 12,242 young people aged from seven to 25. The reports do not make the most reassuring reading, especially in relation to young people's awareness of the provisions of the UNCRC (see Funky Dragon, 2007a, p 105). What is important to note, however, is that a group of young people were able to present the findings of Funky Dragon's research not only in Geneva but also, subsequently, to the Welsh Government's Children and Young People's Cabinet Committee, attended by the First Minister of the day, Rhodri Morgan. In what was an impressive and very moving occasion, the Welsh Government was left in no doubt of the old adage, 'who feels it, knows it', and of the power and value of children and young people's direct participation in the production of public policy at the highest level.

The Rights of Children and Young Persons (Wales) Measure 2011

While the Children and Young People's Scrutiny Committee's judgement of the Welsh Government's record in relation to specific policies and programmes at the end of the Third Assembly was a balanced one (NAW, 2011), it was nonetheless expressly critical of what might be described as the 'implementation gap' between the policy aspirations of the Welsh Government and its achievements 'on the ground' (NAW, 2011, § 179): 'The Committee has voiced its concerns over the past four years that Wales is perceived to be policy rich but implementation poor. External stakeholders have shared the Committee's concerns…'. The question of how far the Welsh Government had 'delivered' on its promises was to be a key debating point during the 2011 National Assembly elections (and not only in relation to policies and programmes for young people). Indeed, concern over the results achieved for young people using the policy framework of previous Assemblies had been expressed much earlier within Welsh Labour, particularly in relation to educational achievement, as measured by pupil attainment, and by progress made in reducing child poverty. These were key themes in Carwyn Jones' campaign to take over the leadership of the Welsh Labour Party during November 2009, following the earlier announcement by Rhodri Morgan of his intention to retire as Labour Leader and First Minister of Wales.

One of Jones' key leadership campaign pledges was to increase spending on education. At the launch of his campaign, he made clear that this pledge was made with the intention of 'raising the bar' in the debate on tackling poverty in Wales, by using education spending as a major 'weapon' in eradicating poverty. He is reported as saying (WalesHome, 2009): 'Education is the route out of poverty. My government would look to increase education spending by at least 1% above the block grant we receive from the UK Government to ensure the best outcomes for Welsh children, with a sharp focus on inequalities in education'. There is some debate about the precise nature of the original pledge (see, for example, *Western Mail*, 3 November 2009). In any event, by the time of the Welsh Labour Manifesto of May 2011, this had been finalised as '[m]ore frontline spending in schools. We will raise schools funding by 1% above the percentage change in the block grant we receive from the UK Government year on year' (Welsh Labour Party, 2011, p 5).

Following Jones' election to the leadership and his confirmation as First Minister (1 and 9 December 2009 respectively), he appointed his campaign manager Leighton Andrews (Labour; Rhondda) as his Minister for Children, Education and Life-Long Learning and one of his rivals in the leadership contest, Huw Lewis (Labour; Merthyr) as Deputy Minister for Children. Lewis' brief, as we have seen, would include child poverty. Lewis would also be responsible for steering through an important piece of legislation that Rhodri Morgan had included in his final legislative programme, announced in July 2009:

We also intend to explore further the possibility of introducing a Measure to embed the principles of the United Nations Convention on the Rights of the Child into law on behalf of Welsh children. Those principles, which are expressed in our seven core aims, already form the basis of children's policy in Wales, and it is my intention that they should also provide the basis for further work to consolidate and reform the law affecting children and young people. (Written Statement by the Welsh Assembly Government, *The Welsh Assembly Government's Legislative Programme 2009-10*, 14 July 2009)

While in many ways, this could be seen as the final affirmation of the UNCRC as the basis for Wales' distinctive approach to children and young people's policy, the legislation had fallen, after Carwyn Jones announced his new Cabinet, to two ministers who did not appear to share the same enthusiasm for children's rights as previous post-holders. Neither had a strong background in children and young people's policies and programmes (unlike previous Welsh Children's Ministers). Moreover, both had pressing issues to address, not least in fulfilment of Jones' own leadership 'manifesto'. Andrews' attention was immediately focused on improving the performance of Welsh schools in the light of imminent and ultimately very disappointing Programme for International Student Assessment (PISA) scores. (PISA tests are intended to measure, for the purposes of international comparison, how far 15-year-olds are prepared for future challenges; whether they can analyse, reason and communicate effectively; and whether they have the capacity to continue learning throughout life. See www.pisa.oecd.org. The 2009 results were made public on 7 December 2010.) Andrews also faced a sudden crisis in higher education funding precipitated by the UK government shortly after it came to office in May 2011. Lewis' had to manage the slow pace of progress in meeting the Welsh Government's child poverty targets and to realign government funding streams to support delivery of a more focused strategy. And, while starting from very different points on the Labour political spectrum, both had new furrows to plough in the post-Morgan Welsh Labour era. Moreover, changes in senior positions within the Welsh civil service, including the recruitment of senior officials more familiar with Great Smith Street in London (the home of the Department for Children, Schools and Families) than with Cathays Park (the 'home' of the civil service in Cardiff), meant that the Measure that was first introduced was perhaps a more timid one than might have been anticipated.

An account of the progress of the Rights of Children and Young Persons (Wales) Measure 2011 would fill a chapter in its own right (see Table 8.1 for a brief account of the timetable for the passage of the Measure). For present purposes, much can be gleaned by simply contrasting the first section of the Measure 'as introduced' and 'as passed'. At the heart of the Measure was the duty that it would convey on the Welsh Government ('Welsh ministers' in the technical language of the Measure) to 'have due regard' to the UNCRC and those protocols in relation to which the Welsh Government had competence (that is, those that were not exclusively the province of the UK Government, such as armed conflict). In debate before Legislation Committee 5, in plenary and beyond, the central issue was how far that 'due regard' duty was to extend.

Table 8.1: Timetable for the Rights of Children and Young Persons (Wales) Measure 2011

Measure introduced	14 June 2010
Stage 1 – consideration and agreement of general principles	
Public consultation and consideration by Legislation Committee	17 June – 22 October 2010
Legislation Committee report published	22 October 2010
Plenary debate on Stage 1 report	2 November 2010
Stage 2 – detailed consideration of the Measure and possible amendments	
Consideration by Stage 2 Committee	3 – 25 November 2010
Stage 3 – detailed consideration in plenary of the Measure and any amendments	Commenced 26 November 2010 Concluded 18 January 2011
Stage 4 – passing of the final text of the Measure	18 January 2011
Approved by Her Majesty in Council	16 March 2011

Essentially, the point at issue was whether the Measure would take one of two forms: either 'everything would be out, unless it was in' or 'everything would be in, unless it was out'. In other words, the duty to 'have regard' either would be applied only to those areas of government that were specifically included in the 'scheme' that was to be attached to the Measure or it would apply to every aspect of the business of government unless it was specifically excluded. In its first iteration (and as described in the *Explanatory Memorandum* published with the first formal draft of the Measure), the Measure was definitely conceived of as a version of the 'everything would be out, unless it was in' option. All that would be included would be those matters that were 'strategic' in their intent:

> *The duty will mean that the Welsh Ministers and the First Minister will have to consider which rights and duties in the UNCRC and its Optional Protocols are relevant to the area or areas of strategic planning they are*

> *looking at, and consider whether and how they can use functions which*
> *are exercisable by them to give better effect to the rights and duties in the*
> *UNCRC. They will have to weigh up these considerations alongside other*
> *relevant factors.* (§ 3.18 *Proposed Rights of Children and Young Persons*
> *(Wales) Measure Explanatory Memorandum* [As Introduced] 2010)

This version of the Measure found little favour beyond the 5th Floor of Tŷ Hywel, where the Welsh ministers have their offices, or Cathays Park. Both in evidence to Legislation Committee 5 and on the floor of the Senedd, a strong lobby was built for the far stronger ('everything would be in, unless it was out') and much more pervasive version of the Measure. Indeed, the debate reached the 5th Floor on more than one occasion, not least in the person of Plaid Cymru AM Helen Mary Jones. In the event, by the time the Measure was passed, it was to be in precisely this form – almost. For, in the time-honoured tradition of governments, a compromise was reached. In order to allow for preparations to be made, including, for example, training civil servants across the whole of the National Assembly and Welsh Government so that they might provide proper advice to ministers and others on how to give 'due regard' to the UNCRC, a delay was built into the Measure. In effect, until the beginning of May 2012 until the end of April 2014, only those matters of a strategic nature are 'in' (that is, legislation; formulation of new policies or the review or change of an existing policy – see section 1(2) of the Measure). Thereafter, the 'due regard' duty will bind on ministers in the exercise of 'any of their functions' (section 1(1) of the Measure). That is to say that from May 2014, everything is 'in'. Needless to say, the Measure was passed unanimously by the members of the National Assembly.

Conclusion

The question was raised at the beginning of this chapter as to how far the Welsh Government could claim to have established a distinctive and coherent 'policy space' for children and young people. While accepting that this cannot fully be considered without reference to a more extensive analysis of the broader political objectives of the Welsh Labour Party, the party that has dominated the first three Assemblies, it is the argument of this chapter that such a space has indeed been constructed.

Children and young people's policy in Wales has been founded on the assumption that children are rights holders with an entitlement to participate in decisions on matters that affect them. Such an assumption has its roots in Welsh radicalism and in the progressive ideals and democratic socialism of the Welsh Labour Party as well as in the emancipatory rhetoric of the specific children's rights 'movement'.

The Welsh Government has used its powers to the full, including showing a willingness to take a different political as well as policy direction to the UK government, to give substance to such an approach. It has institutionalised this commitment in law, culminating in the embedding of the UNCRC in all future legislation and policy making through the 'Rights Measure'. It is difficult to judge at this stage whether the progress of the Measure marks yet another stage in the inexorable progress of a rights-based approach to policy making as it affects children and young people in Wales. It is possible that in an age of 'austerity' the priorities of the Welsh Government in the Assembly's Fourth Term may lie elsewhere. Whether the Measure will come to be seen as a high watermark of children's rights in Wales, time alone will tell.

However, recognition that 'the inherent dignity and ... the equal and inalienable rights of all members of the human family is the foundation of freedom, justice and peace in the world' (Preamble to the UNCRC) has been the principle guiding all of the major political parties in Wales thus far and would seem a reasonable ground for continuing optimism.

References

Archard, D (2004) *Children Rights & Childhood* (second edition), London, Routledge

Blair, T (1999) Beveridge Lecture, 18 March

Butler, I and Drakeford, M (2001) 'Which Blair project? Communitarianism, social authoritarianism and social work' *Journal of Social Work* 1(1), pp 7–20

Butler, I and Drakeford, M (2005) *Scandal, Social Policy and Social Welfare* (revised second edition), Bristol: The Policy Press/BASW

Butler, I and Drakeford, M (2010) 'Children and young people's policy in Wales' in Ayre, P and Preston-Shoot, M (eds) *Children's Services at the Crossroads: A critical evaluation of contemporary policy for practice* Lyme Regis, Russell House Publishing

Butler, I and Drakeford, M (2011) *Social Work on Trial: The case of Maria Colwell and the state of welfare* Bristol, The Policy Press

Croke, R and Crowley, A (eds) (2007) *Stop, Look, Listen: The road to realising children's rights in Wales: Wales NGO alternative report* Cardiff, Save the Children

Croke, R and Crowley, A (eds) and UNCRC Monitoring Group (2006) *Righting the Wrongs: The reality of children's rights in Wales* Cardiff, Save the Children

DfE (Department for Education) (2010) *Review of the Office of the Children's Commissioner (England)* ('The Dunford Report'), Cm 7981 London, The Stationery Office

Drakeford, M (2007) 'Progressive universalism' *Agenda*, Winter, pp 4–7

DWP and DfE (Department for Work and Pensions and Department for Education (2011) *A New Approach to Child Poverty: Tackling the causes of disadvantage and transforming families' lives*, Cm 8061, London, The Stationery Office

Foley, P, Roche, J and Tucker, S (eds) (2001) *Children in Society: Contemporary theory, policy and practice* Basingstoke, Palgrave/Open University

Franklin, B (ed) (2001) *The New Handbook of Children's Rights: Comparative policy and practice* (second edition), London, Routledge

Funky Dragon (2003) *Inventing the Wheel: Annual report and accounts 2002–03* Cardiff, Funky Dragon

Funky Dragon (2007a) *Our Rights Our Story* Swansea, Funky Dragon

Funky Dragon (2007b) *Why Do People's Go Up Not Down?* Swansea, Funky Dragon

Hendrick, H (1994) *Child Welfare England 1872–1989* London, Routledge

HM Treasury (2003) *Every Child Matters*, Cm 5860, London, HMSO

James, A and James, A L (2004) *Constructing Childhood: Theory, policy and social practice* Basingstoke, Palgrave Macmillan

Jordan, B (2008) *Welfare and Well-Being: Social value in public policy* Bristol, The Policy Press

Laming, Lord (2003) *The Victoria Climbié Inquiry: Report of an inquiry by Lord Laming*, Cm 5730, London, HMSO

Marquand, D (2008) 'The progressive consensus: hope for the future or fight to the past? in *Unpacking the Progressive Consensus* Cardiff, Cardiff University and The Institute of Welsh Affairs

Morgan, R (2002) National Centre for Public Policy Annual Lecture, Swansea, University of Wales

NAW (National Assembly for Wales) (2000) *Children and Young People: A framework for partnership* Cardiff, NAW

NAW (2011) *National Assembly for Wales Children and Young People Committee: Legacy report* Cardiff, NAW

Phillips, J, Ajrouch, K J and Hilcoat-Nalletamby, S (2010) *Key Concepts in Gerontology* London, Sage Publications

Prout, A (ed) (2004) *The Future of Childhood* London, Routledge Falmer

Staffordshire County Council (1991) *The Pindown Experience and the Protection of Children* (Allan Levy and Barbara Kahan) Stafford, Staffordshire County Council

Stead, P (2008) 'Progressivism and consensus' in *Unpacking the Progressive Consensus* Cardiff, Cardiff University and The Institute of Welsh Affairs

UNCRCC (United Nations Convention on the Rights of the Child Committee) (2008) *Consideration of Reports Submitted by States Parties under Article 44 of the Convention: Concluding observations: United Kingdom of Great Britain and Northern Ireland* CRC/C/GBR/CO/4 Geneva, United Nations

Waterhouse, R (2000) *Lost in Care: Report of the Tribunal of Inquiry into the abuse of children in care in the former county council areas of Gwynedd and Clwyd since 1974* London, The Stationery Office

WAG (Welsh Assembly Government) (2003) *Wales: A better country* Cardiff, WAG

WAG (2004a) *Making the Connections: Delivering better services for Wales: The Welsh Assembly Government vision for public services* Cardiff, WAG

WAG (2004b) *Children and Young People: Rights to action* Cardiff, WAG

WAG (2005) *A Fair Future for Our Children: The strategy of the Welsh Assembly*

Government for tackling child poverty Cardiff, WAG

WAG (2006a) *Wales's Population: A demographic overview* Cardiff, WAG

WAG (2006b) *Beyond Boundaries: Citizen centred local services for Wales* ('The Beecham Report'), Cardiff, WAG

WAG (2006c) *Keeping us Safe* Cardiff, WAG

WAG (2006d) *Rights in Action: Implementing children and young people's rights in Wales* Cardiff, WAG

WAG (2007) *One Wales: A progressive agenda for the government of Wales* Cardiff, WAG

WAG (2009) *Getting it Right 2009* Cardiff, WAG

WAG (2010) *Wales's Population: A demographic overview* Cardiff, WAG

WAG (2011) *Sustainable Social Services for Wales: A framework for action*, WAG10-11086, Cardiff, WAG

WalesHome, 2009 http://waleshome.org/2009/11/carwyn-launches-manifesto-with-education-pledge (accessed 2 November 2009)

Welsh Labour Party (2011) *Welsh Labour Manifesto 2011: Standing up for Wales* Cardiff, Welsh Labour Party

Written Ministerial Statement: 'Publication of the independent review of the Children's Commissioner' issued by Sarah Teather MP (Minister of State for Children and Families) on 6 December 2010

Chapter 9

Youth Policy and Youth Justice in Wales

Jayne Neal

Introduction

This chapter will consider the way that Welsh Government[1] policy has influenced services for young people in Wales. It will look at the underpinning ethos displayed in its original key policy documents such as *Extending Entitlement* and compare it against Westminster government policies for young people as the political climate has changed. It will then go onto examine a practice example – the youth justice system in Wales.

Due to the piecemeal nature of the original devolution settlement for Wales, Westminster legislation continues to have an impact on social policy in Wales. This is explicitly felt by the Welsh youth justice system as responsibility for criminal justice remains at Westminster. There is a long-held argument over how young people at risk of offending should be treated and this manifests in the 'welfare versus justice' debate. How do youth justice workers in Wales ensure that all young people in their care receive their full rights-based entitlement as required by the Welsh Assembly and, at the same time, meet the central criminal justice concerns of the Westminster government?

This chapter will explore post-devolution developments in youth policy in Wales and compare them against the trends in England. It will then examine issues affecting service delivery in the Welsh context and the impact on service users and professionals involved with the youth justice system.

Policy developments

Post-devolution developments in Welsh youth policy

The Welsh Government signalled its recognition of the needs of young people in Wales early in its development. Only a year after the transfer of powers, the Policy Unit commissioned the report *Extending Entitlement: Supporting young people in Wales* (NAW Youth Policy Unit, 2000). The Welsh Government has sought to underpin its strategies for children and young people with the United Nations Convention on the Rights of the Child (UNCRC) and the report showed a clear emphasis on user consultation; young people's voices were evident throughout the document alongside those of professionals

---

[1] Throughout this chapter, the term 'Welsh Government' has been used in preference to the term 'Welsh Assembly Government', except when used as part of a direct quotation or citation. This reflects current common usage.

working in youth services in Wales. Williams (2003, p 250) sees this as a 'striking development' and something enshrined by Article 12 of the UNCRC whereby '[c]hildren have the right to say what they think should happen, when adults are making decisions that affect them, and to have their opinions taken into account'.

The process had invited over 400 organisations to comment and there was wide publicity through website, youth service and voluntary service publications. The resulting focus groups told a story with a 'powerful theme of disenfranchisement' where young people spoke of 'the lack of respect given by adults, the suspicion they were dealt with in many social settings and the general feeling of not belonging' (NAW Youth Policy Unit, 2000, Annex 3:4).

In its response, the report recommended an 'entitlement model' to create an environment where all young people could be valued and encouraged to achieve their potential (see Box 9.1). As such, services would be available to everyone and, in an attempt to limit stigmatisation or exclusion, those requiring extra help would receive it from an inclusive, rather than targeted service.

Box 9.1: *Extending Entitlement* key principles

- To support and encourage all young people to develop as individuals and to enthuse them with the value of learning.
- To develop a proportionate response to those in need of extra support.
- To focus on what young people can contribute and give them opportunities to influence services that affect them.
- To raise the quality and extend the diversity of what is offered to young people so that they are motivated to participate in learning and as citizens.
- To recognise the diverse nature of Wales' communities in order to produce better outcomes for all our young people.

Source: NAW Youth Policy Unit (2000)

Extending Entitlement justifies this universal approach by noting:

> *Support for young people is likely to be most effective where it is part of a broad network, open to all young people, with opportunities to respond to problems as early as possible and tackle them intelligently and flexibly in the context of the individual's wider needs and those of the group and the community.* (NAW Youth Policy Unit, 2000, 1.8:6)

However, an initial government intention is a long way from the implementation of policy into practice. In their 2004 evaluation report, Haines et al (2004a) see *Extending Entitlement* as 'a comprehensive long-term strategic policy.' They argue (2004a, p 6) that the value of the strategy 'cannot be underestimated' and that it has 'the capacity to not only impact on the lives of individual young people but also on the future economic and social state of Wales as a whole'.

To guide *Extending Entitlement* into practice, the Welsh Government laid out recommendations in the 2000 document *Children and Young People: A framework for partnership* (NAW, 2000). Subsequently, all local authorities in Wales employed a Young People's Partnership (YPP) coordinator in order to set up a YPP committee for their local area. By 2003, the system was in position throughout Wales and the first strategy meetings were taking place. The role of the YPP is to provide and manage a local strategy and evaluation process that brings existing providers together to work towards the same goals (see Box 9.2).

Box 9.2: Young Person Partnership tasks

- Establish a partnership.
- Agree the broad aims of the partnership and begin to identify key objectives.
- Undertake an audit of need, provision and resources.
- Consult with young people.
- Develop a draft five-year strategy.
- Identify a small number of local priorities.
- Produce an annual delivery plan.
- Finalise and publish the strategy.

Source: Haines et al (2004b, p 5)

Clearly, though, this was only a first step as the committees needed to prove they could be effective in achieving their aims. The YPPs rely on the working cooperation between services and require representatives from all welfare agencies and organisations to make up its membership (see Box 9.3). Often those involved come from very different specialisms, with their own particular training and professional ethos. Maintaining the balance of a partnership is particularly difficult where organisations (for example in the charitable sector) are funded or managed differently.

Box 9.3: Membership of Young People's Partnerships

Coherent local frameworks will depend on strong local partnerships which include representatives of all the relevant groups, including local authorities, the NHS, schools, voluntary organisations and children and young people themselves. (NAW, 2000, 4:16)

Example: Membership of Conwy County's Young People's Partnership

Education	Tourism and Leisure	Social Services
NW Police	Health	Youth Offending Team
Voluntary Organisations	ELWa	Careers Wales
Nacro	SureStart	Communities First

Source: Conwy Council YPP Information

In theory, voluntary and community agencies have as much right to contribute to local strategies as anyone else. However, when they are put alongside public sector departments such as social services, an imbalance of power can often be identified, with the statutory agency in danger of leading the decisions. The need for coordinated working practices is widely recognised and supported by research (see Sloper, 2004, p 572) and power imbalance is just one factor that prevents it from being a universal panacea for welfare provision. Sloper (2004, p 572) also recognises that partnership working requires change at all levels and this 'challenges professional cultures'. He notes the resistance to change and defensiveness that may develop. Fortunately, Haines et al (2004b, p 67) do identify projects in Wales that have been successful in their aims for a 'cultural shift amongst all service providers'. These early achievements in youth policy have now gained momentum in Wales and can be seen to have influenced a wider citizen-based agenda that is emerging.

The 2004 Assembly document *Making the Connections* (WAG, 2004b, p 3) aims to bring 'citizens and communities into the centre of the way public services are designed and delivered' and talks about the need to go from 'vision to action'. An important element of Welsh Assembly Government youth policy has been the widespread use of consultation and participation principles. This was achieved locally through Children and Young People's Plan (CYPP) Participation teams and Youth Forums, and nationally with the work of Funky Dragon – the Children and Young People's Assembly for Wales – and the Children's Commissioner for Wales. The approach was recognised as crucial by the Assembly for the transformation of public services in Wales:

> We need to find ways of giving people a stronger voice in their
> communities – both local communities and as communities of interest –
> in shaping services and priorities to meet current and future needs. For
> example, we need to build upon the already excellent, innovative work
> being undertaken to enable children and young people to participate in
> developing and reviewing services they receive in accordance with the
> Assembly Government's commitment to Article 12 of the UN Convention
> on the Rights of the Child. (WAG, 2006, p 12)

Here we see a reassertion of a rights-based agenda and this approach characterises post-devolution Welsh social policy. The 2006 Beecham Review (WAG, 2006, p ii), set up by the Welsh Assembly Government to consider the *Making the Connections* strategy, suggested that Wales now had an opportunity to become an international exemplar. Youth policy in post-devolution Wales led the way in using consultative methods to pull together existing providers and improve relationships. It has been said that a feature of the *Extending Entitlement* ethos was that it was more concerned with the flaws to be found in the working practices of the agencies involved with young people than the much-hyped flaws of young people themselves (Holmes, 2001). This chapter will now go on to investigate the idea that, in contrast, policy in England appears to place more focus on the perceived failures of young people than measures to ensure full entitlement and equality of service.

Westminster developments in youth policy in England

When Tony Blair's Labour government came to power in 1997, it was with great expectations of renewal and regeneration, in particular for the youth of the country. Prominence was given to the relatively young age of the Prime Minister and an air of excitement was encouraged by the 'Cool Britannia' tag and media coverage of pop stars visiting 10 Downing Street for tea and biscuits. Quite early on, this promise turned into something of an embarrassment; the Labour peer, Chris Smith (2003, p 6), assessed that it 'was never more than a rather crude attempt to convey a sense of cultural innovation and because it laid itself open so readily to parody, it failed'. Young people tend to be notoriously good at 'keeping it real' and so positive notions about the relationship between youth and government are soon discarded if actions do not support the rhetorical words. Youth policy and practice have to take full account of this, so when the Connexions youth strategy was launched in 1999, it was of great interest to everyone in the field of youth provision.

In the first place, it was significant that a strategy for a new service was published before an overarching youth policy document and, as such, criticism can be made about a lack of underlying theory or philosophy. Second, its positioning within government was an indicator of where the emphasis would lie. The strategy, although said to be cross-departmental in spirit, came out of the Department for Education and Employment and education, training and employment issues were repeatedly underlined. While a cursory look at the title of the document *Connexions: The best start in life for every young person* (DfEE, 1999) would seem to suggest a universal policy, subtle differences can be identified even before the end of Chapter 1. The concept of 'entitlement' was replaced by a fixation on employability and educational success: 'The key aim of the Service will be to enable all young people to participate effectively in appropriate learning – whether in school, FE [further education] college, training provider or other community setting – by raising their aspirations so that they reach their full potential' (DfEE, 1999, p 32).

Overall, the strategy implied a service that supports young people, not because they have a right to services but because they must not be allowed to fail. Williamson (2006, p 4) writes of the change in young people's transitions from narrow and prescribed routes prior to the 1970s to a complex array of opportunity and options in the late 20th century. As youth transitions have become more complicated, the emphasis on troubled youth and risk of failure has burgeoned. There is a sense that successful transitions now occur against a background of potential troubles and risks. Without a clear statement on entitlement, *Connexions* inevitably fell into a risk reduction youth policy. Although primarily an education welfare document, the strategy's heritage lay in the early Social Exclusion Unit reports (Rough Sleeping, SEU, 1998; *Bridging the Gap*, SEU,1999a; *Teenage Pregnancy*, SEU,1999b and so on). When the Social Exclusion Unit was set up soon after the elections in 1997, the Blair government's growing preoccupation with risk groups was already evident. There was widespread criticism of this and Kemshall (2002, p 120) points to flaws in the ideology of risk reduction: 'Within this approach the primary function of the welfare state is not the alleviation of poverty or the reduction of social exclusion, but the identification, classification and regulation of deviant individuals and groups'.

Bridging the Gap itself was guilty of making false assertions about social exclusion. Colley and Hodkinson (2001, p 342) write about an underlying emphasis on deficits and 'aggregates those individuals as generalized, and pathologised, social groupings'. As they point out, this is somewhat similar to theories of an underclass that were popular in the 1980s when the previous Conservative government was in power. This categorisation of young people at risk of social exclusion provided a marker for the future development of Connexions and this was illustrated by the categorisations used for operational purposes in the 'Connexions triangle' (Figure 9.1).

Figure 9.1: Priority groups for personal advisor intervention

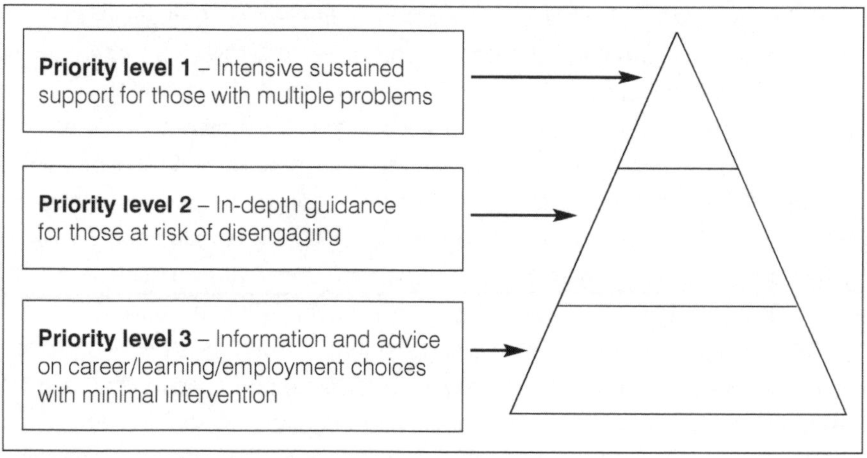

Priority level 1 – Intensive sustained
support for those with multiple problems

Priority level 2 – In-depth guidance
for those at risk of disengaging

Priority level 3 – Information and advice
on career/learning/employment choices
with minimal intervention

Source: DfEE (1999, p 38)

Using Kemshall's analysis of social policy in a risk society, the higher up the triangle the more 'deviant' you become in the eyes of government policy. The more 'deviant' you become the more money the government is willing to spend to ensure that you do not turn out to be a risk to society. Thus, although it is the smallest percentage group, the largest proportion of funding goes to the top triangle for intensive interventions. Jeffs and Smith (2001, internet page) recognise that '[t]his means that resources are being taken away from the vast bulk of young people who do not pose a threat to order and to economic development'. Although there was a considerable amount of money available to Connexions partnerships, it is clear that those at less risk would be in danger of being left out completely when funding became tight.

Operationally, Connexions was to replace the Careers Service in England with a new personal advisory system that would at the low end of need offer basic careers advice and at the high end, present a collection of services offering anything from drug advice and teenage pregnancy support to information on local amenities. Local areas would form Connexions Partnerships with a similar membership to the Young People's Partnerships in Wales. However, in England, the partnerships were to be steered and part-financed by the new cuckoo in the nest of welfare support services. With an influx of funding to the Connexions Partnerships it was inevitable that existing agencies such as the youth service would feel somewhat under pressure. The government again expected partnership working to overcome any problems and issued guidance: *Working Together: Connexions and the statutory youth services*:

> *We would expect to see ALL 13-19 youth work and resources planned,*
> *managed and delivered as part of a joint working agreement between the*
> *Youth Service and the Connexions Partnership* (Connexions et al, 2002, p 13).

This sounds like a rather forced and unequal partnership and it is this type of language that led Davies (1999), in his book on the history of the service in England, to suggest that Connexions could have signalled the end of the universal youth service. As it happens, with the passage of time came the growing awareness that Connexions Partnerships would not be in a position to solve all the problems and would be unable to fully meet Connexions' universal requirement. The Connexions evaluation report by Joyce and White (2004, p 93) supported the view that the service, '[d]espite being introduced as a universal and holistic service for all young people aged 13-19, … is designed to provide more intensive help and support to those young people with multiple barriers to learning and those who are at risk of dropping-out of education'. Joyce and White (2004, p 100) note that their data suggest that 'the service is better equipped to meet the needs of young people with more intensive support needs rather than those following other more straightforward routes', and they discuss how this could lead to problems. Those assessed as priority three one day, if lacking in basic careers advice on jobs and courses, could become a priority one or two case the next. It may be argued that a strongly visionary document such as *Extending Entitlement* (NAW Youth Policy Unit, 2000) could have helped to steer Connexions more effectively but it was not until 2005 that the Westminster government finally produced anything like a comparable document. The *Youth Matters* Green Paper (DfES, 2005) was therefore belatedly launched to a somewhat muted response from academics and youth work professionals. Wylie (2005, p 64) observed that it was 'hard to avoid scepticism regarding another government initiative about young people'. However, there was no doubt that *Youth Matters* did have a different and more inclusive tone to it, even if its ideas were somewhat lacking in innovation. Importantly, it set out a legal duty for all services to work towards five outcomes that had been suggested in consultation with children and young people (see Box 9.4). These had already been seen in the strategy document for children *Every Child Matters* (DfES, 2003) that had been produced in 2003. Wylie (2005, p 64) said of *Youth Matters* that it was 'intended to nest work with young people inside the range of actions which sprang from *Every Child Matters*'.

Box 9.4: *Every Child Matters/Youth Matters* five outcomes

1. Be healthy.
2. Stay safe.
3. Enjoy and achieve.
4. Make a positive contribution.
5. Achieve economic well-being.

Source: DfES (2003, 2005)

Clearly, in the early years of the 21st century, Westminster policy spent some considerable time preoccupied with the re-engagement of disaffected youth. It relied on the introduction of a new agency to lead an integrated service, thus inviting negativity from existing services and difficulties in partnership working. With no strong rights-based agenda, it is even easier to cut or fundamentally change a service when there is a change of government and so public services are more prone to party political challenges. This is illustrated by Connexions' repositioning by the Cameron–Clegg coalition in 2010. After the General Election the Connexions web portal stated that its advice 'may not reflect current Government policy' (accessed March 2011). Subsequently, as part of 'direct.gov.uk', Connexions was clearly realigned within a more traditional jobs and careers role, with a Connexions direct helpline picking up other 'issues'. With an initial emphasis on the role of the one-to-one personal advisor, this was a first step towards undermining the whole service, which over 2010/11 led to inevitable job losses and staff cutbacks. Similarly, Barker (2008) noted that '[s]ince the creation of the Conservative–Liberal Democrat coalition government in the UK in May 2010 there has been a lack of information in relation to the place of the *Every Child Matters* programme and children's services'. Significantly, the only children and family idea that can be properly identified as coming directly from the Cameron–Clegg coalition is the 'Childhood and Family Taskforce', which had undefined parameters and was, on Cameron's own assertion, 'not a Cabinet Committee' (Hansard, 2011). Thus, despite early promises from Nick Clegg, no strong child or youth policy focus emerged during the first two years of the coalition.

In contrast to developments in England, the newly formed Welsh Government declared its full intentions from its inception and went on to justify its position by referring to existing human rights legislation, while utilising traditional services to implement its policy. As Williams (2003, p 252) remarked, '[f]or Wales the key challenge is to meet the gap between the admirable principles and aspirations of the Welsh Assembly Government and the reality for children and young people at local level'. Would universal services be well equipped (and well funded) enough to protect the entitlement of all young people, including those who had disengaged themselves from society and its rules and regulations? Inevitably, these are the young people who often have a multiplicity of problems and can find themselves involved with the youth justice system. It is for this reason that a review of youth justice practice has been chosen to test the efficacy of the intentions of *Extending Entitlement*.

Service delivery in Wales

Wales in context

A review on the implementation process of *Extending Entitlement* within the youth justice system must take into account the fact that there has been a considerable lack of appropriate data on both the current and past experience of youth provision in Wales.

Haines et al (2004b, p 66) noted that evaluation is hampered by the 'patchy and in some cases non existent' availability of data. There is statistical evidence on demographics and this does help to provide a basic picture of young people in Wales. In 2009, the number of young people in Wales (548,871) against the whole population (2,999,300) was just over one in five, similar to ratios in England and Scotland (ONS, 2011). The gender of the youth population was evenly split: 51% were boys and 49% were girls. There was some variation in where young people lived with 18% (550,192) living in Cardiff alone. These figures had not changed much in the 10 years since the previous Census and so projections can be assessed to be fairly stable in numbers. In other words, policymakers in Wales are not expecting any major changes. Therefore, rather than any demographic surprise, it is the geographical spread of the general population in Wales throughout its most rural areas that presents a greater challenge for services dealing with young people (or any welfare service user group for that matter). In addition to this, it is recognised by policy makers and funders alike that a large part of Wales suffers from high levels of social and economic deprivation when compared to its neighbours in the UK and European Union. While this translates into the availability of extra funding for some services related to welfare, it also signals major problems with low income, high levels of economic inactivity and child poverty.[2] Taken alongside the disenfranchisement of young people already identified, the Children & Young People Partnerships face considerable challenges in their quest to ensure full entitlement. Therefore the consultation and participation that has taken place since devolution has been very influential in theories of an emergent Welsh social policy. For professionals working in the youth justice system in Wales, under the direction of a Westminster-based criminal justice policy, there were clearly going to be challenges, not least in the differences in the underpinning ethos of youth policies in Cardiff and Westminster that have already been highlighted.

Implications for service users and professionals in the youth justice system

For social policy in Wales, devolution and the powers held by the Welsh Government in Cardiff have offered an opportunity to develop innovative projects, aimed at meeting the needs of Welsh communities. However, responsibility for youth justice has remained at Westminster and the Home Office and this has created tensions in working practice.

The Home Office drafted legislation to underpin the youth justice system in England and Wales and the Youth Justice Board administered working practice. Using performance management measures, it monitored and gave guidance on effective practice, distributed funding for projects designed to reduce offending behaviour and conducted research into best practice from a 'what works' agenda. Therefore, youth justice practice in Wales has been accountable to a number of different documents all

---

[2] See Butler, Chapter 8, this volume.

with their own key aim and objectives (see Box 9.5). After a report by think-tank Policy Exchange estimated that scrapping the Youth Justice Board would save £100 million over four years, the coalition government decided that in October 2010 the functions of Youth Justice Board would be transferred to the Ministry of Justice over a 12- to 18-month period.

Box 9.5: Early legislative and policy documents relevant to youth justice in Wales

Key Welsh Assembly government documents

- *Extending Entitlement* (National Assembly for Wales, 2000)
- *The Learning Country* (WAG, 2001) + associated education documents
- *Wellbeing in Wales* (WAG, 2002a) + associated health documents
- *A Winning Wales* (WAG, 2002b) + associated enterprise documents
- *All Wales Youth Offending Strategy* (WAG, 2004)

Key Westminster government documents

- Crime and Disorder Act 1998
- Youth Justice and Criminal Evidence Act 1999
- Criminal Justice Act 2003
- Anti-social Behaviour Act 2003
- *Every Child Matters* (DfES, 2003) *and Youth Justice: The next steps* (Home Office, 2003)
- *Youth Offending: The delivery of community and custodial sentences* (2004)

In 2007/08, the 19 Youth Offending Teams (YOTs) in Wales worked with just under 6% (9,330) of total national court disposals for young people[3] (155,856). Comparing this with the London area, which during the same period had over 30 teams working with around 8% of national court disposals (12,886), it is possible to place Wales' youth justice system in some sort of context. Geography has already been mentioned as a factor in the provision of services and this can be further illustrated by considering the differences in size between London (1,579 km²/609 sqmi) and Wales (20,779km²/8,022sqmi). With a population of well over seven million, London holds much more than double the number of people within an area that is only around 8% of the size of Wales. The figures display the disparity between the circumstances in rural Wales and the urban capital. In its research on rural youth crime, the Howard League for Penal Reform (2005, p 9) points out that the 'vast majority of work on crime, exclusion, probation and resettlement fails to incorporate a rural element.' However, in the everyday working practices of youth justice professionals, this difference can be all too evident.

YOTs are responsible for supervising all convicted cases involving 10-to 17-year-olds referred by the courts and are also tasked with preventing young people 'at risk of offending' from following a path into crime. The prevention remit includes children as

---

[3] National as in England and Wales figures. It is important to note that this figure does not correspond with the number of young people who offended in Wales in the period as individuals might be on prevention programmes, pre-court disposals and have committed more than one crime.

young as eight years old, providing they meet the required criteria. Another area of responsibility is young people who fall under antisocial behaviour legislation, which often blurs the lines between criminal and civil justice. Thus, YOTs do not only work with children and young people who have committed a crime but they also work with those who are considered to be a nuisance to society and those who may commit a crime in the future. To place these children in a 'risk of offending' framework is particularly problematical for a rural area such as Wales. The Howard League for Penal Reform (2005, p 31) notes 'visibility' as an issue for rural youth. In a community where everyone knows each other, those who are attending a YOT may be stigmatised as troublesome, when previously they may have been dealt with by educational or social services. The All Wales Youth Offending Strategy (WAG, 2004a, p 3) 'supports the view that there is no contradiction between protecting the welfare of young people in trouble and the prevention of offending and re-offending'. Indeed, Welsh YOTs are supported to some degree by the strong assertion that 'young people should be treated as children first and offenders second' (2004, p 3), something that has never been so explicitly stated in policy produced by any Westminster government.

The robust use of performance management by the Youth Justice Board is one way that the welfare focus from the Welsh Assembly Government can be undermined. The first step in any YOT intervention, whether in Wales or England, is the completion of the standard YOT assessment tool – ASSET (YJB, 2006). This must be completed at the certain points during intervention. A National Audit Commission (2004, p 73) review recognised ASSET as a 'major step forward in providing a comprehensive risk and needs assessment'. However, although the document does identify areas and intensity of welfare need, the focus is on how this affects behaviour and an eventual risk of offending score is used .In the annual Youth Justice Board workload data 2007/08 (YJB, 2007/08, p 25), the Youth Justice Board notes that 'a large proportion of cases show "no change" in scores between the beginning and end of an order'. This could be rather challenging for a practitioner as there is often a correlation between high welfare need and more serious offending and intensive Court Orders (NACRO, 2003). In fact, the chaotic nature of many of these young people would suggest that ASSET scores taken over the period of an order are likely to be just as unpredictable. It is therefore not surprising that while most YOT managers have been positive about using ASSET, practitioners have been more cautious. Using a scoring system might suggest that simple solutions are possible; for example, a young person identified in ASSET as having a mental health problem would be referred to Child and Adolescent Mental Health Services and 'cured' and the risk of offending score would be reduced. Unfortunately, this is not so easy in the real world; for a young person to effect change with a mental health issue, a long road lies ahead, full of ups and downs, and there are no guarantees that when the final ASSET is completed, the news will be positive.

A second way that a welfare approach can be weakened is the access – or lack of it – to other services. ASSET may have identified a mental health issue, but what can the

YOT worker actually do to encourage change? Generally, a YOT cannot buy in services by exchange of money but has to rely on quality standards and policy statements to ensure that its young people gain services. Unfortunately, in a climate of financial constraint and increasing demand, services must have priority groups and criteria to assess who should receive a service. For example, a young person who has a mental health issue and has just been discharged from prison is clearly within a priority group with regard to gaining emergency housing according to local authority guidelines. However, they may not be able to access housing because of challenging behaviour in a previous emergency placement. Thus, they might be deemed intentionally homeless and it would be left to the young person and their worker to prove that their behaviour may not have been intentional and was due to their health condition. That is not to say that these decisions are wholly bureaucratic; the housing worker may very well be prepared to try and place the young person but the landlord of the emergency accommodation is unwilling to take a chance on a difficult young person. Ultimately, whoever owns the housing has the final say and no government pronouncement on who should benefit from the service will make any difference. It is for this reason that the mixed economy of welfare is sometimes unresponsive to extreme social need. The move away from public sector provision towards a mix of providers has diluted the power of policy statements. Unlike the public sector, private or voluntary sector providers have their own agendas and constitutions and, most importantly, the right of refusal. Therefore gaining access to services is all about negotiation and this of course returns to the question of partnership working.

Haines et al (2004a, pp 23/24) found that their respondents are cautiously optimistic about the future of welfare provision for young people in Wales. They identified a 'common multi-agency commitment through the YPPs to achieve *Extending Entitlement* outcomes'. Respondents talked of 'having a common aim', no longer 'working in isolation' and 'it has brought our attention to those groups we were not accessing' (2004a, p 19). Importantly, 21% of the respondents felt that 'Extending Entitlement made a positive difference to youth offending.' Concerns were voiced over resource issues and they stated that this may be an inhibitor to effective implementation of the process. Respondents were clear that universality should not be compromised by the development of targeted interventions and did have some concerns that sacrifices might be made. Haines et al (2004a, p 24) suggested there 'may be a need for reassurances'.

A 2005 Estyn Inspectorate for education and training in Wales report (Estyn, 2005) looked at the quality of education and training for Welsh young people in the youth justice system. It provided valuable information on how devolved educational policy had been translated into practice in Wales. The main findings from the Estyn report on provisions for young people being supervised in the community are summarised in Box 9.6.

Box 9.6: Estyn (2005) report, main findings (supervision in the community only)

✔ There are good examples of informal learning opportunities where young people are supervised by YOTs and remain or return to the community.

✔ Where teaching is good, teachers make use of assessment to plan lessons well and match work to abilities, needs and interests.

✔ Young people receive regular and helpful guidance and support from careers advisors.

✗ YOT education workers do not always have enough influence over schools and local education authorities in order to secure full-time educational placements.

✗ Communication between YOTs, educational settings and the secure estate* is not good enough. This poor liaison leads to a lack of continuity and difficulties with planning effectively for young people.

✗ Standards of achievement are not evaluated or recorded as YJB criteria look at only levels of participation. Therefore, it is not possible to give information on the educational attainments of young people.

✗ Although YOTs show an awareness of YPPs and attend partnership meetings, as yet YPPs have made little contribution to the provision for educational targets.

✗ YOT Annual Youth Justice Plans do not have enough detail and specific targets to improve education and training for young people.

* secure estate = youth justice custodial establishments

Source: (Estyn, 2005, pp 4–6)

It can be seen that practice at that time was far from consistent and did not extend 'an entitlement for all young people in Wales to education, training and work experience – tailored to their needs' (NAW, 2000, p 6). Considering the assertion in the All Wales Youth Offending Strategy that it 'supports the principle of the universal entitlement for all children and young people including those children and young people at risk of offending and those who do offend' (WAG, 2004a, p 3), it can be said that *Extending Entitlement* policy and YPPs still have some way to go.

What *Extending Entitlement* and the welfare ethos of the Wales Assembly Government do achieve is that they give some hope that, in Wales, there is an aim towards universal services focused on social need, rather than targeted services trying to reduce social risk. However, the partial settlement of devolution in Wales has restricted progress towards full universal entitlement. With the extension of powers there is the possibility that some of these restrictions may be removed but, for youth justice in Wales, it is either partial or full devolvement of the system itself that would have most impact. As might be expected, the main concern in Morgan's (2009) report to the Welsh Assembly Government on the question of possible devolution is over cost. A largely rural youth justice service is expensive to run and with a woeful lack of existing custodial facilities for young people in Wales (see Howard League for Penal Reform, 2009), devolution of the system would be an enormous financial challenge to the Welsh Government. In Morgan's (2009, p 90) opinion, it would 'require capital and revenue spending substantially greater than would likely be transferred from the YJB [Youth Justice Board] to the WAG [Welsh Assembly Government]'.

Despite the financial concern, Morgan (2009, p 90) writes that:

> *Almost everyone within the Welsh youth justice favours the rights-based, children first and offenders second, welfare-oriented, WAG policy for children and young people set out in Extending Entitlement. If it were thought that the WAG was able to deliver those policies on the ground for children in trouble then virtually no one would have qualms about devolution.*

Clearly, there has been a determination in Wales among academics, policy makers and practitioners to lead the way in UK youth justice and general youth policy. Maintaining the balance between a strong ideology and economic barriers will be an ever-present challenge. However, the evidence suggests that ideologies about youth in Wales are much more robust than their counterparts in England. As a result, it is hopeful that the rights-based agenda will serve young people and their families well during the transformation of public services in Wales and ensure that they are always fully involved in future developments.

References

Audit Commission (2004) *Youth Justice 2004: A review of the reformed youth justice system* London, Audit Commission

Barker, R (2008) *Making Sense of Every Child Matters: Multi-professional practice guidance* Bristol, The Policy Press, www.everychildmattersbook.co.uk/every-child-matters-and-the-alliance-government

Colley, H and Hodgkinson, P (2001) 'Problems with "bridging the gap": The reversal of structure and agency in addressing social exclusion' *Critical Social Policy* 21(3), pp 335–59

Connexions Service National Unit, the Local Government Association, National Youth
   Agency, Association of Principal Youth and Community Officers (2002) *Working
   together. Connexions and the statutory youth services* Connexions Service National
   Unit, www.education.gov.uk/publications/eOrderingDownload/worktogether.pdf
Davies, B (1999) *From Voluntaryism to Welfare State. A history of the Youth Service in
   England Volume 1: 1939-1979* Leicester, Youth Work Press
DfEE (Department for Education and Employment) (1999) *Connexions: The best start
   in life for every young person* Nottingham, DfEE Publications
DfES (Department for Education and Skills) (2003) *Every Child Matters*, Green Paper,
   Cm 5860, London, The Stationery Office
DfES (2005) *Youth Matters*, Green Paper, Cm 6629, London, The Stationery Office
Estyn (2005) *The Quality of the Education and Training Provided for Welsh Young
   People in the Youth Justice System* Cardiff, Her Majesty's Inspectorate for Education
   and Training in Wales
Funky Dragon (2011) www.funkydragon.org
Haines, K, Case, S, Isles, E, Rees, I and Hancock, A (2004) *Extending Entitlement:
   Making it real* Cardiff, Welsh Assembly Government
Haines, K, Case, S and Portwood, J (2004a) *Extending Entitlement: Creating visions of
   effective practice for young people in Wales* Cardiff, Welsh Assembly Government
Hansard (2011) House of Commons, 14 June, vol 697, Parliamentary Written Answers
Holmes, J (2001) 'The youth service alternative to Connexions' *The Encyclopaedia of
   Informal Education*, www.infed.org/youthwork/extending_entitlement.htm
Home Office (2003) *Youth Justice: The next steps* London, Home Office
Howard League for Penal Reform (2005) *Once Upon a Time in the West: Social
   Deprivation and Rural Youth Crime* London, Howard League
Howard League for Penal Reform (2009) *Youth Justice in Wales: Thinking beyond the
   prison bars* London, Howard League,
   www.howardleague.org/fileadmin/howard_league/user/online_publications/Wales_y
   outh_justice.pdf
Jeffs, T and Smith, M (2001) 'Social exclusion, joined-up thinking and individualization
   – New Labour's Connexions strategy' *The Encyclopedia of Informal Education*
   www.infed.org/personaladvisers/connexions_strategy.htm
Joyce, L and White, C (2004) *Assessing Connexions: Qualitative research with young
   people* BMRB Research Report 577, Nottingham, DfES
Kemshall, H (2002) *Risk, Social Policy and Welfare* Buckingham, Open University Press
Morgan, R (2009) *Report to the Welsh Assembly Government on the question of
   Devolution of Youth Justice Responsibilities* Cardiff, Welsh Assembly Government,
   http://wales.gov.uk/topics/housingandcommunity/safety/publications/youthjustrepor
   t/?lang=en
NACRO (2003) *Some Facts about Young People who Offend – 200* Youth Crime
   Briefing, London, NACRO

NAW (National Assembly for Wales) (2000) *Children and Young People: A Framework for Partnership* Cardiff, NAW,
http://new.wales.gov.uk/docrepos/40382/40382313/childrenyoungpeople/403821/6
23995/q262a360_english1.pdf?lang=en

NAW Youth Policy Unit (2000) *Extending Entitlement: Supporting young people in Wales: A report by the Policy Unit* Cardiff, NAW

ONS (Office of National Statistics) (2011) Census – Wales – population figures [online], www.statistics.gov.uk/census2001/pyramids/pages/w.asp

SEU (Social Exclusion Unit) (1998) *Rough Sleeping* London, SEU

SEU (1999a) *Bridging the Gap* London, SEU

SEU (1999b) *Teenage Pregnancy* London, SEU

Sloper, P (2004) 'Facilitators and barriers for co-ordinated multi-agency services' *Child: Care, Health and Development* 30(6), pp 571–80

Smith, C, Lord (2003) *Beyond Cool Britannia: Destination review 12* London, Locum Publishing, www.locum-destination.com/pdf/LDR12BeyondCoolBrit.pdf

WAG (Welsh Assembly Government) (2001) *Learning Country: A Paving Document. A Comprehensive Education and Lifelong Learning Programme to 2010 in Wales* Cardiff, Welsh Assembly Government

WAG (2002a) *Wellbeing in Wales* consultation document, Cardiff, Welsh Assembly Government

WAG (2002b) *A Winning Wales* Cardiff, Welsh Assembly Government.

WAG (2004a) *All Wales Youth Offending Strategy* Cardiff, WAG and Youth Justice Board

WAG (2004b) *Making the Connections: Delivering better services for Wales* Cardiff, WAG and Youth Justice Board

WAG (2006) *Making the Connections: Delivering beyond boundaries* Cardiff, WAG and Youth Justice Board, www.welshconfed.org/companyData/1898/resources/BeechamResponseEnglish.pdf

Williams, C (2003) 'The impact of Labour on policies for children and young people in Wales' *Children and Society* 17, pp 247–53

Williamson, H (2006) *Spending Wisely: Youth work and the changing policy environment for young people* Leicester, National Youth Agency

Wylie, T (2005) 'Testing a Green Paper' Youth and Policy 89, pp 64–9

YJB (Youth Justice Board) (2006) *ASSET Young Offender Assessment Profile* London, YJB, www.yjb.gov.uk/ (search for ASSET)

YJB (2007/08) *Annual Report and Accounts 2007/08* London, YJB, www.yjb.gov.uk/Publications/Scripts/prodList.asp?idCategory=25&eP=

Chapter 10

Social Services for Adults in Wales

Hefin Gwilym

Introduction

Since the creation of the Welsh Assembly in 1999, new opportunities have emerged for policy makers, academics and practitioners in the field of social care in Wales. The devolution of social care was not new: this had happened previously during the years following the establishment of the Welsh Office in 1963. What was new was the opportunity to expand the Welsh dimension in research, analysis and policy development for creating a specifically Wales social services. The seeds for some of the most significant developments had been planted during the 1980s, with the development of the *All Wales Strategy for the Development of Services for Mentally Handicapped People* (Welsh Office, 1983), subsequently revised in 1993 and still in force today. This Welsh initiative was a pioneering development of international importance and set the scene for the Welsh Assembly Government's vision in social care provision after 1997, most notably to improve services in the areas of mental health and older people. This chapter will discuss these important developments in the provision of social services in Wales, with particular focus on developments since the establishment of the Welsh Assembly. It will seek to clarify the intention of politicians and policy makers in social care policy. But it will also take a critical look at the successes and consider the elusive nature of the challenges that face those who grapple with these issues in Wales.

First, it is necessary to set the scene by looking briefly at the social make-up of Wales. It is in the light of these realities that politicians, policy makers and practitioners have to respond. The services for adults in Wales should correspond to the needs of the people of Wales, and should be tailored to match the specific needs of localities and communities. There is no one size fits all; indeed, there are particular needs in particular areas of Wales. Wales' population of three million is projected to rise to 3.1 million by 2020 (ICSSW, 2010) and 3.3 million by 2034 (Winkler, 2009). Nearly one in four (23%) of Wales' population has a limiting long-term illness. This is slightly lower at one in five (18.4%) among people of working age. Compared to England, the figures in Wales are about 5% higher, and 3% higher than Scotland and Northern Ireland. It has been estimated that 9% of the adult population are being treated for mental illness (WAG, 2006a). Wales has a higher concentration of older people compared with the rest of the United Kingdom (UK). It is anticipated that the 2011 Census will show 19% of the people of Wales as being over 65 (WAG, 2008a). These statistics on their own would be a far too simplistic way of looking at the social needs of Welsh society. Although social services organise their services according to groups, the reality is that there is a web of complex and intricate links between groups and social problems. The issues of mental health cannot be viewed separately from the issues of stigma and discrimination; the issues of learning disabilities cannot be viewed separately from social exclusion and employment; and the issues of older people cannot be viewed separately from age discrimination and the need for social housing. Each group encompasses much diversity in terms of gender, ethnicity, language, income and orientation.

Learning disabilities

The first pioneering attempt at creating a response to some of these needs at a local level started with the 1983 *All Wales Strategy for the Development of Services for Mentally Handicapped People* (Welsh Office, 1983). This was most certainly a radical document that was published by the Welsh Office and noticed internationally. It attempted to address the care needs of people with learning disabilities through a national strategy and became the forerunner of later strategies in other areas. At this time the focus of care for people with learning disabilities was in large hospitals, and most of the resources went to these institutions, despite the fact that the need was in the community where four-fifths of people with learning disabilities lived with their families, with virtually no support (Felce et al., 1998). Many of these people depended entirely on the support of their families, mostly elderly parents, until they were in their forties and the parents had themselves become too frail to look after them.

There was increasing evidence from research showing that people with learning disabilities were capable of living valued lives and even of holding down a job. These ideas were collectively known as the 'normalisation principle' (Wolfensberger, 1992), and influenced the development of the strategy. Another major ideological change at this time was the emergence and growth of the equal opportunities movement and social justice generally. By this time, institutional care in large hospitals, with all the negative connotations of uniformity of routines and restrictions of choice, was becoming less acceptable. In countries such as Denmark, care had shifted much further into the community, with services being as close to normal patterns of living as possible (Felce et al., 1998). In Wales, confidence was further eroded with reports of poor conditions and abuse in some institutions, such as the famous maltreatment of people with learning disabilities in Ely Hospital, Cardiff, during the late 1960s (Butler and Drakeford, 2005).

The strategy's philosophy of normal patterns of life within the community and the right of people with learning disabilities to be treated as individuals heralded a big change of approach at the national level (Drakeford and Williams, 2002). There was an emphasis on advocacy schemes to represent the interests of the service users themselves; the concept of the 'Community Mental Handicap Team' (CMHT) was mooted where there would be an identified named worker to coordinate the care provided; the CMHTs would be multidisciplinary for the first time with social workers, psychologists, family aides, nurses and health visitors working together. It also introduced individual care planning and foresaw the creation of care management, which was later incorporated into legislation in the NHS and Community Care Act 1990.

Implementing the strategy in an equitable and effective way throughout Wales has always been a challenge considering that Wales has 22 unitary authorities and differing traditions of service provision in each area. There were also problems in joint working between health and social services; jealousies were created when social services became the lead authority instead of the health service, which had been dominant in the days of the large hospitals. There was no blueprint for services for the whole of Wales, since services were to be locally determined according to need; this placed a great deal of responsibility for development on the local areas. This helps to explain why some of the ringed-fenced money was not fully utilised and the variability in provision.

The 1993 review of the *All Wales Strategy for the Development of Mentally Handicapped People* resulted in reduced expenditure and far greater emphasis being placed on the closure of the old hospitals. This stage saw the growth of a mixed economy of welfare in this field and the emergence of new voluntary and private organisations who became providers of support services for people with learning disabilities living in ordinary community housing. Many were given tenancy agreements and were supported by the new organisations, which tended to focus on particular localities in Wales, such as Cartrefi Cymru and Mencap. However, independent living did not necessarily lead to new friendships and staff sometimes filled this vacuum by becoming substitutes for the real thing (Ramcharan et al., 1997).

The Welsh Assembly Government after its establishment in 1999 had to address the sense of disappointment that existed about the *All Wales Strategy for the Development of Services for Mentally Handicapped People*. The ideals of the strategy were far from fully met during the early years. It would be easy to underestimate how difficult a task it was to implement any strategy that needed effective collaboration between various institutions and the continued support of service users and their families. The Welsh Assembly Government attempted to address the sense of disappointment about the strategy by publishing the framework document *Fulfilling the Promises* (NAW, 2001a). Despite the strategy's valiant aims of full life opportunities, positive identities and roles, choice and independence, and normal patterns of life within communities, many aspirations and expectations remained to be fulfilled. Other groups such as the Joseph Rowntree Foundation (JRF, 2002), in its response to the framework, identified that the nature of Welsh society had changed and that policy needed to catch up by dealing with the complexities of multiple discrimination in an ethnically diverse society and working in a genuine partnership with people with learning disabilities rather than mere consultation. The framework set out the goals of achieving full citizenship and the right to expect a high quality of life. Moreover, it recommitted itself to the cornerstone of the *All Wales Strategy*, the fundamental importance of individual planning in addressing the needs and aspirations of people with learning disabilities. This latter point had only been achieved in patches throughout Wales, a major problem when it is considered that new services were expected to arise out of the individual care planning process.

The wishes of people with learning disabilities and their families have been for a comprehensive advocacy service in Wales to represent the interests of people with learning disabilities; recognition for the crucial role of individual planning, particularly at times of transitions such as the stage between school and adulthood when many people slip through the net; continued development of day opportunities, particularly in education; real wages for real jobs; and a range of good housing and good locations (Learning Disability Implementation Advisory Group, 2006). A consensus started to form between the organisations representing people with learning disabilities and the Welsh Assembly Government that disability was not just about personal impairment but was also about the way society organises itself. The Welsh Assembly Government's *Statement on Policy and Practice for Adults with a Learning Disability* (WAG, 2007a) reaffirmed the principles of equity and inclusion for people with learning disabilities. The Manifesto of the All Wales People First organisation (AWPF, 2007) called for all people with a learning disability moving out of their family home to be able to live in ordinary housing with support by 2010. However, the current situation in 2011 is uncertain with the end of the Independent Living Fund on the grounds that it is financially unsustainable and uncertainty about the financing of the Advocacy Grant Scheme, which supports independent advocacy services throughout Wales. The present financial climate and constraints present yet another hurdle along the path to an inclusive society with quality of life for all.

Physical and sensory disabilities

The adoption of the social model of disability by the Welsh Assembly Government in 2002 was a watershed moment for disabled people in Wales. The disability model firmly shifts the focus away from the assumption that disability is a personal tragedy, to the requirement that society has to change to allow disabled people to participate fully as equal citizens (Oliver and Sapey, 1999). Equal citizenship was denied by society's discriminatory attitudes and the physical barriers that blocked the access of disabled people to transport services and other public areas. The evidence suggests that disabled people in Wales experience substantial inequality, disadvantage and discrimination in all areas of life. Disabled people experience poverty and social exclusion to a greater extent in Wales, leading to poor health and poor access to care (Winkler, 2009). According to the Welsh Health Survey 2009, 6% of the Welsh population regard themselves as having poor health (Office for National Statistics, WAG, 2010). The Wales Equality and Human Rights Commission notes that 74% of disabled people in Wales are not in employment or full-time education (WEHRC, 2011). These problems are exacerbated as people get older and they are clearly linked to socio-economic problems in certain parts of Wales, where the prevalence of disability continues to be substantially higher, such as in the valleys of South Wales.

The opportunity to participate fully in an inclusive society was seen as a right by the Welsh Assembly Government. Statutory support for this has been enhanced by the Equality Act 2010, with most of its provision coming into force in 2010, and like the previous disability anti-discrimination legislation, requires public bodies including the Welsh Assembly and local authorities to promote disability equality through Disability Equality Schemes. The Welsh Assembly Government's Disability Equality Scheme (WAG, 2006a) required all government departments to produce an equality plan. The Equality Act 2010 gives new impetus towards anti-discrimination with new protection for disabled people in the area of indirect discrimination and in the recruitment process by making it unlawful, in most cases, for employers to ask questions about disability or health before making a job offer. Although a concerted effort has been made to mainstream disability equality into the everyday work of the Assembly and public bodies in Wales, significant problems remain. An area of particular need is the provision of social services for young disabled people in Wales, especially in the area of independent living (Equality of Opportunity Committee, 2007). Recognising the continued weaknesses in this area in 2010, Disability Wales, the national association of disabled people's organisations, called on the Welsh Assembly Government to introduce a National Strategy on Independent Living for Wales, to address the needs and recognise the rights of disabled people to live in their communities, such as through supported housing. The Welsh Assembly Government has responded to some of the concerns with the new Social Care Charges (Wales) Measure 2010, which will protect the 14,000 out of 66,000 disabled and older people who pay for community-based social services. From 2011, there will be a maximum £50 charge for such services, replacing what had been a postcode lottery of widely varying charges throughout Wales.

Mental health

The establishment of the Welsh Assembly saw a new impetus in the development of services for adults with mental health problems. There was an increasing realisation that mental illness was a hidden epidemic in Wales as elsewhere in the UK. The rising suicide rates among young men throughout Wales and farmers in the rural areas were causing serious concern. It was calculated that one in four would experience a mental health problem at one time in their lives and 25% of all general practitioner consultations had a mental health component. Yet the reality about mental health services in Wales was that they had developed with substantial local variations in the type and quality of the services provided. Psychological treatments in many parts of Wales were poorly developed and there were significant variations in staffing levels and skill mix. One of the aims of any strategy was to set a minimum standard of service that was acceptable throughout Wales. The first attempt had been made in 1989 under the old Welsh Office by recognising the importance of establishing multidisciplinary teams in all areas of Wales. Allied to this was the need to plan for the closure of the old asylums of which Wales had its fair share, including Sully Hospital in the Vale of Glamorgan, St David's in Carmarthen and the North Wales Hospital in Denbigh (Michael, 2003).

A far more ambitious strategy was issued in 2001 entitled *Equity, Empowerment, Effectiveness, Efficiency* (NAW, 2001b), which was a 10-year plan to improve mental health services in Wales. Mental good health was no longer seen as dependent on services alone, and the link was firmly made with the social and economic determinants of poor health. The strategy identified social exclusion as a major problem, especially the effects of stigmatisation on people with mental health problems. Wales was lacking an overarching approach to tackling stigma and building social inclusion, which was essential if prejudices were to be overcome and progress made in the areas of employment, education, housing, access and mobility. Support from services in the areas of housing and employment were seen as particularly important steps for social inclusion. The strong association between homelessness and mental illness was accepted. The title of the strategy tried to convey its major thrust:

- *equity* meant that there should be no postcode lottery or discrimination in service provision;
- *empowerment* meant that service users were to be involved in the planning and evaluation of local services;
- *effectiveness* meant that symptoms would improve by following the principles of clinical governance and evidence-based practice;
- *efficiency* meant that organisations would need to work together and be accountable for the use of public money.

According to the strategy, mental health services in Wales for the following 10 years would be characterised by high quality and services responsive to the community. There would need to be:

- a sustained public education programme to reduce stigma by showing the public that mental health problems were treatable and that most people recovered from their difficulties;
- more advocacy services;
- extended hours and outreach services within Community Mental Health Teams and access to services during weekends and public holidays;
- provision of a range of employment and occupational opportunities by linking in to the New Deal for Disabled People and Pathways to Work in Job Centres;
- a comprehensive range of residential accommodation with varying degrees of support.

New services would be developed in partnership between agencies, including health, local authorities, housing associations and the voluntary sector. The Care Programme Approach was adopted to raise standards nationally in response to a patchy situation. Implementing the strategy needed more funds to sustain an increased workforce and finance the process of hospital closures. The aims of the strategy were reinforced by the *National Service Framework for Mental Health* in 2005 (WAG, 2005). Both documents recognised many of the real needs of service users and their families, including the need to work and live ordinary patterns of life without discrimination.

The desire of service users and their families was for a friendly service that was responsive to their needs and accessible outside the normal working hours of 9 to 5, Mondays to Fridays, and staffed by highly skilled workers. However, nationally the achievements of the strategy and framework documents were disappointing, with only limited success in establishing outreach services and health promotion. According to the Wales Audit Office (2005) baseline report, mental health promotion, a key aim in tackling stigma, had been poorly developed. There existed significant variations across Wales in the range and extent of services, for example while some areas had a home treatment service, many other areas had not. Service users and their carers continued to say that support from statutory agencies was only available when a person was in crisis and opportunities for early intervention were missed. The aim of setting up a whole system approach to service development had only been achieved in very few areas. Clearly, there were major weaknesses in the implementation of the strategy, with significant gaps in services.

Part of the problem with the implementation of the All Wales Strategy for Mental Health has been the fact that mental health is often the first service area to be squeezed out when there are conflicting demands for scarce resources. Many of these conflicts exist within the National Health Service (NHS) where mental health is sometimes seen less favourably than other areas of medicine for much-needed resources. Even within mental health services there are tensions between the needs of the acute psychiatric units and the allocation of resources into developing new community services. The hospital-based services are often viewed as bottomless financial pits by people who work within mental health services. But there are other organisational problems when it comes to strategy implementation. Featuring large among these is whether, as creator of the strategy, the Welsh Assembly Government shares the same priorities as those managers and practitioners working at the local level. This gap raises issues about the scale and level of partnership between the two levels and whether there is enough participation in and ownership of the strategy by all concerned.

The other important issue is whether sufficient resources are invested in the strategy and whether these needed to have been more effectively ring-fenced for the tasks intended. Certainly one of the lessons from the *All Wales Strategy for the Development of Services for Mentally Handicapped People* was that a ring-fenced budget was one of its strengths. In a report reviewing mental health services in Wales (Burrows and Greenwell,

2007), many of these deficiencies were recognised. The report called for strong and focused leadership and the creation of a National Strategic Mental Health and Well-Being Board directly accountable to the Minister of Health and Social Services, to take a strategic grip on the implantation of priorities set out in the National Service Framework. Recognising that standards of care and support had been highly variable, the report called for better organisation of services and ring-fencing of mental health resources. However, problems continue in the area of housing, with the Wales Audit Office (2010) reporting that very little progress had been made between 2005 and 2010 in the planning and provision of housing services for people with mental health problems. Only two local authority areas had met more than half the targets for housing set out in the *National Service Framework* and only seven local authorities had action plans for all the housing-related targets. Clearly, the current picture is of continued dissonance between the Welsh Assembly Government's aspirations and delivery in the local areas. The Welsh Assembly made it a statutory requirement for all service users aged 18 or over to have a care plan and for all patients to be able to access independent specialist mental health advocacy, when it passed the Mental Health (Wales) Measure in 2010. Although this was undoubtedly a landmark moment in the evolution of mental health law and services in Wales, it remains to be seen what real effect in improving services the legislation will have when its provisions are implemented between 2010 and 2013. The fact that the Welsh Assembly Government has felt the need to legislate in this area indicates a shift to a more centralist control to achieve better standards. Following a positive outcome in the 2011 referendum on granting direct law-making powers for the Welsh Assembly, it is highly likely that there will be more legislation in social care. However, this in itself might not bring about the desired results unless the legislation has been well drafted and is fully supported at the local level.

Older people

The newest of all the strategies is *The Strategy for Older People* in 2003 (WAG, 2003) followed by the *National Service Framework for Older People* in 2006 (WAG, 2006b). Arguably, developing a strategy for older people is the most challenging of all service areas because of the huge demographic changes that Welsh society faces in the future. Wales' population is ageing with one in four people being over 60, a higher proportion than in England, Scotland and Northern Ireland. Between 1971 and 2006, the number of people over 60 in Wales rose by 30%; the increase was particularly marked among those over 80 (Winkler, 2009). This is obviously something to be celebrated since people are living older and healthier lives. However, by 2026, the number of people in Wales over 60 will rise to about 29%, posing considerable challenges for the provision of social care. There will be a continuous demand for sheltered accommodation and affordable residential and nursing care. There is currently a serious lack of sufficient provision in the area of warden-supported sheltered accommodation for older people in their own locality (Seddon and Harper, 2009). Another area that needs addressing is that of integrated care for older people. While integrated care in England and Wales has been a qualified success, improvements need to be made in the transition from integrated care to home care services. This can be disruptive with a change in carer and a perceived loss in the quality of the service (Scourfield, 2007).

The 2003 strategy sets out a service response to the challenges of an ageing society. It identifies five areas that adversely affect the lives of older people, namely isolation, poverty, exclusion, discrimination and stereotyping. There is a strong emphasis on a whole systems approach in the strategy as it reaches out widely to address a range of social problems as well as specific issues such as hospital care and fall prevention. The need for increased social housing and the development of community services, such as nursing, had already been identified (Wenger et al., 1999). At the centre of the strategy is the requirement to tackle age discrimination, particularly in the area of employment. Continued employment well into old age is viewed as the surest way of tackling both poverty and isolation. The advantages of continuing to work beyond the age of 65 include making and maintaining friends, more social involvement and community activities, an active lifestyle, very significant economic benefits and consequently less dependency on others and services. The aims of continued employment have been given further impetus by the Equality Act 2010, which outlaws discrimination on the basis of age in the employment sphere. The response to the challenge for more quality health and social care research in Wales has come with the creation of Clinical Research Collaboration Cymru (CRC Cymru), drawing together centres of research, such as the Older People and Ageing Research and Development Network (OPAN).

To meet the social and health challenges of an ageing population, the strategy document sets a comprehensive agenda for change. Among the community services to be developed are:

- early intervention services to help people live independently for as long as possible;
- rapid assessment and responses and prompt access to emergency services when required;
- home adaptations;
- support for carers;
- support with activities of daily living;
- sheltered housing;
- integrated transport for older people.

Indeed, one of the early successes of the strategy was the provision of free bus travel for all people over 60 throughout the whole of Wales. The Free Bus Travel Scheme has helped tackle social exclusion, with a 60% increase in the number of trips undertaken by bus. Significantly, a Cabinet sub-committee was set up within the Welsh Assembly to oversee progress and sustain political momentum. All Cabinet members were members of the sub-committee except for the First Minister and the Business Minister. However, recent research indicates areas of significant concerns in service provision for older people, in particular the lack of creative community-based solutions and financial constraints (Seddon and Harper, 2009).

The Strategy for Older People (WAG, 2003a) was the first of its kind for older people in the UK and has attracted interest worldwide. One of its most interesting innovations was the creation of the office of Commissioner for Older People. The Commissioner for Older People (Wales) Act became law in 2006, and the first Commissioner was appointed in 2008. The Commissioner has the power to consider and make representations to the Assembly about any matter relating to the interests of older people in Wales. The scope of the Commissioner's role is wide-ranging, with responsibilities for promoting opportunities for older people and the elimination of discrimination against older people. This was clearly an important innovation that gave considerable clout to the organisational structure of the strategy. It enhanced the already existing structure of the National Partnership Forum, Cabinet sub-committee and Older People's Champions in all the local authority areas in Wales, to ensure that older people are represented in local decisions. However, it soon became clear that there were problems with mainstreaming the ageing agenda within the Welsh Assembly Government and more precisely within the 22 Welsh local authorities, where structures for developing the strategy were deemed to be fragile and too heavily reliant on individuals (AWARD, 2007). Most of the coordinators within the councils are placed within social services rather than within the strategically placed Chief Executive's Department. In 2008, the second phase of the strategy was published, with an emphasis on building on the successes of the first five years, by taking into account older people in all policy areas (WAG, 2008b). There remain enormous challenges for the future in creating community-based and person-centred services that respond imaginatively to individual needs and which are flexible and well coordinated.

Service users and carers

An essential element of the care provision for adults is provided by the vast army of carers, that is, family, friends and neighbours. The 2001 Census identified 12% of the Welsh population as carers; other surveys suggest that the number of carers is higher. Carers provide about 70% of care in the community, with 100,000 people regularly providing over 50 hours of care each week. According to Carers Wales (2010), the overall cost of replacing informal care in Wales would be £5.69 billion. Over 350,000 people experience ill-health, poverty and work-based discrimination as a direct result of being a carer (Carers Wales, 2006). Mental health problems and physical ill-health as a direct result of the stress involved in caring are experienced by 60,000 people. A startling one in three of those providing continuous care live in poverty and struggle to pay food and other bills. A fifth of all carers have had to give up their work to care, significantly compounding their financial problems and increasing their isolation. The problems faced by black and minority ethnic carers are compounded by societal assumptions about their needs and coping abilities (WAG, 2003b). Black and minority ethnic carers are at risk of being isolated and of receiving little help from their families or the state. The common notion that black and minority ethnic families wish to look after their own often disguises inadequate provision and low take-up. The evidence suggests that black and minority ethnic carers would welcome supportive services offered in a culturally sensitive manner (Roulstone et al., 2006).

The 1999 *Caring about Carers* strategy document (DH, 1999) and the subsequent *Carers' Strategy in Wales: Implementation plan* (WAG, 2000) recognised the financial costs on and the social exclusion of carers. Maintaining carer's employment is seen as the most effective way of tackling social exclusion and poverty. To this end, employers would need to be more flexible by allowing flexible working, working from home, career breaks and special leave. A revised strategy was introduced in 2007 called the *Carers' Strategy for Wales Action Plan* (WAG, 2007b), which called for more innovative services and greater control for carers over the types of services provided. The overall evaluation of the Carers' Strategy in Wales is mixed, with a gap between staff positive perceptions of expanding and more innovative services and carers' first-hand experiences of problems in the organisation and delivery of these services where they exist (Seddon et al., 2010). The Welsh Assembly Government has taken the landmark step of trying to deal with some of the problems through legislation in the Carers Strategies (Wales) Measure 2010, which provides for more information and consultation for carers.

The service user involvement movement has increased in influence since the 1980s. All the strategies have good intentions about involving service users and their carers. The strategy for learning disabilities states that service users and their families must play a full part in decisions taken about them. The mental health strategy sees the views of service users and their carers as a fundamental principle of the strategy. *The Strategy for Older People* states the case most powerfully of all when it calls for older people to be able to participate fully as citizens in all aspects of society. However, all the strategies have had difficulties in achieving their ideals in this area. The overall picture is varied across Wales, with patchy development of advocacy services and systems for the involvement of service users and their families and carers. The most promising area for user involvement is in the field of services for older people with the creation of the National Partnership Forum to provide advice to the Welsh Assembly and statutory bodies in Wales. However, it has been difficult for older people to be heard directly by the Assembly without having to pass through several organisational layers where representation may consist of people who have made a career of the user involvement role (Walters, 2005). It is unfortunate that service user involvement is not more successfully implemented in Wales since it can involve users as active citizens within organisations and bring about positive strategic changes (Carr, 2007). More needs to be done to facilitate open dialogue between service users and frontline staff as a tool for change in practice.

Challenges for social services providers

The area of greatest change in policy following 1999 is in driving forward joint working, especially between health and social services. Terms such as 'partnership' and 'collaborative working' are used interchangeably to refer to the process of blurring the boundaries between health and social provision. The Care Programme Approach (CPA) was introduced in the early 1990s following the high-profile death of a social worker by her client in a London hospital (the Campbell Inquiry – see Sharkey, 2007). It was intended to improve interprofessional communication and collaboration, both of which had been lacking, and would remove the need for separate assessments by health and social services. It became the cornerstone of service delivery for people with serious mental illness who had often slipped through the net (DH, 1995). Its main features are an assessment before people with serious mental illnesses are discharged from hospital; a care plan; a key-worker to coordinate care; and regular review of cases. In this respect, the CPA is similar to Care Management, and both exist side by side, with the CPA being a more specialist approach for people with serious mental illness. Chief among the problems with the CPA in England were that key components of the CPA were not being fully implemented, with wide variations between agencies (Simpson et al., 2003). In Wales, access to and eligibility for adult social care seems to be for the most part fair and consistent, however, it is questionable whether local authorities are defining levels of eligibility in an equitable way (CSSIW, 2010).

The CPA is generally seen as a specialist assessment within the Unified Assessment Process (UAP) for people with serious mental health problems. The UAP was implemented in Wales between April 2005 for older people and April 2006 for the other adult groups. The UAP is an attempt to standardise eligibility criteria for social care services throughout Wales and to end the duplication in the assessment process between health and social care agencies. Many service users were being asked the same assessment questions more than once by different agencies and this became known as the problem of serial assessments. The UAP consists of one assessment document for each service user and the information gathered is shared with all agencies concerned. While there is broad agreement that the UAP has facilitated some positive changes to practice, there remain considerable problems, such as resistance by practitioners to the domain approach of assessment and inconsistencies in the amount of information gathered (Seddon et al., 2008).

The Welsh Assembly Government has continued to strive towards improving standards of social care for adults in Wales since its creation in 1999. The latest attempt, *Sustainable Social Services for Wales: A framework for action* (WAG, 2011), makes a commitment to more coherent and focused improvement measures, with more accountability and strong national outcomes. The stakes are raised with the spectre of new legislation should this be necessary. The Framework incorporates the recommendations of the Independent Commission on Social Services in Wales report (ICSSW, 2010), which recommends better regional partnerships involving social services departments, with 'regional' being defined as adopting the footprint of the seven Local Health Boards. In time, the report will come to be seen as a prerequisite for full local government reform, with a reduction from 22 to seven local authorities. The changes in social services in Wales will be staged and will not follow the same pattern as that taking place in England following the Social Work Task Force report (DCSF, 2009; see Chapter 11, this volume).The reforms in both countries are in response to similar problems, and it remains to be seen how tenable the different solutions will be at a time of economic constraint and a continued rise in the demand for social services.

Conclusion

The establishment of the Welsh Assembly in 1999 was a great impetus in the evolution of a Wales social services. The problems in developing a Wales social services are in the area of delivering equitable services throughout Wales without unnecessary variations in quality and accessibility. There are, of course, huge challenges that Wales shares with other countries, such as the ever-ageing society. The socio-economic position of Wales is a further complication with some areas with particular structural deprivation, such as areas within the South Wales valleys and some rural communities. The Welsh Assembly Government is attempting to deal with the situation in Wales by setting out national standards within strategy and framework documents. It is also imaginatively introducing social policies that are easier to implement in countries with small populations, such as a limit on the cost of community-based social services. However, a pattern is emerging that should cause some concern as well as interest. This is the Welsh Assembly Government's commitment to raising the stakes when standards at the local level do not meet its standards. The latest step is to legislate for social problems in areas where local provision has been poor. With new powers granted in the 2011 referendum, the Welsh Assembly is almost certain to increase its use of legislation in the social care field. Yet placing too much hope in legislation can disappoint, as Westminster knows only too well. Wales continues to move further down the road of a distinctive Wales social services. This in itself is an interesting adventure but its success will be judged by achieving the elusive prize of high-quality social care that is accessible and affordable at the point of need.

References

AWARD (All-Wales Alliance for Research and Development in Health and Social Care) (2007) *Strategy for Older People in Wales: An interim review: Final report* Swansea, University of Wales

AWPF (All Wales People First) (2007) *Manifesto*, www.allwalespeople1st.co.uk/pdfdownloads/Manifesto.pdf

Burrows, M and Greenwell, S (2007) *The Other End of the Telescope: A refocusing of mental health and well being for service users and carers: All-Wales review of mental health services* Cardiff, Welsh Assembly Government, http://new.wales.gov.uk/dhss/publications/health/reports/2278708/mentalhealthrevie we.pdf?lang=cy

Butler, I and Drakeford, M (2005) *Scandal, Social Policy and Social Welfare* Bristol, BASW/The Policy Press

Carers Wales (2006) *Looking After Someone: A guide to carers' rights and benefits* Cardiff, Carers Wales

Carers Wales (2010) *Carers Strategy (Wales) Measure 2010: Policy briefing* Cardiff, Carers Wales

Carr, S (2007) 'Participation, power, conflict and change: Theorizing dynamics of service user participation in the social care system of England and Wales' *Critical Social Policy* 27, pp 266-76

CSSIW (Care and Social Services Inspectorate Wales) (2010) *National Review of Access and Eligibility in Adults' Social Care: Overview report* Cardiff, CSSIW

DCSF (Department for Children, Schools and Families) (2009) *Building a Safe, Confident Future: The final report of the Social Work Task Force* London, DCSF

DH (Department of Health) (1995) *Building Bridges* London, HMSO

DH (1999) *Caring About Carers: A national strategy for carers* London, HMSO

Drakeford, M and Williams, C (2002) 'Social work in Wales' in Payne, M and Shardlow, S M (eds) *Social Work in the British Isles* London, Jessica Kingsley Publishers, pp 156–85

Equality of Opportunity Committee (2007) *Why Is It that Disabled Young People are Always Left Until Last?* Cardiff, WAG

Felce, D, Grant, G (1998) *Towards a Full Life: Researching policy innovation for people with learning disabilities* Oxford and Boston, MA, Butterworth Heinemann

ICSSW (Independent Commission on Social Services in Wales) (2010) *From Vision to Action: The report of the Independent Commission on Social Services in Wales* Cardiff, ICSSW

JRF (Joseph Rowntree Foundation) (2002) *Fulfilling the Promises: A response from the Joseph Rowntree Foundation to the proposed framework for services for people with learning disabilities in Wales* York, Joseph Rowntree Foundation

Learning Disability Implementation Advisory Group (2006) *Proposed Statement on Policy and Practice for Adults with a Learning Disability* Cardiff, Welsh Assembly Government

Michael, P (2003) *Care and Treatment of the Mentally Ill in North Wales 1800-2000* Cardiff, University of Wales Press

NAW (National Assembly for Wales) Learning Disability Group (2001a) *Fulfilling the Promises: Report to the National Assembly for Wales* Cardiff, NAW

NAW (2001b) *Equity, Empowerment, Effectiveness, Efficiency: Strategy document* Cardiff, NAW

Oliver, M and Sapey, B (1999) *Social Work with Disabled People* Basingstoke, Palgrave Macmillan

Ramcharan, P, McGrath, M and Grant, G (1997) 'Voices and choices: mapping entitlements to friendships and community contacts' in Ramcharan, P, Roberts, G, Grant, G and Borland, J (eds) *Empowerment in Everyday Life* London, Jessica Kingsley Publishers, pp 48–70

Roulston, A, Hudson, V, Kearney, J, Martin, A and Warren, J (2006) *Working Together: Carer participation in England, Wales and Northern Ireland* Stakeholder Participation Position Paper 5, London, SCIE

Office for National Statistics, WAG (2010) *Welsh Health Survey 2009* Cardiff, Welsh Assembly Government

Scourfield, P (2007) 'Issues arising for older people at the "interface" of intermediate care and social care research', *Policy and Planning* 25(1), pp 57–67

Seddon, D and Harper, G (2009) 'What works well in community care? Supporting older people in their own homes and community networks' *Quality in Ageing* 10(4), pp 8–17

Seddon, D, Robinson, C and Perry, J (2008) 'Unified assessment: Policy, implementation and practice' *British Journal of Social Work*, Advanced Access, 19 June, pp 1–19

Seddon, D, Robinson, C, Tommis, Y, Woods, B, Perry, J and Russell, I (2010) 'A study of the Carers Strategy (2000): Supporting carers in Wales' *British Journal of Social Work* 40(5), pp 1470–87

Sharkey P (2007) *The Essentials of Community Care* London, Palgrave

Simpson, A, Miller, C and Bowers, L (2003) 'The history of the care programme approach in England: Where did it go wrong?' *Journal of Mental Health* 12(5), pp 489–504

WAG (Welsh Assembly Government) (2000) *The Carers' Strategy in Wales: Implementation plan* Cardiff, WAG

WAG (2003a) *The Strategy for Older People in Wales* Cardiff, WAG

WAG (2003b) *Challenging the Myth 'They Look After their Own': Black and minority ethnic (BME) carers* Cardiff, WAG

WAG (2005) *Raising the Standards: The revised Adult Mental Health National Service*

Framework and Action Plan for Wales Cardiff, WAG

WAG (2006a) *Disability Equality Scheme* Cardiff, WAG

WAG (2006b) *National Service Framework for Older People in Wales* Cardiff, WAG

WAG (2007a) *Statement on Policy and Practice for Adults with a Learning Disability* Cardiff, WAG

WAG (2007b) *Carers' Strategy for Wales Action Plan 2007* Cardiff, WAG

WAG (2008a) *A Statistical Focus on Older People in Wales* Cardiff, WAG

WAG (2008b) *The Strategy for Older People in Wales, 2008-13: Living longer, living better* Cardiff, WAG

WAG (2011) *Sustainable Social Services for Wales: A framework for action* Cardiff WAG

Wales Audit Office (2005) *Adult Mental Health Services in Wales: A baseline review of service provision* Cardiff, Wales Audit Office

Wales Audit Office (2010) *Housing Services for Adults with Mental Health Needs* Cardiff, Wales Audit Office

Walters, V (2005) *The Strategy for Older People in Wales: A framework for evolution* Swansea, University of Wales

WEHRC (Wales Equalities and Human Rights Commission) and WISERD (Wales Institute of Social and Economic Research, Data and Methods) (2011) *An Anatomy of Economic Inequality in Wales* Cardiff, WEHRC and WISERD

Welsh Office (1983) *All Wales Strategy for the Development of Services for Mentally Handicapped People* Cardiff, HMSO

Wenger, G C, Barholt, V and Scott A (1999) *Bangor Longitudinal Study of Ageing* Bangor, Centre for Social Policy Research and Development, University of Wales

Winkler, V (ed) (2009) *Equality Issues in Wales: A research review* Manchester, Equality and Human Rights Commission

Wolfensberger, W (1992) *A Brief Introduction to Social Role Valorization as a High-Order Concept for Structuring Human Services* Syracuse, NY, Syracuse University

Chapter 11

Social Work in a Devolved Wales

Charlotte Williams

Introduction

> *We must create a culture whereby there is a feeling that staff are working*
> *for Wales Social Services, which reinforces the principle of social care*
> *being one sector with one workforce.* (Garthwaite, 2005, p 16)

I was trained as a social worker in Wales in the early 1980s in a period of great uncertainty and change. The Barclay Report (Barclay, 1982) on the roles and tasks of social workers pointed to a radical reshuffle of local authority social services departments and their relationship to the communities they served, a locality model which although rejected may have been eminently suited to the realities of rural social work we were experiencing in practice. The Thatcher administration had begun what we later came to understand as a radical restructure of the whole context of welfare delivery, opening with a period of retrenchment of services and financial stringency. Academic forecasters quickly focused on the 'crisis in welfare' (Munday, 1989). If the enemy was not yet named we were led to expect the concomitant 'crisis in social work' (Munday, 1989, p 34). Brewer and Lait (1980) had presented a trenchant critique of the utility of social work, pointing to the lack of empirical rigour guiding interventions and it had long been clear to us that what we had to offer was not what service users wanted (Mayer and Timms, 1973). In the face of this onslaught we were weak, adrift in a sea change – rudderless and anchorless, graduating into a profession that had clearly lost its way. Things happened to social work and they happened to us in Wales by dint of distant forces. We were relatively powerless to affect our fate or to shape anything that might approximate a 'social work in Wales'. Meanwhile, the experimental initiative of the *All Wales Strategy for the Development of Services for Mentally Handicapped People* (Welsh Office, 1983) rolled out novel multidisciplinary teams and new ways of working with users and carers that provided a glimmer of hope. As students we were becoming increasingly politicised as the strategies of the largely English-driven anti-racist agenda were deployed towards an emerging Welsh language agenda in social work and social care. Yet despite the potential of these latter initiatives we held little sense of ourselves as a social work service *for* Wales and little confidence to articulate our specific concerns.

In post-devolution Wales, the 'crisis of social work' sentiment is somehow still with us. Despite widespread changes in workforce management over almost a decade, far-reaching reforms that impinge on the nature and functioning of the social work role are once again proposed at home (WAG, 2011) and away (Social Work Reform Board, Munro Review, ongoing). This should not be seen so much as troubling as inevitable. Economic uncertainties, organisational changes, new government priorities, social work scandals and media panics will always conspire to 'unsettle' social work. Social work is, as Harris (2008) has argued, a contingent activity, subject to the exigencies of complex environments and pressures of the time. It will therefore of necessity be contested; an unfinished business subject to flux and change. Accordingly, Dickens (2011, p 36) has suggested that 'it is important that social work keeps a sense of being on the cusp, aware of the constraints and contradictions, moving forwards but never expecting to arrive'.

In this chapter I will explore the nature of the changing context for practice under devolution and consider this notion of the perennial 'crisis', that 'being on the cusp' that besets contemporary social work. I will draw out some of the implications of constitutional change for the development of a 'Wales social services' and the idea of 'social work in Wales' (Garthwaite, 2005) or indeed the search for something as distinctive as 'social work for Wales'.

Continuity and change: 'learning from the journey'

Social care services in Wales are a huge enterprise, currently accounting for £1.418 billion in public spending, employing more than 70,000 people, some 27,000 of which are directly employed by local authorities and supporting over 150,000 people (WAG, 2011). In 2010, there were some 44,000 referrals concerning children and young people and 88,000 assessments of need for adults. The demand side of the welfare equation is set to rise exponentially. Social care services in Wales have faced unsustainable increases in demand against a shrinking financial base and difficult choices are having to be made about priorities in service delivery. There is little doubting that social work is operating in a climate of considerable flux and change and in setting the framework for action the Welsh Assembly Government has been guided by evidence garnered from a number of reports in the first decade of the devolutionary settlement (WAG, 2011).

Devolution has seen the introduction of wide-ranging policy changes that not only have resulted in new legislative mandates but also have led to changes in organisational arrangements and to changes in philosophy, approaches and ways of working. Few areas of social work practice remain untouched by a plethora of strategies that have emanated from the Welsh Assembly in relation to specific groups, such as *The Strategy for Older People in Wales* (WAG, 2003), *A Fair Future for Our Children* (WAG, 2005) and the *Review of Service Provision for Gypsies and Travellers* (WAG, 2007), and in relation to key areas of need such as homelessness and drugs. New approaches to working have been rolled out within policy documents such as *Making Connections* (WAG, 2006) and *Fulfilled Lives, Supportive Communities* (WAG, 2007), signalling a distinctive value base for the operation of 'Welsh public service values' (WAG, 2011, p 5). *Fulfilled Lives,*

Supporting Communities (WAG, 2007) provided the agenda for change with targets set for a modernised social services in Wales by the year 2018. It reinforced the 'single workforce' ideas and the idea that 'the social services workforce needs to be involved in the local authority's decision making' was established as a principle (WAG, 2007, p 9). The document, which received widespread support, embodied the following key conclusions:

- that social services should remain a core responsibility of local authorities, in order to place social workers at the heart of a range of wider services, such as housing and education, on which their users need to draw;
- that local authorities should remain key providers of social services, as well as taking responsibility for overall planning, and commissioning some services from others;
- that the focus of social work and allied professionals should be re-orientated towards preventative strategies, wherever possible, in relation to both children's services and social care. The Welsh Assembly Government will set specific targets for reducing the proportion of children received into the 'looked after' system, and invest in new services for older people, designed actively to counteract the loss of independence;
- that new arrangements will be put in place to strengthen the influence of users, and carers, on what services are provided, and how they are delivered;
- that the staff needed for the future of social services should be regarded as a single workforce, well trained, well motivated and informed by up-to-date evidence and research. Workers in social services in Wales will be capable of exercising *critical judgement* and expected to do so in the unique circumstances of each individual user;
- that the new powers of the Government of Wales Act 2006 should be used actively, where these lead to better outcomes for users.

Taken together, these conclusions set out a future for social work as an occupation in its own right, actively involved in influencing national and local policy through speaking up alongside users; utilising and developing the wider community and neighbourhood networks that strengthen the wider social fabric; and enabling individuals and their families to obtain the help they need. The Welsh Assembly Government philosophy of greater collaboration, partnership and the primacy of 'voice over choice' lies at the heart of the approach set out in this document, which opens up considerable opportunities for the profession to be proactive in shaping change.

New regulatory bodies have been established, in particular the Care Council for Wales (CCW), the Social Services Inspectorate for Wales (SSIW) and the Care Standards Inspectorate for Wales (CSIW). Statutory registration of social workers and student social workers has been embedded following the Care Standards Act 2000 based on a robust Code of Practice and is gradually being rolled out to sectors of the social care workforce. Efforts have been made to coordinate research activity across health and social care in Wales with the establishment of the Clinical Research Collaboration Cymru under the auspices of the National Institute for Social Care and Health Research (NISCHR), which is developing a coherent approach to research and development across the nation. In social work education, the transition from the Diploma in Social Work to the three-year degree programme has seen eight programmes up and running at both undergraduate and postgraduate levels. Comprehensive reviews of workforce need have been undertaken, which seek to tie training more securely to employer requirements in Wales (CCW, 2007) and major inspection reviews of the delivery of services have provided key messages about the state of play (CSSIW, 2008). Not all of these activities emanate from within Welsh governance structures. Changes to social work education and the regulation of the profession are standard across the United Kingdom (UK) and the re-engineering and gearing up of social work to be responsive to national context is happening elsewhere (for example, on Scotland, see Asquith et al., 2005; Ferguson et al., 2005). Major reviews of the roles and tasks of social work are currently being undertaken in England (Social Work Reform Board, Munro Review, ongoing), which are likely to have some impacts on social work in Wales. What is interesting to explore, however, is the emergence of the idea of a 'social work in Wales' as a coherent entity and to consider how this is being constructed, what the nature of the distinctiveness is and what this might mean for a wider conceptualisation of the profession.

While it is difficult to delineate social work in Wales historically in the way for example it is possible to do in the Scottish context, there are nevertheless ways of viewing the 'old' and the 'new'. The story of social work in Wales emerges from a number of sources. There are the insights of the welfare historians, who have for example illustrated aspects of the treatment of people with mental illness in Wales (Michael, 2003) or provided early glimpses of social welfare delivery in rural communities (Grant, 1978). Fascinating, if under-explored, archives exist from the last century of the experiences of people in Butetown, Cardiff, which although controversial, provide the earliest account of the nature of social work with minority groups in Wales (Sherwood, 1991). The legacy of scandals in the Welsh context and concomitant reports, such as Lord Howe's Report (1969) into the conditions and treatment of patients in Ely hospital in the 1960s, the Waterhouse Inquiry (2000) into the abuse of children in North Wales in the 1990s and the case of Andrew Cole who following discharge from a mid-Wales hospital in 1996 murdered William Crompton and Fiona Ovis, illustrate aspects of the highly contentious nature of the terrain and some of the more fundamental failings of social work practice (Butler and Drakeford, 2003). The history of local government reorganisation serves to indicate something about the legacy of fragmentation and problems of coordination that beset service delivery in particular in relation to children's services (Drakeford et al., 1998). An important historical account exists on the endeavours to establish the principles of Welsh language equality in service delivery, practice and in terms of the representation of Welsh speakers in the social work workforce (Huws-Williams et al., 1994). The Wales office of the Central Council for Education and Training in Social Work (CCETSW) under the direction of Rhian Huws-Williams from the early 1990s onwards developed a forthright programme on the Welsh language, which included a range of publications and training materials and the facilitation of networks of Welsh-speaking social workers across Wales.

Despite these factors, the organisation of social work in Wales largely followed Seebohm lines as in England. The coming of the *All Wales Strategy for the Development of Services for Mentally Handicapped People* (Wales Office, 1983) (see Chapter 10, this volume) and the strategy on mental illness (Welsh Office, 1989) represented a major departure in service delivery and one that was well researched and provided groundbreaking lessons on multidisciplinary working, user involvement and mobilising local resources (Ramchuran et al., 1997). While many policy strategies subsequently emanated from the Welsh Office pre-devolution, it would be difficult, however, to sustain the argument that they represented any consistent departure from the approach taken in England. In fact, all the evidence suggests that social work in Wales was as subject to the vicissitudes of the Thatcher era as much as anywhere else in the UK, as the series of studies conducted by a team of researchers in the Centre for Social Policy Research and Development (CSPRD) of the University of Wales Bangor in the mid-1990s revealed (McGrath et al., 1996a, 1996b; Parry-Jones et al., 1996). These CSPRD studies are significant in that, although they focused on a survey of workers in adult services and an analysis of their roles and tasks, they highlighted the nature of increasing demands on staff under the new care management arrangements and the tensions between their perception of their traditional social work roles and the imposition of market principles on frontline work with users. The studies gave voice to the fears of social workers that they were being deskilled, that they were becoming distanced from service users given the emphasis on 'paperwork', of them experiencing high levels of stress due to lack of support, and a training regime that ill-equipped them for the new roles. A study conducted in 2001 by Parry-Jones and Soulsby in Powys reiterated the discrepancy between the aim to provide a needs-led service and the realities on the front line, confirming the ongoing tensions in practice.

The findings apparent in the CSPRD studies resonated some 10 years later with the predicament of workers and their concerns expressed in the Garthwaite Report (2005, p 13):

> *Increased scrutiny, joint reviews, inspections and publicly available annual performance evaluations are moving local authorities towards increased target setting often based on process indicators. This is contributing to a*

shift in the emphasis of the social work role from direct work with clients. Social workers and their managers are expressing concern about increased levels of bureaucracy in their roles which do not necessarily translate into improved outcomes for service users and carers.

What might be deduced from the parallels between the accounts in the CSPRD studies and those documented in the Garthwaite review is that the neoliberal agenda of managerialist and market-driven approaches to social work that have prevailed for over a decade have led to a demoralised workforce and one in which there is serious attrition. While the crisis was formulated as one of recruitment and retention related to pay and conditions in the early 2000s, there can be no running away from the fundamental expression of discontent at the mismatch between the motivations for becoming a social worker as a wish to work directly with people and enhance their well-being, the skills and values as social work professionals, and the realities of the changed nature of the job itself.

In this respect, social workers in Wales in the mid-2000s were saying nothing different from their colleagues elsewhere in the UK. In Scotland, Wilson et al. (2003) noted the predominance of the managerialist over the professional ethos as a source of frustration to workers. Jones' (2001) study, 'Voices from the front line', exploring state social work in England, provided a powerful insight into the nature of these transformations to the social work role under neoliberal policies. Jones (2001, p 359) concluded that the 'fragility of state social work' has meant that social service managers have been 'particularly compliant in accommodating the neo-liberal agenda'.

The Garthwaite Report, *Social Work in Wales: A profession to value*, which arose from concerns raised by a task and finish group of the Assembly, which reported in 2001, acknowledged these trends. The task and finish group on social care workforce issues identified inadequate pay levels as contributing to social workers leaving the sector. As a result of this, they suggested that a fragmented sector had emerged with individual local authorities responding to staff shortages with initiatives such as 'golden hello' packages to staff to join or stay with them. A system of competition prevailed, which it was felt was detrimental to the principle of what the task and finish group termed '*one sector, one workforce*'. Data on the social care workforce of Wales had traditionally been sparse and inconsistent and it was only in 2003 that the Skills Foresight Plan described for the first time the social care sector workforce of Wales. In 2007, the CCW published the outcome of its workforce review (CCW, 2007). A number of particular characteristics on the registered social work workforce emerged from the data. Most social workers in Wales were state social workers (62%). The analysis by the CCW of those on their register revealed them to have, perhaps unsurprisingly, a broadly white, female, middle-aged and monolingual profile. A large proportion of social workers were noted as approaching retirement age, with 40% of them being over the age of 50 (CCW, 2007) and there was apparent a substantial under-representation of disabled people (2.2%), people from minority ethnic groups (3%), men (23%) and Welsh speakers (17% for the sector as a whole). This under-representation was a feature of both the workforce and the student trainee population.

Today, the figure for the total number of registered social workers is 4,500, which excludes the registered social work students. The Garthwaite Report (2005) noted that other than teachers, social workers form the largest single group of qualified workers employed by local authorities and that the demand for social workers was well in excess of supply and likely to remain so for some years to come. The vacancy rate of almost 15%, coupled with an equivalent turnover rate as social workers moved through a revolving door between authorities, was regarded as having a damaging effect on the capacity of local authorities to deliver services to those in need. High turnover rates and sickness levels were particular acute in children's services, where the vacancy rate ran at 18.8% (CCW, 2007). Indeed, the recruitment and retention of social workers continues to present the greatest difficulties for local authorities of any of its occupational groups. Factors affecting the retention of staff were discussed in the Garthwaite Report (2005) and among the reasons given for leaving the job were heavy workload, the stressful nature of the job, low pay, lack of appreciation and being taken for granted. The quality and nature of leadership, supervision and support were also cited by many as a reason for leaving. The Garthwaite Report (2005, p 16) called for 'a universally applicable set of definitions of roles and responsibilities for social workers' and the development of minimum standards on working conditions and a common approach to workload management. The CCW (2007, p 47) report on the social care workforce referred to these workers as a 'national asset' and pledged to respond to some of the workforce challenges that had become apparent.

This commitment has been manifest in a number of initiatives. Guidance has been produced for social workers and their managers for the first year of practice resulting in a slowdown in the turnover of social workers. A new qualifications and credit framework – the Continuing Professional Education and Learning (CPEL) framework – with defined career pathways and programmes of support for professional development, has been launched. Efforts have been made to strengthen the leadership and management of social workers. Now experienced social workers can work in consultancy roles while remaining at the front line and programmes of leadership training are being rolled out. In addition, a lot of publicity effort has gone into attracting people to the profession, enhancing the public profile of social work and creating a forum (actual and virtual) for giving the profession a collective sense of itself (CCW, 2011). The stated ambition is to create a 'safe and confident' profession.

The notion of 'crisis' that dominated the policy agenda of the mid-2000s was of course highly contestable. That change for the profession in Wales was under way is undisputed. What is perhaps more disputable are the drivers of that change and the discourse as to what the nature of the change should be. The prevailing discourse on the 'crisis' focused on the recruitment and retention issues. The workforce agenda argument suggested the need to attract and retain more social workers in order to respond to growing demand, and as such tended to focus on the malaise rather than the symptoms. The voice of the workforce told a different story. Professional formulations of the agenda coined nebulously as 'increasing bureaucracy' as the Garthwaite Report (2005, p 86) indicated, or feelings of being devalued, reflected the clear unease in practice with being key participants in a neoliberal welfare framework that is, in Jones' (2001) words 'degrading and damaging' to social work practitioners and those whom they seek to serve. The report flagged the International Association of Schools of Social Work (IASSW) and International Federation of Social Workers (IFSW) agreed international definition of social work as part of the bedrock values and principles of social work:

> *The social work profession promotes social change, problem solving in human relationships and the empowerment and liberation of people to enhance well-being. Utilising theories of human behaviour and social systems, social work intervenes at the points where people interact with their environments. Principles of human rights and social justice are fundamental to social work.* (Garthwaite, 2005, p 53)

While these social justice ambitions, 'fundamental to social work', were left suspended in the report, the commitments laid out in *Fulfilled Lives, Supporting Communities* (WAG, 2007) resonate with these ideals. It has been argued (see Chapters 1 and 2, this volume) that devolution heralds a welfare regime significantly different in many respects from that of England, with an emphasis on the redistributive and integrative potential of welfare policies. Further, it is advanced that this diversity goes beyond policy differences between nations to incorporate the idea of differences in philosophy (values), style and relationships. Welfare measures in these contexts have become a major instrument in reaching citizens and in defining the contours of national difference.

After a decade of devolution, this rhetoric of resistance to market-driven principles in welfare is writ large across a range of government reports aimed at developing the modernised social services post devolution. The report of the Independent Commission on Social Services in Wales (2010), *From Vision to Action*, endorses the philosophy of partnership, collaboration, high user and citizen involvement and the Welsh Assembly Government's *Sustainable Social Services for Wales: A framework for action* (WAG, 2011, p 11) opens by underscoring these 'Welsh public service values'. The latter document speaks directly to professionalism, outlining a framework for the development of a 'confident and competent workforce'. It locates social work at the heart of the aspiration for citizen-focused service delivery:

> *Whilst leadership, collaboration and integrated services and the focus on performance make a huge impact, it is the way in which frontline staff deliver the day-to-day work with citizens that ultimately makes the*

difference. We see the quality of professionals and their professionalism
as central to responsive and sustainable social services.
(WAG, 2011, p 24)

Building on the foundations laid down by the Care Council for Wales in developing a new model of professionalism, the report argues for a refreshed focus on 'professional practice and judgement': 'We will ensure that the workforce is more confident and is supported in applying its own professional judgement, using evidence that works as professionals instead of an over-reliance on government guidance' (WAG, 2011, Summary) … and it signals a commitment to an 'overall reduction in the burden of guidance, regulation and inspection'. This positioning has accordingly placed professionalism at the heart of public services in stark contrast to a pervading neoliberal trend in UK social work to strip away the space for professionalism and professional judgement.

In such a context it is now possible to consider the possibilities and potential for social work to demonstrate 'acts of resistance' and to develop creative practices that translate this distinctiveness into real effects, to develop a welfare *style* that will benefit users and move the profession beyond the perennial sense of 'crisis'.

Practising nation: tensions and possibilities for social work in a devolved Wales

The way in which social work has evolved in the UK reflects both its positioning and its role. The central state – the welfare state – defined social work, both given social work's central location within state institutions and the way in which relationships between state services and the independent sector have developed in the mixed economy of welfare. Since the imposition of neoliberal principles from the early 1980s, the welfare state has increasingly been subject to transformations and, within it, social work has been reshaped and subject to the constraints of a state-led institution. In times of recession, governments across the UK have had to make choices about whether retrenchment or renewal represents the best way forward. It is frequently argued that social work has been a passive participant in these transformations, unable to muster a level of autonomy necessary to effect critical re-interpretations of government dictat. Writers such as Lorenz (2001) have urged the profession to realise its autonomy by defining its role more clearly and thus being less subject to the contingent and shifting nature of political decisions. Lorenz draws attention to the interplay of welfare regimes with social work methodologies. He argues that welfare regimes reflect the histories and traditions of particular countries and suggests that social work methodologies form a nexus with these regimes, contributing to the development of particular 'welfare cultures' (Lorenz, 2001, p 606). The notion of welfare culture or what have been called 'ways of life' within a nation (Mooney and Williams, 2006) is key to an understanding of how social work can engage with the re-engineering of the welfare state that is under way.

Devolution has brought considerable potential for a repositioning of social work and current political rhetoric suggests that the profession has a central place at the heart of local government services. Opportunities for direct involvement in the political process have been opened up in a number of ways. In a small country, direct access to politicians and civil servants is assured not only at constituency level but also the Assembly has sought out ways to make its deliberations more open, transparent and subject to a range of influences, such as through regional committees, through the establishment of a plethora of consultation fora and through the widespread use of stakeholder representatives in task and finish groups. The Child Poverty Task Group mentioned in Chapter 5, this volume, is but one example, drawing its membership largely from practising social workers involved in an existing collaboration between voluntary agencies across Wales (the End Child Poverty Network); consultation on *The Strategy for Older People* is another. Much of this networking and partnership working is not new and comes from a long tradition of close working relationships across agencies, albeit ad hoc, and based on voluntarism rather than strategic thinking. As a small country, professional groups have built up a certain familiarity with each other alongside informal processes of working across agencies. Some of these existing ways of working are now being mobilised to greater effect and given a strategic push. Social workers can be effectively engaged in lobbying as key stakeholders in the activities of a range of decision-making institutions at local, regional and national levels. *Sustainable Social Services for Wales* (WAG, 2011, p 26) argues: 'We want social work to be listened to widely'. In the emergent welfare framework the state is no longer the principal agent of social policy delivery, as its functions are complemented, augmented or replaced by other key stakeholders. The opportunities presented by the shift towards governance (see Chapter 2, this volume) and away from government can be illustrated diagrammatically as in Table 11.1

Table 11.1: Policy development pre and post devolution

	Pre devolution	Post devolution
Relationship to the centre	Strong, top down	Two-way between multiple centres (transnational)
Institutional context	England (centre) focus	Realignment/networks
User involvement	Low	High
Innovations	Emanate from the central state	Emanate from multiple actors in the field
Outcomes	Rational planning	Experiential and emergent (based on evidence from the field)
Goals	Standardisation	Particularist

Within this new framework, social work is reconfigured and located within new policy networks that are highly differentiated and in which there are multiple actors. Policies are much more the subject of negotiation and emerge from experiences and evidence on the ground. The search is for responsive, localised and particularist solutions rather than standardisation based on rational planning from the centre and this is a trend set to increase. The possibilities for greater user engagement and for developing new partners and allies are greatly increased. However, it must be noted that this shift away from government to governance (see Chapter 2, this volume) brings with it its own challenges and concerns. In such a pluralist framework, inevitably some voices will be heard and others muffled and the appearance of involvement and engagement may be more apparent than real.

Undoubtedly, however, more open government has provided a plethora of opportunities for social welfare professionals. There are also increased possibilities for research alliances to be developed with academic institutions and research institutes. Think tanks such as the Institute of Welsh Affairs and the Bevan Foundation welcome contributions, commentary and involvement from those at the front line of public service delivery. *Sustainable Social Services for Wales* (WAG, 2011) highlights the importance of evidence-based practice and has signalled the establishment of a Centre of Excellence for Social Care Research. As research practices themselves become more inclusive, academics seek partners among practitioners and user groups in determining research agendas, undertaking research and disseminating findings. Voluntary agencies often find themselves at the forefront in identifying research needs, undertaking small-scale studies or acting as partners in academic research. In this way, social workers and other welfare professionals can be actively involved in the production of knowledge and influencing policy.

Above all, however, social welfare practitioners are the key implementers of the new public provision model. In Chapter 7, this volume, I indicated their critical role in translating equality principles into practices that matter to users and their carers. The underpinning principles of the new approach to public services in Wales (see Chapter 2, this volume) have a strong resonance with the fundamental values of social work and with the aspirations of the profession towards social justice ideals. If this is to move beyond political rhetoric it will largely be down to the everyday actions of social welfare practitioners at the front line of services. The leverage this broad approach provides for well-judged 'acts of resistance' to the dictates of neoliberal managerialism to be tested, and has clear support in the infrastructure being laid down in Wales for a renewed professionalism.

In many respects, social work in Wales is well poised for a refreshed role. A renewed politicisation builds on a history of collective action in social welfare, for example in relation to Welsh language policies, international activism and a history of innovations in practice, such as the All Wales Strategy for the Development of Services for Mentally Handicapped People (Welsh Office 1983). The fact that many social workers have been trained in Wales, worked within Welsh institutions for many years and that most are state social workers, affords them not only familiarity with key decision-making processes but also the potential to build a strong collective identity for the profession. The 'One Sector' approach enhances this by rejecting individualism and competition in favour of collaborative practices and a sense of common purpose. While some have argued that registration can be a double-edged sword, it nevertheless provides for a corporate identity at national and transnational levels. The CCW is steering a clear agenda of support and development and promotion of the profession alongside its regulating roles. It has established a number of national fora for closer cooperation and consolidation of a sense of social work in Wales and even a sense of Welsh-*style* social work Traditionally, *All*-Wales coordination and cooperation has foundered on both sides of the Brecon Beacons as efforts to endure the discomforts of north/south transport links ultimately deter even the most enthusiastic. Now the virtual environment of the internet is being exploited to provide a sense of proximity. While Wales is resisting the establishment of a National College of Social Work in Wales, the retention of the CCW means that this will be the key body designated to drive arrangements to deliver on this renewed professionalism.

In their discussion of social work in Wales since devolution, Scourfield et al. (2008) offer some discussion of what they consider the distinctiveness of the Welsh context for social work. They suggest four factors:

- the particular social and economic characteristics of Wales;
- the bilingual character of Welsh society and institutions;

- Wales-specific law and social policy;
- the role of national, ethnic and local identities.

The CCW has done much in its regulating role to steer attention to these factors in the training of social workers. The explicit plans of the Welsh Assembly Government to have a more integrated and people-centric social services delivery model suggest a particular role for social work. To this agenda therefore it may now be pertinent to add the emerging shift from bureaucratically led to more professionally led public services and the emphasis on valorising the role of the profession in meeting user need and defining flexible and accessible service delivery. It will be interesting to track how this development unfolds vis-à-vis social work elsewhere in the UK. This notion of 'trusting the professionals' is not without criticism and it clearly must be supplemented by an expectation of high standards, strong accountability and an explicit value base.

Social work education and training will need to keep apace of the new style requirements as laid out in Sustainable Social Services (WAG, 2011). Welsh social policy and attention to aspects of Welsh social life, language and culture have been afforded a profiled place in the social work education curriculum and increasingly so since the inception of the degree qualification. Recruitment of students who are Welsh speakers is being carefully monitored by the CCW in line with workforce demand, as is representation from other minority groups. Social work education programmes will also have to work to reflect the particular public service ethos of social policy in Wales, to underscore its social justice concerns and to develop students' skills in working strategically in the new governance framework.

While opportunities proliferate under devolution, there are also a number of issues that must remain of concern to welfare practice. Large policy swathes that fundamentally affect the well-being of citizens in Wales lie outside the remit of the Welsh Assembly Government. Issues of criminal justice, immigration, income support and thus income poverty are some key examples. In some areas of social work practice, for example youth justice (see Chapter 9, this volume) and with some areas of children's work (see Chapter 8, this volume), social workers will be obliged to struggle with 'serving two masters'. It would be easy to overstate the power of the Welsh Assembly Government in this respect. Neither, as I have argued elsewhere, is the Welsh Assembly Government immune to the flow and influence of overarching neoliberal ideas, nor significantly as yet shown itself to be in direct conflict with them (Mooney and Williams, 2006). This may well change with the attainment of increased law-making powers from 2011 and is a trend to be analysed in the forthcoming years.

Devolution also brings to the fore a number of social justice issues as indicated in Chapter 1, this volume. Territorial inequalities will inevitably become more acute as factors of place and access to welfare resources (or not) are now flagged more significantly. Some have argued that superficial 'boutique policies' might generate migrations towards hot-spots as people move in search of the good life. Issues of access to key welfare resources such as jobs and housing may become increasingly tied to pre 'national' credentials in ways that may exclude as well as include. For these reasons, social welfare professions should develop a critical questioning of national narratives and sufficient confidence and autonomy to critically inspect notions of Welsh citizenship as they develop inclusionary and exclusionary dimensions. In the endeavour to participate in the nation-building project there will always be a danger of losing sight of the ways in which social issues transcend the national boundary, for example, issues such as asylum, racism and other discriminations, child poverty, human trafficking and contemporary slavery. In a globalising world, fundamental inequalities between nations can also be ignored in clinging to the certainties of the parochial, to the cosy securities of nation. 'Grasping at nationalistic verities' (McDonald, 2002, p 508) may mean we lose sight of those who are on the real fringes of societies; those communities subject to persistent and unremitting poverty, excluded from citizenship rights and exploited for the benefit of wealthy nations (Midgely, 2000).

Arguably, a more confident social work in Wales will be in a better position to engage with these concerns, looking outward as well as inward.

Conclusions: 'the social work project'

The social work project under devolution is intricate and complex. It will require a careful balancing act on the part of the profession. I have suggested that the so-called 'crisis of social work' has been manifest epoch after epoch, foregrounding often differing discourses to explain the overriding tale of a profession that drifts helplessly in the ebb and flow of political tides. In the early 1980s, as I undertook my training, the search was on for a better ship in which to sail – the reorganisation of social services. In the late 1980s under Thatcher, came the crisis of role as social work functions were up for grabs by a range of associated professionals, and in the late 1990s the modernisation mantra emerged, which compromised the fundamental values on which the profession was built under the 'Blair project' (see Butler and Drakeford, 2001). To find ourselves in the 2000s under devolution in a political climate conducive to the aims, values and purposes of social work is one thing. But it may prove to be equally transient if social work in Wales is unable or unwilling to seize the opportunities to gain a more enduring collective sense of role and purpose. At the same time there are tensions to negotiate. Does the development of a Welsh-style social work represent a fundamental fragmentation of professional identity and the political power beyond national boundaries? Will devolution prove to be an even more effective method of technocratic control of the profession? Will it represent a fragmentation of political issues that require a UK or international response? Will constitutional change serve to pave the way for a break-up of the ideology of the welfare state, in particular its integrative potential to build social solidarities?

A strong body of work has admonished social work for acquiescence and collusion in the new managerialism of the neoliberal agenda (Jones, 2001; Ferguson 2005) and for the failure to engage with social justice concerns. The social justice manifesto for a new engaged practice developed by Jones et al. (2006, p 1) argues that social work in Britain has lost its way and suggests that 'we need to find more effective ways of resisting the dominant trends within social work and map ways forward for a new engaged practice'. They speak of 'new resources of hope that have emerged in recent years' (Jones et al., 2006, p 2). These resources, it is suggested, lie in new engagements with user group movements, with a culture of protest and new-style alliances with service users. Alongside this, Butler and Drakeford's (2005) review of the direction of contemporary social work offered up a plea for the profession to be a confident participant in what they refer to as 'the social work project' for the 21st century, one which, they suggest, will rely heavily on the development of trust: 'the most urgent need is to rehabilitate the concept of trust as a social good and as an integral part of a progressive, co-operative practice' (Butler and Drakeford, 2005, p 649). Their argument relies on renewed and productive alliances between practitioners and service users: 'The way to ensure we have a form of social work that combines sensitivity to individual needs and circumstances with the confident and articulate pursuit of equality is to understand the contribution both users and workers make to social work encounters' (Butler and Drakeford, 2005, p 650).

Opportunities have been opened up within the welfare context and within a new and strengthened recognition of social work in Wales in which social work will have to play a part in asserting itself with a renewed confidence. Devolution represents, in the words of one commentator, the opportunities for experimentation in 'new policy laboratories' (Jeffrey, 2005, p 5). As key implementers of the new public provision model there is a responsibility to develop new practices and new cultures based on productive alliances with a range of stakeholder groups, including service users and their carers, other professional groups, social work students, the army of workers who make up the social care sector, academics as well as politicians and civil servants. In developing a distinctive 'welfare culture' and style, the notion of a Welsh social work can emerge.

References

Asquith, S, Clark, C and Waterhouse, L (2005) *The Role of the Social Worker in the 21st Century: A literature review* Edinburgh, Scottish Executive, www.21csocialwork.org.uk

Barclay, P (1982) *Social Workers: Their role and tasks* (the 'Barclay Report') London, Bedford Square Press

Brewer, C and Lait, J (1980) *Can Social Work Survive?* London, Maurice Temple Smith

Butler, I and Drakeford, M (2001) 'Which Blair project: Communitarianism, social authoritarianism and social work' *Journal of Social Work*, 1(1), pp 7–20

Butler, I and Drakeford, M (2003) *Scandal, Social Policy and Social Welfare* Bristol, BASW/The Policy Press

Butler, I and Drakeford, M. (2005) 'Trusting in social work' *British Journal of Social Work* 35(5), pp 639–53

CCW (Care Council for Wales) (2007) *Workforce Development Report* (see updated October 2010), Cardiff, CCW, www.ccwales.org.uk/publications-and-resources

CCW (2007/08) *Annual Report* Cardiff, CCW, www.ccwales.org.uk

CCW (2011) *Newsletter* Cardiff, CCW, www.ccwales.org.uk

CSSIW (Care and Social Services Inspectorate Wales) (2008) *The Report of the Chief Inspector: Reviewing social services in Wales 1998–2008: Learning from the journey* Cardiff, CSSIW and Wales Audit Office

Dickens, J (2011) 'Social work in England at a watershed – as always: From the Seebohm Report to the Social Work Task Force' *British Journal of Social Work* 41, pp 22–39

Drakeford, M, Butler, I and Pithouse, A (1998) 'Social services' in Osmond, J (ed) *The National Assembly Agenda: A handbook for the first four years* Cardiff, Institute of Welsh Affairs, pp 266–80

Ferguson, I (2005) 'Social work and social care in the "new Scotland"' in Mooney, G and Scott, G (eds) *Exploring Social Policy in the 'New' Scotland* Bristol, The Policy Press

Ferguson, I, Lavelette, M and Whitmore, E (eds) (2005) *Globalisation, Global Justice and Social Work* London, Routledge

Garthwaite Report (2005) *Social Work in Wales: A profession to value* Cardiff, ADSS (Association of Directors of Social Services) All Wales Support Unit, www.allwalesunit.gov.uk/garthwaitereport

Grant, G (1978) 'The provision of social services in rural areas' in Williams, G (ed) *Social and Cultural Change in Contemporary Wales* London, Routledge & Kegan Paul, pp 61–75

Harris, J (2008) 'State social work: Constructing the present from moments in the past' *British Journal of Social Work* 38, pp 662–79

Howe, G (Chair) Report of the Committee of Inquiry into Allegations of Ill-Treatment of Patients and other Irregularities at Ely Hospital, Cardiff (Ely Report) 1969 Cmnd 3975 London, HMSO

Huws-Williams, R, Davies, E and Williams, H (1994) *Social Work and the Welsh Language* Cardiff, University of Wales Press

ICSSW (Independent Commission on Social Services in Wales) (2010) *From Vision to Action: The report of the Independent Commission on Social Services in Wales*, Cardiff, ICSSW, www.wlga.gov.uk/english/library/independent-commission-on-social-services-in-wales-from-vision-to-action/

Jeffrey, C (2005) *Devolution: What difference has it made?* Swindon, ESRC Research Programme on Constitutional Change, www.dev.ac.uk

Jones, C (2001) 'Voices from the front line: State social workers and New Labour' *British Journal of Social Work* 31(4), pp 341–82

Jones, C, Ferguson, I, Lavalette, M and Penketh, L (2006) *Social Work and Social Justice: A manifesto for a new engaged practice* Liverpool, University of Liverpool, www.liv.ac.uk/sspsw/Social_Work_Manifesto.html

Lorenz, W (2001) 'Social work responses to 'New Labour' in Continental European countries' *British Journal of Social Work* 31(4), pp 595–609

Mayer, E and Timms, N (1973) *Client Speaks: Working class impressions of casework* London, Routledge

McDonald, D (2002) 'Life on the fringe: Nationalism and social work' *British Journal of Social Work* 32(4), pp 503–8

McGrath, M, Grant, G, Ramcharan, P, Caldock, K, Parry-Jones, B and Robinson, C (1996a) *Care Management in Wales: Perceptions of front line workers*, CSPRD Report, Bangor, University of Wales Bangor

McGrath, M, Grant, G, Ramcharan, P, Caldock, K, Parry-Jones, B and Robinson, C (1996b) 'The roles and tasks of care managers in Wales', *Community Care Management and Practice* 4(6), pp 185–94

Michael, P (2003) *Care and Treatment of the Mentally Ill in North Wales 1800–2000* Cardiff, University of Wales Press

Midgely, J (2000) 'Globalisation, postmodernity and international social work' in Tan, N and Envall, E (eds) *Social Work around the World* Geneva, International Federation of Social Workers

Mooney, G and Williams, C (2006) 'Forging new "ways of life"? Social policy and nation building in devolved Scotland and Wales' *Critical Social Policy* 26(3), pp 608–29

Munday, B (ed) (1989) *The Crisis in Welfare* Hemel Hempstead, Harvester Wheatsheaf

Parry-Jones, B and Soulsby, J (2001) 'Need-led assessment: The challenges and the reality' *Health and Social Care in the Community* 9(6), pp 414–28

Parry-Jones, B, Grant, G, McGrath, M, Caldock, K, Ramchuran, P and Robinson, C A (1996) *Stress and Job Satisfaction among Social Workers, Nurses, Community Psychiatric Nurses: Implications for the care management model*, CSPRD Report, Bangor, University of Wales Bangor

Ramcharan, P, McGrath, M and Grant, G (1997) 'Voices and choices: mapping entitlements to friendships and community contacts' in Ramcharan, P, Roberts, G, Grant, G and Borland, J (eds) *Empowerment in Everyday Life* London, Jessica Kingsley Publishers, pp 48–70

Scourfield, J, Holland, S and Young, C (2008) 'Social work in Wales since democratic devolution' *Australian Social Work* 61(1) pp 42–56

Sherwood, M (1991) 'Racism and resistance: Cardiff in the 1930s and 1940s', *Welsh History Review* 15(3), pp 51–70

WAG (Welsh Assembly Government) (2003) *The Strategy for Older People in Wales* Cardiff, WAG

WAG (2005) *A Fair Future for Our Children* Cardiff, WAG

WAG (2006) *Making Connections* Cardiff, WAG

WAG (2007a) *Fulfilled Lives, Supportive Communities* Cardiff, WAG

WAG (2007b) *Review of Service Provision for Gypsy and Travellers*, Report LD2070, Cardiff, WAG

WAG (2011) *Sustainable Social Services for Wales: A framework for action* Cardiff, WAG

Waterhouse Report (2000) Lost in Care – Report of the Tribunal of Inquiry into the Abuse of Children in Care in the Former County Council Areas of Gwynedd and Clwyd since 1974, London, The Stationery Office

Welsh Office (1983) *All Wales Strategy for the Development of Services for Mentally Handicapped People* Cardiff, Welsh Office

Welsh Office (1989) *Mental Illness Services: A strategy for Wales* Cardiff, Welsh Office

Wilson, M, Walker, M and Stalker, K (2003) *Career Pathways in Scottish Social Services* Stirling, Social Work Research Centre, University of Stirling